LET THEM EAT

MARKETING LUXURY TO THE MASSES— AS WELL AS THE CLASSES

PAMELA N. DANZIGER

Trade Publishing

A **Kaplan Professional** Company

This publication is designed to provide accurate and authoritative information in regard to the subject matter covered. It is sold with the understanding that the publisher is not engaged in rendering legal, accounting, or other professional service. If legal advice or other expert assistance is required, the services of a competent professional person should be sought.

Vice President and Publisher: Cynthia A. Zigmund
Acquisitions Editor: Michael Cunningham
Senior Managing Editor: Jack Kiburz
Interior Design: Lucy Jenkins
Cover Design: Design Solutions
Typesetting: the dotted i

Published by Dearborn Trade Publishing
A Kaplan Professional Company

Printed in the United States of America

05 06 07   10 9 8 7 6 5 4 3 2

Library of Congress Cataloging-in-Publication Data

Danziger, Pamela N.
    Let them eat cake : marketing luxury to the masses—as well as the classes
/ Pamela N. Danziger.
    p. cm.
    ISBN 0-7931-9307-9 (6x9 hardcover)
    1. Affluent consumers—Psychology. 2. Luxuries—Marketing.
3. Consumer behavior. I. Title.
HF5415.32.D357 2005
658.8'343—dc22

                         2004023142

Dedication

This book is dedicated to my father, Edmund Newton Jr., who passed over on Christmas Day, 2002. While he is gone, I drew strength from his spirit through the course of researching and writing this book.

Contents

PART TWO

The Five Ps of Luxury Marketing

PART THREE

Putting the Insights to Work in Luxury Marketing

WHY LUXURY NOW?

Wal-Mart seems to be taking over the world! Or at least that part of the world that controls retailing in 21st-century America. With its sales over $256 billion in fiscal 2004, Wal-Mart is within striking distance of dominating a 10 percent share of the total $2.9 trillion U.S. retail market, excluding motor vehicles and parts. When it reaches this pinnacle, and I suspect it will unless the government moves in to break up what increasingly looks like a monopoly, it will mean that Wal-Mart alone takes in one of every $10 spent in this country at every retail and food service establishment, including car dealers, gas stations, convenience stores, restaurants, gift stores, grocery stores, and drugstores. It is unthinkable that an economy as broad and wide and diverse as 21st-century America could have nurtured a single company that controls so much of the U.S. national pocketbook.

As Sam Walton's juggernaut siphons hundreds of billions of dollars out of everybody else's pockets and into its own, is it any wonder that the rest of the nation's retailers figure the only way to get a little piece of the pie is by following Sam's lead? The thinking goes, "If 'everyday low pricing' works for Wal-Mart, then it's got to work for me." So like lemmings running to the sea, retailers everywhere rush to discounting and sales with catastrophic results for everybody. History has shown, and Kmart is learning it along with Montgomery Ward, Service Merchandise, and Ames, to name a few, that you can't beat a dominant competitor by playing his game. Wal-Mart with its near monopolistic control of its vendors and enormous diversity of product offerings can outlast anybody anywhere playing the markdown discounting game. Today, if you want to win in consumer marketing, whether you are a manufac-

> New luxury taps into a new consumer psychology that transcends the product or the thing being bought or consumed to reach a new level of enhanced experience, deeper meaning, richer enjoyment, more profound feelings.

turer, marketer, or retailer, you have to play a different game.

In 2003, Michael Silverstein and Neil Fiske in *Trading Up: The New American Luxury* proposed a "new luxury" strategy hinged on going in the opposite direction: upmarket to more exclusivity, higher prices, and higher margins. Their case was strong, and they had the success stories to back up their claims. They showed how Starbucks coaxed virtually the whole country into paying two, three, even four times more for a "cuppa joe." They investigated the strategy Boston Brewing used to create a new market thirsty for luxury beer, an oxymoron if there ever was one.

But new luxury is more than a savvy business strategy or brand management tool. It taps into a new consumer psychology that transcends the product or the thing being bought or consumed to reach a new level of enhanced experience, deeper meaning, richer enjoyment, more profound feelings. In my last book, *Why People Buy Things They Don't Need,* I returned again and again to the simple fact that when consumers buy anything they don't strictly need, they are in reality buying that thing to achieve a feeling or to enhance an experience. So the thing (i.e., a noun) they buy becomes a means to an end, and that end is experienced or felt (i.e., a verb).

In the luxury market it's the same, only more so. Luxury consumers are seeking new experiences and valuing them more rather than pursuing materialism for the sake of materialism.

EVERYONE EVERYWHERE WANTS MORE LUXURY

Today consumers everywhere at every income level want more luxury and are willing to pay for it. Further, everything is up for grabs and consumers are willing to accept totally new, unexpected definitions of what luxury is and where luxury can be found.

Because so much is at stake, the only strategy that will really work and take a company and its brand into the future is to continually enhance and build more and more luxury value into the company's products, its service, the brand. No matter where your product is on the luxury price continuum, from lowest to highest, you must continually reinvent your brand and keep it moving upward. In marketing today, the watchword is perpetual motion. We must keep moving our brands, our products, and our services to keep them vital and alive. So we can move more up-market by adding more luxury value. Other companies are shifting downmarket by taking the essential luxury brand proposition to a more moderate price point, as Mercedes-Benz or Jaguar is doing. And some marketers are extending their brand across new product categories while maintaining the brand's core emotional values. Or we can make all three moves simultaneously. All represent real-world strategic opportunities in today's luxury marketplace. In fact, the most dangerous strategy of all for any luxury brand or aspiring luxury player is to simply stand still.

> Everything is up for grabs, and consumers are willing to accept totally new, unexpected definitions of what luxury is and where luxury can be found.

Why? Because the natural evolution of all luxury concepts is from class to mass. First, luxury is introduced and embraced by the affluent; then, inevitably, it is translated and reinterpreted down to the masses. Thus today's luxuries become tomorrow's necessities. Luxury marketers, therefore, have to stay out in front of the luxury consumers, discovering new and different ways to give expression to consumers' growing luxury fantasies and desires. This is "luxflation"—the need for marketers to continually inflate or enhance the luxury value of their brand in order to counteract the inevitable downward gravitational pull to the mass market.

> The natural evolution of all luxury concepts is from class to mass. First, luxury is introduced and embraced by the affluent; then, inevitably, it is translated and reinterpreted down to the masses. Thus today's luxuries become tomorrow's necessities.

Further, if you really want to predict the future, you need to watch what the affluent market is doing and how it is spending its money, because it is what I call the *early adopters,* the bellwether that predicts where the rest of society will be in the near future. One of my guiding principles in trend forecasting: First the rich do it, then everybody else. What does today's luxury market foretell for the future of the mass market? Simply, the consumer economy is going experiential with people everywhere craving enhanced experiences rather than more things.

Today, with the rising affluence of the American consumer and the instantaneous transmission of information, the speed with which luxury companies must enhance their luxury values has accelerated even more. Ironically, the increasing velocity with which luxury evolves from the classes to the masses is less a result of rising affluence and consumers' greater ability to buy luxury. Rather, it is a function of consumers having new information and a greater awareness of how the "other half" lives. They see it on the telly or in pages of a magazine and they want it too. That leads us into a discussion of the metaphysics of luxury—that luxury is always the unattainable, that which we desire but can never really achieve.

METAPHYSICS OF LUXURY: LUXURY IS ULTIMATELY THE UNATTAINABLE

When consumers talk about luxury and why they buy luxury, they often explain it in terms of fantasy fulfillment. Through their consuming fantasies, consumers imagine how they will enhance their life by their luxury purchase. They fantasize how it will taste, feel, smell, look, and sound once they achieve their desire. They are visceral in their fantasies and use them to build excitement and anticipation toward the purchase. Thus luxury takes on a transcendent quality linked to the person's hopes, wishes, and dreams. Because luxury is played out in the fantasy realm, once it becomes a reality, something one has attained and achieved, this interesting transformation occurs. The extraordinary becomes the ordinary, and one's fantasies turn to striving and desiring something else more luxurious and even more special. A luxury consumer expressed this increasing desire for ever greater and greater luxury: "The more you have, the more you want. It's all about the individual and his or her perspective, where the individual is in his or her life."

It's human nature: that which is unattainable is also overwhelmingly attractive and desirable. Once the unattainable is attained, it loses its mystique, it becomes known, it becomes ordinary. So it is with luxuries. We all know this experience. After years of longing for a Mercedes, we finally achieve an income level that can support our purchase. You feel wonderful that first time you drive off the car lot in your brand new car. There is that wonderful new car leather smell, the seats and floor are spotless, and the exterior just sparkles. But after a couple of weeks, that feeling of excitement and specialness you got the first time you drove the car is gone. Your spotless car has accumulated the debris of daily living, and you can't get it to the car wash as often as you would like, so a fine layer of dust is on the hood. You don't even notice the smell anymore. What was once extraordinary becomes ordinary, and so it goes with every single luxury thing you buy.

Luxury is ultimately about the unattainable. This is what I call *the metaphysics of luxury*. It's about the consumers' fantasies, hopes, and dreams and not really about the physical or material realm. Luxury marketers will do well to connect with those fantasies, because the fantasies are often far better and more fulfilling than the ultimate reality.

BRANDING CONNECTS CORPORATE STRATEGY WITH CONSUMER PSYCHOLOGY

As we pursue an understanding of luxury brands and branding, whether we are talking about mass luxury brands (e.g., Isaac Mizrahi for Target) or class brands (e.g., Cartier) or something in

Luxury brands' essential role is to perform luxury fantasy fulfillment for the consumer, with a focus on the word *perform*, because it is through luxury brand performance that the real action lies.

between, branding is ultimately the way companies connect corporate strategy with consumer psychology. It's on an emotional level that consumers interact with luxury brands. They don't need any of it in reality. In fact, the one dominant definition of luxury among all the luxury consumers and luxury company executives that I have talked with is "that which nobody needs but desires." The word *luxury* comes from the Latin "luxuria," which means "excess" or "extras of life." A consumer in a focus group described it this way: "A luxury is more than extra. It's more 'more.'"

Luxuries are the extras in life that make it more fulfilling, more rewarding, more comfortable, more enjoyable, more "more." Branding is how companies communicate and deliver those emotional fantasies, promises, rewards, and fulfillment to the consumer. In other words, luxury brands' essential role is to perform luxury fantasy fulfillment for the consumer, with a focus on the word *perform*, because it is through luxury brand performance that the real action lies. Although the idea of a luxury brand's performance fits when talking about a car, a watch, or even a luxury hotel, it is a foreign concept in relation to a piece of art, an evening gown, a diamond necklace. But performance, no matter what the product or service, is the key: how the luxury brand delivers fulfillment in the emotional and physical realm for the consumer.

FINDING A NEW DIRECTION TO LUXURY: FROM MASS TO CLASS *AND* CLASS TO MASS

With the whole world jumping on the discounting bandwagon, you have to go against the flow. You have to find a new direction toward luxury for the masses, the classes, and everyone in between. What's remarkable about this strategy is that it is doable for any company or retailer at any place in the economic or pricing spectrum. The luxury market is no longer something out there, circumscribed by income levels, personal wealth, or spending budgets. Today, everyone is part of the luxury market. Luxury is for you, for me, for people living in trailer parks, inner-city projects, 1,500-square-foot tract homes, suburban "McMansions," gated enclaves, estates, and everywhere in between.

In America's 21st-century information economy, luxury is where the action is, no matter where you start. If you are marketing to the masses today, the big opportunity comes in moving from mass to class by making your product more luxurious and moving it upmarket. If you are marketing luxury to the classes, then the strategic direction is downmarket to capture luxury-enabled and desiring consumers on the fringes. Luxury in all its dimensions is the optimum way to grow a brand and build a sustainable business for the future.

Left-brained dominant, industrial age economic theories can't fully explain today's emotionally based, right-brained dominant consumer market culture. Some other factor is at work that isn't represented in traditional economic equations. This x factor is related to consumer passion, desire, and feelings and how those feelings can be massaged to increase desire for the product or the brand.

This is a book for marketing practitioners. It is a guide book for how to take your simple product, your basic brand, your retailing or service concept and add value and uniqueness to make it more special, unique, and more luxurious to satisfy consumers' emotional desires. By drawing on a major two-year quantitative and qualitative consumer research study of the luxury market, conducted in part in association with *House & Garden* magazine and profiling exceptional companies that get it right when marketing luxury to their customers at all levels of the market, this book will lay down the marketing strategies that work to bring a new luxury value proposition to your customers.

Let your customers go to Wal-Mart to get their plain white bread, but when they come to you, "let them eat cake!"

PREVIEWING WHAT'S TO COME

This book is divided into three parts. Part One describes this mysterious concept of luxury. Chapter 1 traces the history of the "new" luxury that began to come onto the national stage around 1984. Chapter 2 then defines exactly what we mean by new luxury in terms of consumer perspective.

In Part Two, which encompasses the bulk of the book, I analyze the luxury marketing paradigm around the basic Ps of marketing: the missing fifth P—People—and the other four Ps—Product; Pricing; Promotion; and Placement, or retailing. Chapter 3 explains who makes it into today's luxury class. Chapter 4 is an overview of luxury consumers' behavior, including what luxuries they buy and how much they spend. Chapter 5 is a field guide to the four distinctive personalities of the luxury consumer, including the iconoclastic Butterflies, the indulgent X-Fluents (extreme affluents), the Luxury Cocooners, and the Luxury Aspirers. Chapter 6 delves more intensely into the category of home luxuries; Chapter 7 into personal luxuries; and Chapter 8 into the experiential luxuries, such as travel, dining, spa and beauty services, and home services. Chapter 9 picks up a discussion of pricing and how to maintain a pricing premium when all the rest of retail is going discount. Chapter 10 tackles the myths and mysteries of luxury branding, and Chapter 11 probes the trends in luxury retail.

Part Three is also the final chapter, Chapter 12, which encapsulates the insights and learning from the previous chapters into 11 key lessons for success in the luxury market in the future, as well as a final case study of chocolate marketing that illustrates the transition of chocolate as it has moved from class to mass and then back to class again.

> Let your customers go to Wal-Mart to get their plain white bread, but when they come to you, "let them eat cake!"

If you want to read the ending first, go to Chapter 12 and start there, but please circle around to the other parts of the book to see exactly where these important lessons in luxury marketing originated.

As those of you who know me and know my work, and for those of you who haven't yet experienced my writing, you will find I cling pretty closely to the data, not just summarizing the top line but sharing the data with you so you can draw your own conclusions. As a result, some of the more data-intensive sections might be better taken in "sips" than in "gulps." Although I enjoy writing books as a bully pulpit to express my ideas and opinions, I consider this the start of a dialogue between us. I am first and foremost a researcher, and so I am continually striving for greater and deeper understandings. That happens best in a collegial environment where we can bounce ideas and theories around and bend and shape ideas in new directions. So I invite you to visit me at my Web site, http://www.unitymarketingonline.com, sign up for my online newsletter about new research on the luxury market, and write me your thoughts and ideas at pam@unitymarketingonline .com. I hope to hear from you soon.

1

TODAY'S LUXURY MARKET

THE YEAR 1984 MARKS THE OFFICIAL BIRTH OF "NEW" LUXURY

If we were to identify an official birth year of "new" luxury, it would be 1984. That year marked President Reagan's landslide victory for his second term in office. The economic lethargy and the "small is beautiful" philosophy that characterized the Carter years were history. By 1984, the economy had fully rebounded from a national recession, and go-go American consumerism came back in full force, driven by pent-up demand and expanding wallets.

The presidential couple set the trends for the hoi polloi to follow. The Reagans blew $11 million hosting the most extravagant inaugural celebration in history. Mrs. Reagan's passion for expensive designer clothes was legendary, but in a bow to frugality, she only borrowed, not bought, the designer "rags" she wore. Then Nancy hit up her friends and others on the social register for $44 million in private donations to renovate the White House. Taking conspicuous consumption to new heights, Mrs. Reagan spent $209,000 buying a 4,372-piece set of china trimmed in red for the White House.

Encouraged by President Reagan's infectious enthusiasm and his commitment to free-market policies, Americans felt confident in the economy and good about their personal financial situations. Rising consumer confidence drove exuberant consumer spending so that the economy grew a record 7.2 percent in 1984, the highest rate since 1951, according to statistics compiled by the Bureau of Economic Analysis.

Set against a backdrop of the Reagan presidency and vigorous economic growth, two landmark events occurred in 1984 that gave birth to the modern age of luxury as it has evolved today. That year Bernard Arnault acquired the luxury fashion house Christian Dior, which became the cornerstone of the world's largest luxury goods conglomerate LVMH. Today, the LVMH empire extends across wine and spirits, jewelry and watches, fashion and leather goods, perfumes and cosmetics, and luxury retailing. It is one of the international pacesetters of global luxury goods marketing and includes such heritage brands as Louis Vuitton bags, Moet and Dom Perignon champagne, Donna Karan fashions, and TAG Heuer watches.

Also in 1984 American Express launched its superpremium American Express Platinum Card to an exclusive group of high-flying existing cardholders. Priced at a premium over its gold and green cards, the American Express Platinum Card was designed for luxury consumers passionate about travel. The Platinum Card provided superior service through an exclusive full-service travel agency available 24/7 toll-free from virtually anywhere in the world.

American Express's Sylvia Bass
Luxury Is a Higher Level of Service for Those with Discriminating Taste

"There are cards in the marketplace that are painted platinum, and then there's the original Platinum Card from American Express. The Platinum Card represents style, sophistication, and access to a certain lifestyle through the services and benefits it provides. Our Platinum Card is designed to not just meet card member expectations but exceed them—and we've been doing just that for 20 years," says Sylvia Bass, vice president, Platinum and Centurion Product Management, American Express. Who doesn't know American Express and its classic brand tagline "Membership has its privileges"?

As the consumer economy has gotten more affluent with a rising tide of luxury expectations, American Express has continued to refine its service offerings to target the needs and desires of the more discriminating luxury consumer. "We target frequent travelers and people who have a specific mindset—those who appreciate the benefits of luxury goods and services and are willing to pay more when they see the values," Bass explains. Bass is responsible for two cards that aim at this upscale customer: Platinum Card with a $395 annual membership fee for a bevy of travel and shopping services; and Centurion Card (the famous black card) with a $2,500 fee that pushes the boundaries of what a card can offer and gives access to a personal assistant and luxury travel agent—available to meet members' toughest demands. Both cards are marketed primarily by invitation only, thus maintaining an exclusivity that is part of the luxury of the cards. Bass says, "Membership exclusivity drives a component of the emotional value and cachet that is created in supporting the identity of the product. The notion of a higher level of service for Platinum Card members and personalized service for Centurion members are two key pillars that support the experiential aspect of the brand."

The added-value services provided by these premium cards could include helping the luxury consumer plan a complex travel itinerary, locating a hard-to-find gift, or offering invitation-only special events to create a once-in-a-lifetime experience for their members, from sporting events and fine dining to visual and performing arts. Some recent to-die-for events that American Express arranged for its members were a Sting concert where members could get up close and personal with the star and an exclusive wine-tasting event where a private jet transported visitors into the vineyard to meet the cultivators and taste wonderful wine.

Enhancing luxury experiences is the real focus of the Platinum and Centurion Card platform, and the experiential is becoming more important to their members. Bass explains: "The luxury consumer has shifted from caring about the material element to the unique experiences that make them feel special. We have embraced this trend over the years by offering amenities and experiences exclusively to the super-affluent. This doesn't mean the super-affluent don't care about buying that luxury item, but they want the purchase to be surrounded by the ultimate, unique shopping experience."

A key value of Platinum and Centurion Card services is their time-savings aspects. Nature gives each of us, no matter how rich or poor, only 24/7, and you can't add to that. But Platinum and Centurion Card members can do more with less time through the support given by the cards' concierge service. "Time is more valued than money with this particular audience. Saving time is considered a luxury. Through our concierge service, you can pick up the phone and make three reservations, plan a party, and send a gift with only one phone call rather than a dozen, and that saves time," Bass says.

"Because time is so scarce among this group, they are more likely to go all

> "Time is more valued than money with this particular audience," says Sylvia Bass, American Express.

out to make sure their travel experience or vacation includes unique and exclusive elements that they will be able to remember and cherish for a long time," Bass continues.

For the future, Bass foresees the need to focus on more personalization and innovative ways to add value and ease the busy lives of these luxury consumers. According to her, "The pressure is on to keep innovating in the luxury market. Things that are luxury today quickly become the standard tomorrow, and it is happening much faster than in the past. It is a continuous challenge as luxury becomes more and more mainstream. But as marketers we have to stay ahead of the game."

THE 1990S WERE GO-GO YEARS FOR LUXURY MARKETERS

Following these two luxury marketing trendsetters—Bernard Arnault and American Express—many other world-class marketers ventured into the new luxury space during the latter part of the 1990s. The decade of the '90s was one of special excitement for marketers who staked their claim to luxury. Among the traditional luxury goods companies, revenue growth averaged in the double digits throughout most of the decade. Contributing to the phenomenal decade-long string of good fortune for these luxury goods marketers were the development and expansion of company-owned retail establishments that gave brands direct distribution to their customers. For goods sold in company-owned stores, these marketers got a double boost to profits and four times the bump in revenues, because they were selling their own goods at full list price, not at the discounted wholesale price paid by independent retailers. (See Figure 1.1 for luxury marketers' revenues from 2000 to 2003.)

FIGURE 1.1

Luxury Marketers' Revenues 2000–2003 in Millions of Dollars

	'00	% CHG '00–'99	'01	% CHG '01–'00	'02	% CHG '01–'02	'03	% CHG '02–'03
Pinault-Printemps-Redoute	$23,308.0	22.4%	$24,623.9	5.6%	$28,692.2	16.5%	$30,577.7	6.6%
Christian Dior	11,174.0	26.7	11,131.8	–0.4	13,801.4	24.0		
LVMH	10,909.0	27.0	10,900.0	–0.1	13,303.5	22.1		
Richemont**	2,792.3		3,237.5	15.9	3,358.2	3.7	3,941.2	17.4
Luxottica Group	2,268.9	20.2	2,731.8	20.4	3,284.1	20.2	3,551.1	8.1
Swatch	2,563.3	12.5	2,419.5	–5.6	2,834.5	17.2		
Gucci*	2,258.5	82.7	2,285.0	1.2	2,738.2	19.8	3,227.0	17.9
Polo Ralph Lauren*	2,225.8	14.2	2,363.7	19.2	2,439.3	3.2		
Tommy Hilfiger*	1,880.9	4.9	1,876.7	–0.2	1,876.7	0.0	1,888.1	0.6
Tiffany & Co*	1,668.1	14.1	1,606.5	–3.7	1,706.6	6.2	2,000.0	17.2
Prada/I Pellettieri d'Italia**			1,553.6	1.4	1,635.0	5.2	1,635.0	0.0
Giorgio Armani	973.6	11.6	1,126.7	15.7	1,362.5	20.9		
Hermes	1,090.9	16.8	1,086.8	–0.4	1,302.1	19.8		
Waterford Wedgwood	1,021.3	15.1	902.0	–11.7	1,036.5	14.9	1,036.5	0.0
Bulgari	636.6	17.9	678.6	6.6	810.9	19.5	953.0	17.5
Coach	548.9	8.1	616.1	12.2	719.4	16.8	953.2	32.5
Burberry Ltd.**			605.9		711.7	17.5	934.3	31.3
IT Holdings/Ittierre	432.9	12.9	466.5	7.8	686.8	47.2		
Versace**	425.5	1.5	450.0	5.8			485.0	
Movado*	320.8	8.7	299.7	–6.6	300.1	0.1	330.2	10.0
Dolce & Gabbana**			188.3		276.3	46.7	276.3	0.0
Average	**$3,694.41**	**18.66%**	**3,388.12**	**4.37%**	**4,143.80**	**17.08%**	**3,699.19**	**12.23%**

*Fiscal year ends early in year so sales reported represent sales year.
**Previous year data unavailable.

While these trends were afoot and were expanding the availability of luxury goods to a wider audience of consumers, the emergence of a younger, more affluent luxury consumer was transforming the luxury market from its traditional conspicuous consumption model. These young luxury consumers brought both a passion for self-indulgence and an iconoclastic world view that disdained conspicuous consumption for the sake of conspicuous consumption. The model for the new luxury market is based on a highly individualistic luxury consumer driven by new needs and desires for experiences.

While these trends were afoot and were expanding the availability of luxury goods to a wider audience of consumers, the emergence of a younger, more affluent luxury consumer was transforming the luxury market from its traditional conspicuous consumption model.

BABY BOOMERS ARE THE NEW LUXURY GENERATION

The paradigm shift in the luxury market from the old conspicuous consumption model to the new experiential luxury sensibility that started in 1984 and has now reached full expression, is marked by a change in the way consumers define luxury. *Old luxury* was about the attributes, qualities, and features of the product, and much of its appeal was derived from status and prestige. *New luxury* defines the category from the point of view of the consumer. Today's new-luxury consumers focus on the experience of luxury embodied in the goods and services they buy, not in ownership or possession itself. So new luxury is about the experience of luxury from the consumer's perspective, whereas old luxury remains focused on the traditional status and prestige ideal of luxury.

So new luxury is about the experience of luxury from the consumer's perspective, whereas old luxury remains focused on the traditional status and prestige ideal of luxury.

What has brought about this paradigm shift in luxury marketing? In a word, the baby boom generation, made up of 76 million Americans born in the postwar boom years from 1946 to 1964. This generation has transformed consumer markets at every generational life stage through which it has progressed. From the counterculture hippies in the 1960s to the career-driven yuppies in the 1980s to today's luxury generation, the baby boomers, with their tradition-bending value system, express luxury today by rejecting the traditional status symbols of wealth, while fully embracing the power and privileges that their tremendous affluence and spending power give them. They want to experience the good life and all that goes along with it, but they simply do not care if anybody else notices. Rejecting status and prestige, today's new luxury consumer embraces a democratic ideal of luxury—that it's *for* everybody and *different* for everybody.

P *e r s o n a l* **P** *e r s p e c t i v e o n* **L** *u x u r y*

House & Garden's Dominique Browning
Luxury Is Creative Expression

As editor-in-chief of Condé Nast's *House & Garden* magazine since 1995 and author of the recently published *The Well-Lived Life* (New York: Assouline, 2003) as well as several other titles, Dominque Browning has been a keen observer of the shifts and turns in the luxury market, particularly as they are expressed through the home. A hallmark of *House & Garden* magazine every year is its luxury issue published in September. In a shelter book so tied to wonderful things for the home, its choice of themes for the annual luxury issues are decidedly experiential—luxury of time, luxury of space, luxury of quiet, luxury of dreams. Browning explains thus:

Nearly ten years ago when we were starting up *House & Garden* again, I thought about doing a luxury issue. But at the time, we weren't even sure if we could call it the luxury issue, because *luxury* for a while was a dirty word. We started asking around and discovered that there was a quiet resurgence of interest in luxury. And people saw luxury as all those intangibles—luxury of time, luxury of space, luxury of quiet, luxury of simplicity—that seem to disappear the harder you work for luxury. But even though there was this revolutionary focus on interpreting your own experience of luxury, people were also very much focused on buying the right things. Luxury is what is uniquely your own and your unique experience of a thing. It's not anti-materialistic so much as it is interpretive.

> "Luxury is what is uniquely your own and your unique experience of a thing. It's not anti-materialistic so much as it is interpretive," says Dominique Browning, *House & Garden* magazine.

From the perspective of luxury, Browning sees the well-lived life as an expression of personal creativity. "There is a sense of wanting to integrate things into a larger tapestry of life, and that is true luxury. It's not only that you have a wonderful car, but that [the same] car takes you to your wonderful house. You have a surround-sound experience of luxury. Your self-expression is how you stitch all the pieces together. You have the icons of luxury, but the trick is to present yourself as not caring about these things. They are just there, mixed in with your personal and found treasures."

The "icons of luxury" Browning refers to are largely luxury brands:

In June [2004] we did an issue called "The Well-Lived Life." This issue is filled with people living wonderful lives surrounded by friends, family, nature. We asked each person to tell us about their luxuries, and we got very specific so that they would tell us about their shoes, their pocket-book, their watch. It's really interesting that everybody said basically the same luxury brands. They say Cartier. They say Tiffany. They say Bulgari. These are the touchstones that indicate where they are in the class structure and what they can afford and what they believe is luxurious. These are also the same people who talk about the luxury of time, sleep, a good book, a hot bath.

Regarding the appeal of these luxury brands, Browning says that "they are not just empty names. They stand for quality. This is how we justify buying them. We are a generation that needs to think 'I'm investing,' as opposed to 'I'm spoiling myself.'"

For Browning the home is where luxury originates and finds its fullest expression. "I feel the zeitgeist moving to seeing luxury as the ability to design your dream—your dream life and dream home. The home, after all, is the stage for your life. Living well begins at home. Home is where you show that you are living well. It's where you display the trophies of your travels. Your trip to Tibet is the carpet on the floor," she says.

But with all this striving for the icons of luxury, Browning comes back to ask the essential question for us all: What does it really mean?

There is something that I've been puzzling over that runs counter to everything we have said. But I feel it and my friends feel it. Our closets are filled with little black suits from Helmut Lang, and we all have a lot of stuff. When is it too much? It's not antiluxury, but there is something going on culturally where people want life to mean more. I see dissatisfaction arising, like finally you can afford the Valentino handbag, and you go out and buy it. Then it becomes a "so what else?" We seem to be getting into that "so what?" era. It doesn't mean we stop buying. It means the focus is changing.

I think more of us have a sense of spiritual yearning, a sense that there has to be more in life than material success. Maybe it is related to getting older—in which case it is going to be a huge shift. It means luxury marketers will have to sell the deeper meaning of their products. I feel slightly disoriented these days when I see a $2,000 price tag on a skirt. I think more of us are saying, "I'd rather go to Gap." That's behind the huge popularity of places like Crate & Barrel and Target for people who can afford to shop anywhere in the world. But it doesn't mean I don't want a $2,000 handbag or, for house junkies, a $2,000 vase. It just means there is a weird and constant calculation about choosing which luxuries are meaningful to you—again personal expression. It means, I think, that people are going to become even more selective in their purchases; they're going to edit their luxury living more rigorously. I always feel if I am carrying the right bag, even if I am only wearing blue jeans, then I am OK.

DEMOGRAPHICS ARE DESTINY IN 1984 AND 2004

The story of the new luxury market is the story of the baby boomer generation. In a landmark article in 1984—"What the Baby-Boomers Will Buy Next"—*Fortune* magazine predicted that the boomers would mature into the most affluent generation ever seen and that they will spend a greater share of their wealth.

While marketers were predicting increasing wealth and spending power among the baby boomers, the boomers were only 20 to 38 years old in 1984 and had not yet hit their stride in terms of earning power and spending potential. The generation's income in 1984 was only 6 percent above the nation's median, or $23,735.

It was the older generation of households, those born from 1930 to 1939 and aged 45 to 54, who were earning the most money back then.

Now aged 40 to 58, baby boomers are the luxury generation today. See Figure 1.2. In 1984, luxury marketers were targeting a different generation, the "swing" and World War II generations born before 1946. This older generation, many of whom experienced the nationwide impoverishment of the Depression and years of sacrifice during World War II, basked in the enjoyment of material things. They measured their success in what they had and what they owned and eagerly sought out the status symbols of wealth. It was a reflection of this more materialistic generation that Malcolm Forbes proclaimed, "He that dies with the most toys wins!"

The baby boomer's life experiences were completely different from those of the generations that came before. The generation as a whole was raised largely in middle-class circumstances and never faced the deprivations of a national Depression or a war economy demanding the magnitude of sacrifice of World War II. The generation at once rejected the blatant materialism of their parents during the hippie era of the 1960s and 1970s. But they found as they matured from adolescence to adulthood that the realities of living in 20th-century America demanded compromise. So they turned their youthful energy toward building careers, getting married, having children, and accumulating the trappings of wealth.

FIGURE 1.2

Median Household Income by Age 1984 and 2002

AGE	1984	2002	% CHG
Under 24	$14,028	$27,828	98%
25 to 34	23,735	45,330	91
35 to 44	29,784	53,521	80
45 to 54	31,516	59,021	87
55 to 64	24,094	47,203	96
65 and older	12,799	23,152	81
Total	**$22,415**	**$42,409**	**89**
Current Dollars			

Source: U.S. Bureau of the Census

Today the boomers' drive to affluence and luxury is very different from that of their parents' generation. For this generation it's not about keeping up with the Joneses or sporting the latest status symbol of wealth; it is a more self-directed, inward-focused desire for living the good life. An article in the November 27, 2000, *New Statesman*, titled "The Rise of Stealth Wealth—Perceptions of Luxury" explains how the concept of luxury in the present age is decidedly inconspicuous and a rejection of the status-symbol-obsessed 1980s: "It's about private pleasure as opposed to public swank." Stealth wealth, in other words, is about luxury on the inside (i.e., the experience) rather than on the outside (i.e., conspicuous consumption), such as fur worn on the inside of your coat rather than on the outside for all to see.

> For this generation, luxury is not so much what I have or what I own but how much I enjoy it . . . the pleasure it gives me . . . the experience of luxury, not the thing in and of itself.

For the boomers, it is not so much what I have or what I own but how much I enjoy it . . . the pleasure it gives me . . . the experience of luxury, not the thing in and of itself. Being privileged to have inside information and to be in the know is one way luxury is measured, according to the senior vice president of marketing at Bergdorf Goodman: "This group's notion of status is being ahead of the curve, the first in knowing, seeing, experiencing, and then acquiring a particular piece of merchandise." The luxury consumer today is an opinion leader, an innovator, one used to thinking outside the box.

FUTURE VISION OF LUXURY—CONSUMER MARKET WILL INCREASINGLY POLARIZE WITH GROWTH AT LUXURY AND BUDGET EXTREMES

Fashion designer for the new luxury age Isaac Mizrahi has a clear vision of the future of the luxury market, and he is carefully

For marketers in the future, the middle will continue to shrink while opportunities at the lower, bargain end of the market and those targeting the upper luxury end will flourish.

crafting a marketing strategy for it. Following the lead of Martha Stewart, who became an icon in issues related to the home, Mizrahi is grounding his new luxury fashion empire on television through his *Isaac Mizrahi Show* that airs weekdays on the Oxygen network. His captivating personality and deliciously wicked wit make him a natural on TV, but he is also so unpresuming and approachable when it comes to fashion that women of every age and every shape can connect with him. That's no mean feat in today's fashion world. But where his future vision of luxury is playing out is through his selection of business partners for fashion. With much fanfare Mizrahi launched his affordably priced Luxury for Every Woman Everywhere line with Target in March 2003. Now he is taking his couture fashion to the "classes" with shoes at Neiman Marcus and clothes at Bergdorf Goodman.

Mizrahi sees the future of luxury and recognizes it is polarizing with lots of growth at the lower-priced end—targeting a more moderate income but still luxury-leaning consumer as well as a more affluent shopper who simply craves a bargain for her luxury indulgences—and lots of growth at the high end for the fashion-forward, affluent baby boomers. Given the demographic trends taking hold in the marketplace over the next 10 to 20 years, there won't be a lot of growth in the middle market, where the U.S. economy has traditionally been strongest. For marketers of the future, the middle will continue to shrink while opportunities at the lower, bargain end of the market and those targeting the upper luxury end will flourish.

For consumer marketers, demographics is destiny. This applies even more to the luxury marketers who target the most affluent members of our culture. Today, four major generations are active in the consumer marketplace:

1. World War II and swing generations, born before 1946 and who in 2004 are 59 years old and older
2. Baby boomers, born between 1946 and 1964 (40 to 58 years old)
3. Generation X, born between 1965 and 1976 (28 to 39 years old)
4. Millennials, born after 1977 (27 years old and younger)

The two generations that will have the longest and strongest impact on the luxury market in the near and distant future are the boomers, some 76 million strong, and the millennials, the babies of the baby boomers who number about 71 million. The generation X group is far smaller in comparison with the boomers or millennials, and so they are not going to dominate consumer markets in the same way that the boomers have and will continue to or as the millennials are about to. See Figure 1.3.

FIGURE 1.3
Consumer Generations in Millions

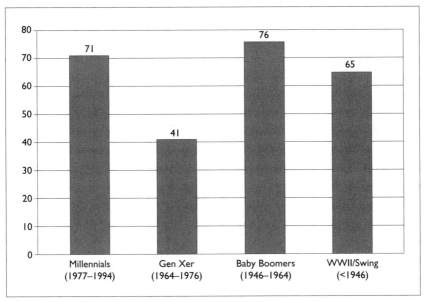

What these generational trends foretell is a market structured very differently from anything our economy has ever experienced before. The big opportunities will emerge for marketers who go after the aging baby boomers, now officially the luxury generation. The other immediate opportunity is toward the younger millennial generation, who are just starting in young adulthood. They will likely follow patterns similar to their baby boom parents'—a fierce appetite for fashion, entertainment, technology, and personal indulgences of all kinds while they are single that will turn into a hunger for home and baby goods once they settle down and start a family. But the millennials are marrying later than their parents did, so marketers still have plenty of time to appeal to their self-indulgent, self-expressive side.

For the next 10 to 20 years, the baby boom generation is the target for luxury marketers. At the same time savvy marketers like Isaac Mizrahi recognize that consumers with limited cash also have a taste for luxury. Marketers that have prospered in the past by firmly targeting the middle, such as Sears and JCPenney, will find they need to pick a side—either the market's upside (as it appears JCPenney is pursuing with new home licenses under decorator Chris Madden) or the economy shopper at the lower end. But marketers that start down the discounting pathway will need a strategy that incorporates enhanced luxury value at an affordable, not necessarily the cheapest, price. Nobody can beat Wal-Mart at its own game, so the key is to change it, as Target is doing through its affiliation with designers like Mizrahi.

2

NEW LUXURY— OLD LUXURY IS ABOUT THE "THING," NEW LUXURY IS DEFINED BY THE EXPERIENCE

DEFINITION OF LUXURY DEPENDS ON WHOM YOU ASK

The definition of luxury depends on whom you ask. An official dictionary definition is: (1) Something inessential but conducive to pleasure and comfort. (2) Something expensive or hard to obtain. (3) Sumptuous living or surroundings: *lives in luxury.* (*The American Heritage Dictionary of the English Language*, 4th ed.). During a focus group, a consumer put it simply: "Luxury is more 'more.'" Our modern word is derived from the Latin *luxuria,* which means "excess" or the "extras of life."

Widely recognized as the opposite of necessity, *luxury* is an emotionally charged word that carries a lot of baggage along with it. The synonyms for the word hint at just how "hot" the term *luxury* really

> "Luxury has been railed at for two thousand years, in verse and in prose, and it has always been loved," said Voltaire (1694–1778), philosopher.

> "The state is suffering from two opposite vices, avarice and luxury; two plagues which, in the past, have been the ruin of every great empire," said Titus Livius (Livy) (59 BC– AD 17), Roman historian.

is: sybaritic, voluptuary, epicurean, deluxe, opulent, sumptuous, self-indulgent, princely, languorous, Babylonian, posh, ostentatious, palatial, pampered, titillating, tantalizing, tempting. At its root, luxury is experienced sensually as voluptuous self-indulgence.

During the past century, *luxury* lost much of its implied decadence and moral taint. But with that loss, it became disconnected from the sensate experience to which the original term alludes. So during the 20th century, *luxury* became a word that described a product, an industry, an objective thing. It came to mean something expensive, affordable only to the rich, an object of transcendent quality, the best of the best. With a focus on the intrinsic quality of the item itself, luxury came to be an object that costs a lot and exhibits elegance and sumptuousness, as in a "deluxe car" or a "luxury apartment."

For most of the 20th century, luxury has described the lifestyle of the elite, the things they buy, and the places where they live. Carriage trade retailers, like Tiffany, Bergdorf Goodman, Barneys New York, and Saks Fifth Avenue, were its purveyors. Luxury was available only to the rich, and the price of entry into the luxury lifestyle was a big, fat bank account.

But during the mid-1980s, the way the culture defined luxury started to shift from a focus on a description of a thing back to an experientially based view. The baby boom generation was the force behind this paradigm shift in how luxury is perceived and experienced.

NEW LUXURY DESCRIBES THE EXPERIENCE

The term *new luxury* is freely bandied about today without any clear-cut definition of what it means. New luxury usually refers to more recent luxury concepts and those that are more affordable, as

opposed to old luxury, which is understood to be the iconic heritage luxury
brands, such as Mercedes-Benz, Tiffany,
Cartier, and so on. New luxury is often
closely associated with talk of the "democratization of luxury" or "mass-tige" brands,
referring to new, more affordable luxury.

"I love luxury. And luxury
lies not in richness and
ornateness but in the
absence of vulgarity," said
Coco Chanel (1883–
1971), fashion designer.

But the real paradigm shift occurring
in the luxury market that signifies new luxury is the consumercentric way people are defining luxury as an experience or feeling.
In other words, old luxury is about the thing (i.e., a noun), whereas
new luxury is about the consumer's experience (i.e., a verb.)

In yesterday's old luxury world, luxury was defined from the
point of view of the thing itself. Luxury was intrinsic to the object,
and it was by its intrinsic qualities that luxury was defined. In old
luxury, the product's attributes, qualities, and features qualified
the item as worthy of the luxury label. Only the best of the best
earned the name of luxury.

But today's new-luxury consumer doesn't necessarily buy the
old luxury definition. Returning to luxury's sensual roots, the baby
boomers put their own unique spin on luxury: "If it feels good,
then it must be luxury." From an experiential perspective, luxury
is all about how the consumer feels and experiences luxury. For
example, a company might design a product that encompasses
best-of-class features in the product category. But if those features
that make the product special or best in class are irrelevant or just
not that important to the target consumer, then there is no justification for spending more for the specialness that confers little
or no extra value.

The consumercentric definition of luxury focuses on the experience, the feeling, the personal dimensions of luxury. Consumers describe luxury this way:

- How you experience it is all part of the package. Everything
  comes together. It's not just one particular aspect of a lux-

---

O *ld* **L** *uxury* **I** *ntrinsic* **C** *hecklist*

- Consistent delivery of *premium quality* across all products in the line, from the most to the least expensive
- Heritage of *craftsmanship,* often stemming from the original designer
- *Recognizable style or design* so that the savvy customer doesn't have to look at the label to know the brand
- *Limited production* run of any item to ensure exclusivity and possibly to generate a customer waiting list
- Marketing program that supports, through limited distribution and premium pricing, a market position that combines *emotional appeal* with product excellence
- *Global reputation*
- Association with a *country of origin* that has an especially strong reputation as a source of excellence in the relevant product category
- Element of *uniqueness* to each product; for example, the imperfections in a hand-blown Waterford crystal vase that provides an assurance of exclusivity
- Ability to time design shifts when the category is *fashion intensive*
- Embodies the *personality and values of its creator* (Luxury brands hold a higher share of market in product categories where the brand used conveys social status and image.)

Based on criteria developed by Professor Jose Luis Nueno

ury. It's how you experience your home luxuries or how you experience your personal luxuries. So they're all interchangeable and all about the experience.

- Quality is in the eye of the beholder. We often associate quality with expensivevess, but they don't necessarily have to go hand in hand—sensual experience, a massage, a wonderful dinner, travel, a treat, something very special you do for yourself.
- A state of mind, being able to do something that I couldn't do before
- Luxury means I can live my life in such a way that I don't have to worry about money. Luxury doesn't mean labels. It

means comfort. If I want to go somewhere and am able to do it, that is luxury.

- Luxury to me is not a necessity but a privilege. It means being able to do things with regard to services, time, material things.
- The most luxury ever is to have enough time to do whatever you want and be able to afford it.
- I buy what I like and what I want. It is nice to have the feeling that you can do what you want when you want.

When we talk about luxury from the consumers' experiential perspective, the brand itself is irrelevant. All that matters is how the brand delivers the luxury feeling or luxury experience promised to the consumer.

FOUR DIMENSIONS OF LUXURY PUT NEW AND OLD LUXURY INTO PERSPECTIVE

Ultimately, the final arbiter of luxury, what it is and what it isn't, is the individual consumer. When the discussion turns toward more affordable luxury in my conversations with executives from luxury goods companies, people often proclaim, "But that brand isn't luxury," as they comment on companies like Viking or Jenn-Air or Coach or any other brand they perceive doesn't measure up to their standard of luxury. The answer to the question, Who is the ultimate authority on luxury? clearly isn't the people making it, but rather the people buying it. Luxury has taken a decidedly personal turn. Let's look at the four dimensions of luxury identified and described by luxury consumers themselves.

Dimension #1: Luxury as a Brand

Only 24 percent of luxury consumers agreed with the statement, "Luxury is defined by the brand of the product, so if it isn't

FIGURE 2.1
The Four Dimensions of Luxury

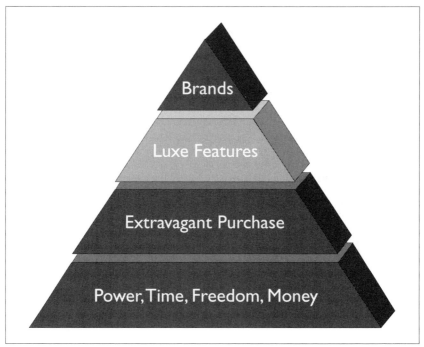

a luxury brand, it isn't a luxury." A few iconic brands, although not defining luxury in the product category, at least benchmark luxury for the competing players. Brands like Mercedes-Benz, Rolls Royce, Cartier, Tiffany, Rolex, St. Johns knits, Prada, Hunter Douglas, and Gucci are among those mentioned by luxury consumers that have captured the popular imagination and represent luxury within their category.

When asked to describe how the brand defines luxury, a luxury consumer said, "Designer names mean status. If I carry a Prada bag, it comes along with lots of other feelings. The better brands are usually better quality. You feel good carrying that bag. But it is about the perception of others. If you spent $600 on a bag, you got to feel good carrying it."

These iconic luxury brands have effectively communicated both their superior intrinsic features and their emotional attributes to the target market. Few iconic luxury brands are created overnight; it may instead take decades for a brand to connect emotionally with the consumer and achieve a true identification as a luxury. Many luxury brands have a heritage that extends nearly a century. Cartier was founded in 1847; Tiffany dates from 1837; Rolex originated in 1908; and Gucci dates from 1923.

Although some brands may have achieved iconic luxury status, they still may not be the personal luxury of an individual. In a recent focus group, a luxury consumer expressed the need to have a personal connection with a luxury brand: "Luxury might be driving around in a Mercedes-Benz. But that isn't necessarily luxury for everyone. Someone might not feel they're in luxury with a Mercedes. It might be a sports car or a Cadillac depending upon your personal taste." Luxury brands have the potential to make deep and lasting connections with consumers. At the same time, a luxury brand only epitomizes luxury when it connects with the individual's passion.

Dimension #2: Luxury as Luxe Product Features

People are more likely to describe luxury as specific features, qualities, and attributes that are generally recognized as luxurious within the product or service category; thus platinum jewelry is luxury whereas gold plate is not. Category specific, these qualities may include handcrafting; careful attention to detail; superior quality; cutting-edge design; radiant colors; distinctive textures; long lasting; made from natural, nonsynthetic materials; and so on. For experiential luxuries, like travel or fine dining, qualities include exceptional décor, a soothing atmosphere, attentive service personnel, and other amenities. Within this dimension, those intrinsic product features that transform the ordinary into the extraordinary define luxury. They are the product cues and clues that signal superior quality. Nearly 90 percent of luxury consumers agree with the statement, "When you buy a luxury item, you expect it to be noticeably a cut above the average."

For example, a person might select an ordinary brand of car but equip it with all kinds of luxury features to create a "virtual" luxury model. So instead of buying Nissan's luxury Infiniti brand, you buy the Nissan Altima model with the full luxury package, including leather seats, power sun roof, wood grain trim, Bose® am/fm radio and 6-disc CD changer, with xenon lights and fancy steel wheels just for fun. Your car might not have the badge value that the Infiniti label brings and thus might be less impressive to passersby on the street. But driving around the city with the sun roof open and your favorite CD playing on the stereo system, you feel in the lap of luxury. And maybe you even feel more self-satisfied because you paid under $25,000 for your virtual luxury car, whereas the other guy spent $50,000 and got the same basic car only with the Infiniti name plate.

It's to compete more effectively for the value-oriented luxury customer that Mercedes and Jaguar brands are using their formidable luxury brand heritage to extend down into the near-luxury price range. Their thinking is that rather than eliminate a Mercedes luxury brand car entirely from consumers' consideration, why not deliver Mercedes-brand qualities and features at a more moderate price? This is a luxury marketing strategy conceived with a long-range vision. Their goal is to build lifetime brand loyalty by meeting automobile consumers at nearly every price point throughout their life stages. Thus, the 30-something C-class buyer turns into a 40-something E-Class driver, then on to a 50-something S-Class consumer and then back again to a C-Class model after retirement.

Dimension #3: Luxury as Nonnecessities

Moving beyond a consideration of intrinsic product features, as expressed in the previous two dimensions of luxury, another perspective on luxury is one expressed by this consumer: "Luxury is more of what you want than what you need. Luxury is different for different people. What's luxury to me is somebody else's everyday way of living." This is the dimension of luxury explored in depth in my last book, *Why People Buy Things They Don't Need* (Dearborn Trade Publishing, 2004). From this perspective, luxury is anything you buy that you don't strictly need. It has virtually nothing to do with the thing itself, whether it is a luxury brand or incorporates specific luxe features or costs more or less; rather, it is how the consumer perceives the item that makes it a luxury. That personal interpretation of luxury is totally subjective and highly individualistic.

Keeping with our car examples, my family will be buying two luxury cars this year, but these cars will be luxuries only because they are discretionary. My first-born son starts college this fall. He has a car, an old beat-up Subaru Legacy station wagon with 145,000 miles that our "car guy" assures me is just now broken in, but I would feel better if he were driving around in something a little newer and a little more substantial. Although our son has tried to convince us that a used Mercedes is the perfect first car for college, his father and I are not swayed. So he has settled on a 2000 Jeep Wrangler. Luxurious? No, but this is a luxury purchase for him as the Subaru can still get him around.

My luxury car purchase this year will be a Ford Escape Hybrid. I will add a few "bells and whistles" to the basic model, but it would be a real stretch to call it a luxury model. I definitely don't need another car, but I feel compelled to vote for the hybrid concept to do my small part to get out from under the tyranny of the Middle Eastern oil sheiks. After years of driving a monster gas-guzzling SUV around, the Escape Hybrid is my penance. Together, our luxury cars will cost under $50,000, but they will be personal luxuries because their purchases are definitely not driven by need but by desire.

Dimension #4: Luxury as the Power to Pursue Your Passions

The ultimate expression of luxury is defined as the power to pursue your passions. This dimension encompasses the "intangibles" that Dominique Browning of *House & Garden* magazine refers to in the "luxury of time, luxury of space, luxury of quiet, luxury of simplicity, luxury of dreams." In our society, money is often equated with power, and so more money means you have more freedom and power to do your choosing. But this may not necessarily be the case, as Browning says; the intangibles of luxury are the ones we often lose first in our pursuit of the luxury lifestyle.

Luxury as the power to pursue your passions is the ultimate experiential dimension of luxury. Totally divorced from the intrinsic product-based definitions of luxury, this dimension turns us inward to find that place deep inside where true luxury resides. It's not about the external thing at all but how one experiences the luxuries of life. More than 80 percent of luxury consumers agree with the following statements that reflect this experiential dimension of luxury:

- Luxury is buying those extras in life that make it more comfortable and meaningful. (86 percent)
- Luxury is having the feeling I can do what I want when I want to. (84 percent)
- Luxury is being able to pursue my passions and interests. (83 percent)

LUXURY IS A VERB

The closer we get to consumers' perspective of luxury, the further removed we get from the luxury marketers' point of view.

Luxury ultimately does not reside in the object, the product, the brand. Luxury is all about the consumers' experience of it. So luxury is no longer a noun but a verb connoting the action and the delivery of the luxury experience and feeling to the consumer. Active rather than passive, luxury isn't luxury until it is experienced by the individual. The object, thing, brand that delivers the luxury feeling is a catalyst for the feeling, but it isn't the cause of the feeling. The luxury feeling comes from how the consumer personally interprets the luxury.

In understanding luxury from the perspective of consumers, luxury marketers must turn themselves around 180° and look at their products not as the wonderful, beautiful, luxurious things they are but as the delivery mechanism through which they transmit a luxury experience to the consumer. The luxury marketer's challenge is to maximize the way the consumer experiences the luxury.

There are two basic ways marketers can make that delivery of a luxury experience happen. They can design their products with the right combination of product features and attributes that carry an expectation of a luxury experience. In certain product categories, notably fashion, luxury is often delivered through look and

Words That Describe Luxury

Comfort	Made Well	More Convenient
Expensive	Quality	Looks Beautiful
Pampering	Design	Makes Life Easier
Not Practical	Nonessential	The BEST
Extravagant	Reputation	Sensual
Unique	No Worry	Privileged
Not Ordinary	What I Want	Indulgence
Craftsmanship	Pleasant	Hard to Find
Allure	Beyond the Basics	Exclusive
Special	Softness of Life	Freedom

feel, design flash, and product sizzle. In other categories—think of electronics and kitchen appliances—luxury must be carefully engineered into the product so it is less about looks and more about substance. But even in these highly engineered goods, attractive and unique styling takes you far in the luxury world. Why is the KitchenAid standing mixer *de rigueur* in everyone's luxury kitchen even though only Martha Stewart wannabes or food channel junkies still use mixers? Because they come in such great colors, and they look so retro cool on the granite counter.

KitchenAid's Brian Maynard
Luxury Is Personal Transformation

As brand director for integrated marketing at KitchenAid Home Appliances, a division of the Whirlpool Corporation, Brian Maynard has seen the evolution of the luxury market from conspicuous consumption to today's experiential paradigm. But now he believes luxury has taken another step toward personal transformation (or as I would phrase it, "self-actualization"). "For many years luxury was identified as expensive things, like big cars, big homes with massive things in them. Then luxury evolved to experiences and the experience of having and using. But today I see luxury as evolving to something even more personal. It is now about expert, insider knowledge," he says.

> "Luxury is about personal transformation and reinvention," says Brian Maynard, KitchenAid.

"True luxury today is being an expert at something. It's being a wine expert, a cooking expert, a golf expert, because you have the time and wherewithal to take the time to study, to learn, to travel, and to become an expert. Luxury is about personal transformation and reinvention," Maynard declares.

"In terms of our brand, KitchenAid is for people who love to cook, who have that expert knowledge and love to use it. If it has anything to do with a cooking passion, we provide a product for that. And while we have these wonderfully engineered products that perform expertly, we talk about the brand by communicating *why* someone would want convection cooking or a wine cellar with temperature zones. We communicate why the product is important to the consumer," he says.

Sponsoring "brand experiences" is a key component of KitchenAid's commitment to consumers' personal transformation through KitchenAid's products and usage. Maynard says:

> Some companies might call it public relations, but we term them *brand experiences*. We sponsor events like the Aspen Food and Wine Classic. We just held a KitchenAid Book and Cook event in Philadelphia where we bring in influencers like celebrity chefs, book authors, food writers, and kitchen designers so that people can come and meet the brand. We associate the brand with influencers like Jacque Pepin and Julia Child because these individuals represent that expert knowledge.

The KitchenAid brand has a unique historical perspective within the luxury market. Founded more than 80 years ago toward a decidedly down-home market, KitchenAid started with the masses, but today is marketing to the "classes." "Our first product was the stand mixer back in 1919; then in 1949 we introduced the dishwasher. At first the mixer was a fixture in the farmhouse kitchen. It was totally utilitarian, and mixers were bought at the grain elevator or hardware store. The story of our mixer in the luxury market is from mass to class since we were retro long before retro was cool," Maynard says.

Maynard concludes:

We look at our products as classics in terms of design and performance. Our products, while they are kept current with different colors and patterns, are really designed to last for a long time. We emphasize the experience of using them. For example, years ago we introduced our first line of coffeemakers. We designed the little door on the coffee-maker that holds the grounds to click when it was closed. The way people perceived the noise was like a precision piece of equipment closing and locking into place. It doesn't need that functionality to operate, but it was an experience that the people felt and perceived as important.

LUXURY MUST TRANSCEND THE ORDINARY TO BECOME EXTRAORDINARY

The key for marketers is to transcend the ordinary and create an extraordinary experience in and through their products. They must infuse the luxury products they make and the luxury brands they craft with the consumers' personal dimensions of luxury. That means linking their luxury products and brands with emotional values that epitomize and resonate with the hopes, wishes, and dreams of the consumers when they envision a luxury life-style. For example, it is not about the quality of leather seats in a car; rather, it's the way sitting on leather seats makes the consumer feel—wrapped in comfort and luxury, pampered, and made to feel special through the sensation of this luxurious experience. The importance of luxury branding, its myths and mysteries, is explored in much more depth in Chapter 10.

3

WHO IS A MEMBER OF THE LUXURY "CLASS"?

THE MISSING "P" OF MARKETING: PEOPLE

We all remember our first introduction to marketing back in college. Undoubtedly, the most indelible mark that our Marketing 101 class made was inculcating the Four Ps of marketing—product, price, promotion, and placement. The Four Ps gave structure to the course discussion and provided the theoretical underpinnings toward a deeper understanding of marketing strategies. The only problem with the Four Ps of marketing was they missed the most important P—the people.

All the marketing strategies that manipulate product, price, promotion, or placement count for nothing without the people to buy the product. It is so ironic, yet so understandable, why the most important P—the people side of the marketing equation— is ignored in introductory marketing classes. Getting your hands around product, price, promotion, and placement is fairly straightforward when compared with the contradictory, confusing, and confounding inner life of the consumer.

If the people side of marketing even comes up in your college course, it's usually in the context of demographics, the study of large populations and the facts and figures that describe those populations. But the sheer enormity of demographics and our human inability to get our heads around the numbers in order to grasp the implications of what those numbers really mean render demographics increasingly marginalized by the working marketer. As a result, demographics are left in the province of the "experts," who are called in occasionally to expound on macro demographic trends. In other words, demographics become irrelevant for addressing day-to-day marketing challenges. Can you picture 111 million U.S. households or the 288.4 million people that make up the U.S. population?

Yet if "demographics are destiny," nowhere is that truer than in the luxury market. From now until 2010, the number of affluent households and their influence will continue to grow. The rising tide of affluence is driven by the 76 million baby boomers who range in age from 40 to 58. This is the age of empty nesting, when consumers are earning the most money in their life but no longer have to stretch their paychecks across the demands of a growing family. Empowered with the most discretionary income ever in their life, empty nesters feel free to spend on those luxuries they denied themselves when their children were younger.

Because people are the fulcrum on which all luxury marketing hinges, this chapter focuses on their role in the luxury market. In Chapter 3 I examine the demographics that define and describe the affluents; in Chapter 4 I look at their shopping behavior as consumers of luxury. In Chapter 5 I explore the psychographics that describe the inner life of luxury consumers, their motivations and drives toward luxury that propel them into the marketplace. After the people, the rest of Part Two addresses the other Ps in the luxury marketing equation—product, price, promotion, and placement.

LUXURY CONSUMER DEMOGRAPHICS: CONSUMERS' GREATEST LUXURY SATISFACTION COMES FROM EXPERIENCES

Luxury is going experiential. When asked where they derive their greatest luxury satisfaction as luxury consumers from, the greatest share of luxury consumers (41 percent) said that experiential luxuries provide their greatest source of luxury satisfaction and happiness. By comparison, 31 percent of luxury consumers get their biggest kicks from home, followed by 28 percent who said that personal luxuries are their preferred luxury. The question was phrased: "When thinking about all your luxury purchases in the past year, which provides you with the most personal satisfaction and happiness?" They were then asked to distinguish between three types of luxury purchases:

1. Home luxuries, such as luxury art and antiques, electronics and/or photography equipment, fabrics, wall and window coverings, furniture and floor coverings, garden products, kitchenware and housewares, kitchen appliances, bath and building products, linens and tabletop products, and dinnerware (31 percent)

2. Personal luxuries, such as luxury automobiles; luxury beauty items, cosmetics, and fragrances; luxury apparel and fashion accessories; and luxury jewelry and watches (28 percent)

3. Experiential luxuries, such as luxury travel, fine dining and restaurants; entertainment (including theatre, shows, and concerts); and beauty, spa, and massage services as well as such home luxury services as housekeeping/housecleaning, home decorators, and landscape and gardening services (41 percent)

WHY DO EXPERIENCES PROVIDE
THE GREATEST LUXURY SATISFACTION?

New research coming out of academia provides insights into why experiences are the source of greater happiness and satisfaction. Leaf Van Boven and Thomas Gilovich wrote an article entitled "To Do or to Have? That is the question," published in the *Journal of Personality and Psychology* (vol. 85, no. 6, 2003). The subject of their research, stated simply, is this: "Do experiences make people happier than material possessions? . . . The thesis examined in this article is that happiness is advanced more by allocating discretionary income toward the acquisition of life experiences than toward the acquisition of material possessions. 'The good life,' in other words, may be better lived by doing things than by having things."

To prove the hypothesis, they conducted a series of experiments asking consumers to measure their happiness and enjoyment of either "spending money with the primary intention of acquiring a life experience—an event or series of events that you personally encounter or live through" [i.e., an experience] or "spending money with the primary intention of acquiring a material possession—a tangible object that you obtain and keep in your possession [i.e., a thing]." Note: In none of Van Boven and Gilovich's research was the concept of luxury introduced nor were their survey samples drawn from luxury consumers. However, the basic conclusions from their work clearly apply to the luxury market.

Although the researchers recognized that there may be some fuzziness between what is interpreted as an experiential purchase versus a material purchase—for example, is a flat-screen television or a car a possession or an experiential purchase?—their findings from three different experiments conducted to tease out various key factors in the consumer equation were that experiential purchases have it all over material goods in making the consumer happier. In one of their surveys conducted among a national sample of 1,263 consumers, nearly 60 percent (57 percent) said that their experiential purchases made them happier than their material purchases. Even more interesting, across every demographic segment (e.g., gender, employment, age, marital status, political affiliation, region, etc.) the experiential purchases get the vote as primary motivator of consumer happiness.

Even more significant, rising levels of household income corresponded to higher ratings for experiential happiness. In other words, the richer you are, the more likely you are to find greater satisfaction in life experiences. Authors Van Boven and Gilovich hypothesize that consumers are more likely to have "increasingly favorable interpretations over time" related to life experiences. For example, as we get farther away from a specific experience, such as a hike in the Alaska wilderness, we are more likely to remember the good feelings of accomplishment and the beauty of the experience than the blisters we got on our feet or the aches in our calf muscles. That's because we tend to focus on the more abstract, higher-level meanings of an experience in retrospect as opposed to the lower-level features that are more peripheral in nature (e.g., the hassles and inconveniences).

The authors conclude: "These results suggest that experiences have particular appeal when construed from the higher level of abstraction that comes with temporal distance, implying that experiences are more open to favorable interpretations over time." That means, simply, that we are free to relive our life experiences, embellishing them as we go to make them even more pleasant in retrospect. We selectively forget the annoyances and distractions (i.e., the low-level features) that take away from our favorable memories. We don't create these embellished fantasies for material possessions after we own them because "people adapt to material advances, requiring continued increases to achieve the same level of satisfaction." As a survey respondent is quoted as saying, "Material possessions, they sort of become part of the background; experiences just get better over time."

Another reason why experiences give more happiness is that experiences are more central to one's identity. They explain:

> A person's life is quite literally the sum of his or her experiences. The accumulation of rich experiences thus creates a richer life. The same cannot be said of material possessions. As important and gratifying as they sometimes are, they usually remain "out there," separate from the individual who attained them. Experiences, then, can provide greater hedonic [Note: this word is from the same root that gives us hedonism, which is sensualism, gratification, enjoyment, indulgence] value because they contribute so much more to the construction of the self than material possessions.

In other words, experiences are central to self-actualization and help people realize their ultimate identity and self-expression, as described by Abraham Maslow. This drive for self-actualization is even more pronounced among the more affluent, as Van Boven and Gilovich say: "We suspect that wealthier, more educated people may have been acculturated and educated in a system that emphasizes self-actualization, which might help them reap greater psychological benefits from experiences."

Finally, experiences provide greater happiness because relating to one another's experiences has greater social value. Social relationships can be enhanced by sharing stories about one's experiences, whereas the same cannot be said for stories related to your material possessions. It's one thing to talk about your trip to Paris and quite another to talk about all the stuff you bought while you were there. As the authors explain: "Because experiences are more likely to have a typical narrative structure with a beginning, middle and end, both listeners and storytellers may enjoy conversing about experiences more than about possessions. And because being 'materialistic' is viewed negatively whereas being 'experiential' is viewed positively, telling stories about experiences one has acquired may portray the storyteller in a more favorable light than telling stories about acquired possessions."

With some final caveats to the research, such as the fact that some material possessions may have greater sentimental value (e.g., a wedding ring, an heirloom) and so provide greater happiness and that the research does not state that things don't make people happy but only that experiences make them happier, Van Boven and Gilovich conclude: "Our research suggests that people will live happier lives if they invest in experiences more than material possessions. By the same token, communities will have happier citizens if they make available an abundance of experiences to be acquired. Both individuals and communities would thus do well to heed the slogan of the Center for the New American Dream, "More fun, less stuff!"

WHO QUALIFIES FOR THE LUXURY MARKET?

Confusion reigns when describing the luxury market, which is variously defined as the top 2 or 5 percent of earners or the upper 10 percent of household incomes. Others define affluence as high-net-worth consumers, such as those with $1 million in investible assets. The trading-up model based on mass-tige, or cheaper luxuries, presents a more fluid, less rigid description of the luxury market that defines luxury at the $50,000 income level, in recognition that middle-income consumers are selectively buying luxury.

The simple fact is that luxury living is within the means of more and more Americans. Throughout the whole history of the world, there has been a huge gulf between the way the rich folks lived and everybody else. That gulf is not nearly so wide today in 21st-century America. Even the poorest in our society enjoy a standard of living far exceeding basic subsistence, and they widely partake in many luxuries like air-conditioning, cell phones, DVD players, color TVs, designer sneakers, and more. Even though the affluent in American society can afford to buy lots more stuff and pay a higher ticket for their favorite experiences, they really don't live all that differently from the typical American in terms of food, shelter, health care, and education. Just think about the difference between the way the peasants lived in medieval England in dirt floor hovels with the farm animals providing supplemental heat to the open fire hearth and the lord of the manor on his country estate sleeping in feather beds with woolen blankets, with tapestries on the walls, glass-covered windows, fireplaces, and kitchens equipped with all of the latest medieval kitchen appliances. Today, the rich may have bigger and more nicely appointed homes, but the rich and poor both have all the same standard-of-living basics, like running hot water, toilets, showers, tubs, electricity, refrigerators, stoves, and indoor heat; and most have some form of cooling. So today's luxury market in very real terms includes everyone from the hip-hop teenager driving around town in a Cadillac SUV and wearing a Burberry jacket to the Fifth Avenue ladies who lunch.

As a researcher, I favor defining the luxury market behaviorally, or strictly by its participation in luxury. In other words, if they buy luxuries, then de facto they are luxury consumers. So if someone believes he or she is buying a luxury, whether that person makes $25,000 and is shopping at Wal-Mart or making $250,000 and shopping on Rodeo Drive, then he or she qualifies for membership in the market segment called "luxury consumer." But my natural egalitarian approach to defining the luxury market doesn't cut it with my luxury goods clients. They require far greater specificity in the demographics that quantify and qualify for membership in the luxury market. The simple fact is that just as the definition of what is luxury is highly subjective, the way we define the luxury market is also up for grabs.

In search of a reliable, defensible, and nonarbitrary definition of the luxury market, I turned to the government and the Bureau of Labor Statistics (BLS) consumer expenditure survey (CEX). The CEX is the definitive survey of consumer spending used by the government for making policy. The CEX breaks down the nation's

111 million households into quintiles, or fifths, based on household income. The start of the upper quintile, or top 20 percent of U.S. households included in the CEX survey, is about $75,000 for 2002. Using the CEX as our authority, therefore, I define the luxury market as those households with income within the upper quintile of the BLS model. The average income for upper-quintile households is $121,367.

Now to totally confuse you, when you take the BLS income model and overlay it on the household income data from the Bureau of the Census, we find that about 25 percent of total U.S. households have household incomes of $75,000 and above. The reason why the BLS top 20 percent translates to the census bureau's top 25 percent is simple: Not all households at all income levels are represented in the BLS consumer expenditure survey, so the difference is the share of non-reporting households. But why I strongly favor the BLS definition is that the CEX survey provides definitive data on what the affluent consumer households buy. If we used any other income cutoff of affluence, we wouldn't have detailed data of affluent household spending or be able to compare it to how other households at other income levels spend their money.

As shown in Figure 3.1, of the total 111 million U.S. households, approximately 27.9 million, or one-quarter, have an income of $75,000 and above. At $100,000 and above, there are approximately 15.7 million households, or 14 percent of households. And at the $150,000 level and above, there are 5.6 million households. To provide further refinement of the discrete segments in the luxury market, I further subdivide the market by income:

- **Near-affluents.** Households at the lowest range of the income scale—that is, household income (HHI) from $75,000 to $99,999—is an important segment for the future of the luxury market, as these near-affluents are likely to see their incomes rise in the coming years. These households may be more or less affluent depending on household composition

FIGURE 3.1
U.S. Households by Income

U.S. HOUSEHOLDS BY INCOME (IN THOUSANDS)	2002	% SOM
$49,999 or less	63,057	57%
$50k to $74,999	20,315	18
$75k to $99,999 (Near-Affluents)	12,230	11
$100,000 to $149,999 (Affluents)	10,073	9
$150,000 to $199,999 (Super-Affluents)	2,977	3
$200,000 to $249,999 (Super-Affluents)	1,154	1
$250,000 and above (Super-Affluents)	1,472	1
Total	111,278	100%

Source: U.S. Bureau of the Census

and in what part of the country they live. Also, this segment will reach luxury in specific product and experiential categories; a total of 12.2 million households fall within this range.

- **Affluents.** Those households with incomes of $100,000 to $149,999; 10.1 million households.
- **Super-affluents.** Households with incomes of $150,000 and above are super-affluents; 5.6 million households.

THE AFFLUENTS ARE A LOT ALIKE DEMOGRAPHICALLY

Demographically, the top-income households share many characteristics, one of the more notable being their origin in the decidedly middle class. In the latest Unity Marketing luxury-tracking study, we asked over 1,000 affluent luxury consumers surveyed to describe the financial status of their family of origin. Today's affluents are living the American dream with 90 percent coming from middle-class roots, as shown in Figure 3.2.

The affluents exhibit far less demographic diversity than is exhibited in any of the lower-income segments of the population. Their key demographic characteristics include the following:

FIGURE 3.2

Financial Status of Family of Origin

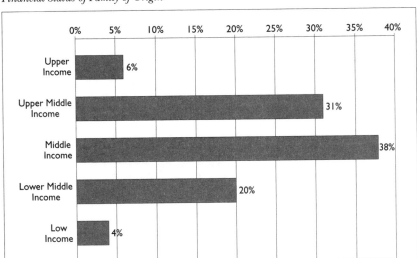

- **Larger households.** The typical affluent household has 3.2 members, as compared with the total population of 2.5. Married couples predominate at the higher-income level.
- **More workers in household.** The affluent household has 2.1 earners, as compared with 1.4 earners in the typical household.
- **Own more cars.** They own 2.9 vehicles, as compared with 2.0 for the typical household.
- **Nearly all own homes.** Ninety percent of affluents own a home, as compared with two-thirds of typical households.
- **Mostly white.** African-American households make up only 6 percent of the affluent households, as compared with 12 percent of the total.
- **Higher education levels.** A key demographic characteristic of the affluent is higher education. The heads of some 80 percent of affluent households have some or more college attainment compared with 56 percent of typical households.

- **Middle-aged.** Most distinctive, the affluent are members of the baby boom generation. In 2002, the average income, at $74,934, is highest among households aged 45 to 54. This income peak is flanked by age groups above and below. The 35- to 44-year-old households have an average income of $68,310; the average income of the 55 to 64 households is $64,118.

FUTURE VISION OF LUXURY—RISING TIDE OF AFFLUENCE: BOOMERS KEY TO GROWTH THROUGH 2010

Taking aim at the rising tide of affluence, The Conference Board recently completed a study of the affluent market with projections for its growth and changes in it through the year 2010. See Figure 3.3 for household growth in general between 2002 and as projected through 2010. Lynn Franco, director of The Confer-

FIGURE 3.3
Household Growth, 2002–2010

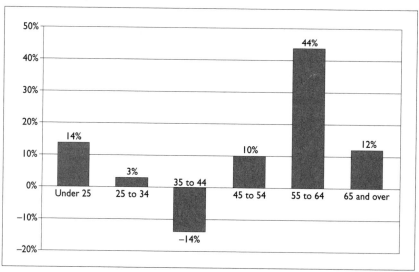

Source: Census Bureau and The Conference Board

ence Board Consumer Research Center, reports that "over the past 20 years, America's middle- and lower-income classes have slowly been working their way into the ranks of the well-to-do. As the country steadily moves toward a society with more top-heavy incomes, average household earnings will top $63,500 in 2010, up from about $50,000 in 1990."

Although it focused on the income segment of $100,000 and above as its definition of the affluent market, The Conference Board's conclusions are definitive:

> With the 78 million aging Baby Boomers expanding the peak earning years beyond the traditional 35–54 period, the result will be a larger and more mature affluent market. The high number of well-educated boomers is a major reason behind the growth of affluent households. In fact, older affluent boomer households—headed by those aged 55–64—are expected to increase by more than 60 percent over the next several years. By 2010, this older segment will top 4.2 million, up from less than 2.7 million today. Over the same period, their spending power will increase from $455 billion to more than $750 billion.

The boomers are either already in, or rapidly approaching, the empty nest life stage, when consumers are earning at the peak of their lifetime but no longer have to stretch their paychecks across the demands of a growing family. This frees up discretionary spending for luxuries that they might have denied themselves when their children were younger. It also means mature couples have more free time to spend outside the home connecting in their social sphere. These boomers will also expand the peak earning years beyond the traditional 35-to-54 period as they delay retirement en masse and continue to contribute as workers in the increasingly information- and knowledge-oriented economy.

But the prospects for luxury marketers are also clear: Better get it while it's hot, because the Generation X population's smaller size will leave a growth gap in the affluent market. The Conference Board thus predicts: "The graying of the boomers will leave a void in the 35–44 age market that members of . . . Generation X will not be able to fill completely. By the end of this decade, Generation X will have declined in relative importance and account for less than a quarter of the affluent, down from 28 percent in 2002."

Though after the year 2015, the Board expects the millennial generation (i.e., the babies of the baby boomers born from 1977 to 1994 and numbering about 72 million, nearly as many as in the baby boom generation) to be poised to make an impact on the luxury market. Of the millennials, The Conference Board says they "could very well produce another surge in affluence."

Remarking in its study on the affluent's distinctive spending patterns, The Conference Board Report finds affluent households spent

- four times the national average for housekeeping services, care for the elderly, catered affairs, and accounting fees;
- more than three-and-one-half times the average household's budget on vacation homes, jewelry, and gardening and lawn care services; and
- over two-and-one-half times the norm for recreational vehicles and new cars.

It predicts that through 2010, "the growing number of affluent, the graying of the population, and the increase in empty-nesting households combine to produce a favorable outlook for the luxury, travel, entertainment, household furnishings, and housing industries."

AFFLUENTS MAKE MORE, SPEND MORE, AND SAVE MORE

Although the affluent households have after-tax income nearly 2.5 times the typical household ($113,044, as compared with $46,934, according to the BLS CEX survey of 2002), their spending is less than twice that of the average ($79,199 versus $40,677); they therefore have more money left over for saving and investing. In effect, they have 0.5 times the nation's average income left over to invest and save. The luxury consumers are highly motivated to protect and preserve their luxury standard of living. What they don't spend, they save and invest.

In general, the spending gap between the typical American household and the most affluent hovers around 2.0 times in most categories of spending—that is, the highest-income households spend roughly twice as much as the typical household in most budget items tracked. The spending gap is slightly lower in the category of health care and insurance, where the most affluent spend only 1.4 times the average of the typical household. Food, where the affluents spend 1.7 times more, transportation (1.7 times more), and personal care (1.8 times more) are also categories where the spending gap is less.

On the other hand, the affluents spend 3.0 times as much on personal insurance and pensions, including Social Security, than the typical American household. With more to protect, they tend to spend more money on insurance that provides security for their standard of living. They also spend more on education (2.3 times as much), household furnishings (2.2 times), the category that includes textiles, furniture, floor coverings, appliances, housewares, and other decorative spending for the home, and entertainment and recreation (2.2 times the average). See Figure 3.4.

LUXURY CONSUMERS FEEL FAR BETTER OFF FINANCIALLY NOW THAN THEY DID IN 2002, BUT THEIR SPENDING LAGS THEIR CONFIDENCE

Consumer confidence plays an important role in giving consumers permission to buy luxuries. At the end of 2003, the luxury consumers surveyed said they felt considerably better off finan-

FIGURE 3.4
Annual Expenditures, 2002

AVERAGE ANNUAL EXPENDITURE, 2002	TYPICAL HOUSEHOLD	HIGHEST 20%	DIFFERENCE
Income after Taxes	$46,934	$113,044	2.4
Avg. Total Expenditure	40,677	79,199	1.9
Food	5,375	9,083	1.7
Food Away from Home	2,276	4,554	2.0
Housing	13,283	24,541	1.9
Shelter	7,829	14,690	1.9
Household Furnishings	1,518	3,484	2.3
Apparel & Services	1,749	3,617	2.1
Transportation	7,759	13,769	1.8
Health Care & Insurance	2,350	3,262	1.4
Entertainment	2,079	4,608	2.2
Personal Care	526	947	1.8
Reading	139	271	2.0
Education	752	1,729	2.3
Personal Insurance and Pensions	3,899	11,967	3.1
Other	2,389	4,589	1.9

Source: BLS

cially than they did in 2002. Perhaps owing to the 2003 year-end rise in their stock portfolios, some 43 percent of luxury consumers said they felt better off financially in 2003. An equal percentage, 43 percent, said they felt equal to their financial position in 2002, and only 14 percent said they feel less well off.

But renewed feelings of luxury consumer confidence are not translating into increased spending on luxuries. Although a near majority of luxury consumers felt better off financially at the end of 2003 than they did the previous year, they are not increasing their spending commensurate with their renewed feelings of confidence. Only 30 percent of luxury consumers said they spent more on luxury in 2003 compared with the previous year; 21 percent said they spent less than the year before.

There is a 15 percentage point gap between those who feel better off financially and those who are translating that better financial feeling into more spending on luxuries.

The profile of the luxury consumer that emerges is one of caution. These are consumers who give careful consideration to their spending. Even though these consumers could spend more money buying luxuries, they are not about to put their lifestyle at risk. Rather than spend it all, they are more likely to spend a little on luxuries they desire and save or invest the rest. As opposed to viewing the luxury consumer as a spendthrift, marketers need to see them as they are: cautious, risk adverse, and protective of their financial resources. They know the value of a dollar and clearly are predisposed to conserve their resources rather than spend them too freely.

> As opposed to viewing the luxury consumer as a spendthrift, marketers need to see them as they are: cautious, risk adverse, and protective of their financial resources.

4

LUXURY CONSUMERS— THE LUXURIES THEY BUY, HOW MUCH THEY SPEND, AND WHY THEY BUY

SHIFTS AND TURNS IN LUXURY CONSUMER PURCHASE BEHAVIOR

Through annual luxury consumer behavior surveys, as well as through quarterly luxury-tracking studies that enable luxury marketers to keep their fingers on the pulse of the luxury consumer market, Unity Marketing has compiled a database of key research findings about luxury consumers— what they buy, where they shop, how much they spend, and why they buy. In this chapter I summarize major findings from Unity's latest luxury consumer surveys about what luxuries consumers buy and why they buy them.

LIFESTYLE CHANGES TRIGGER
LUXURY SPENDING

Specific life stage or lifestyle changes predispose luxury consumers to buy more luxury. For example, redecorating one's home
is an important trigger for the purchase of luxury home products.
As shown in Figure 4.1, the top lifestyle changes that impacted
luxury consumers in the past two years are these:

- **Redecorating home.** About half of the luxury consumers
  have redecorated their home in the past two years, whereas
  some 44 percent of luxury consumers expect to redecorate

FIGURE 4.1

Luxury Purchase Triggers

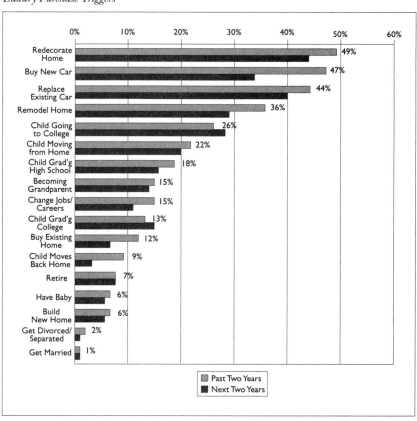

their home in the next two years. That means nearly all luxury consumers are involved in some aspect of a home decorating project, either recently completed or in the planning phase.

- **Buying new car.** This was a lifestyle change for 47 percent of luxury consumers. Only about one-third expect to buy a new car in the coming two years.
- **Replacing existing car.** Some 44 percent of luxury consumers surveyed said they replaced an existing car in the past two years; 40 percent expected to replace an existing car in the coming two years. In other words, the luxury consumers are more likely to be buying a car to replace an older model rather than adding a new vehicle to the household's collection.
- **Remodeling home.** Just over one-third of the households (36 percent) remodeled their home in the past two years. Remodeling, being a major home project involving hammers, nails, and saws as opposed to redecorating (which is more about paint and paint brushes), usually gives rise to redecorating as well. Some 29 percent expect to remodel their home in the coming two years.
- **Child going off to college.** Sending a child off to college is usually the "official" start of the empty nest lifestage. Although college-aged kids are still tied to the nest for subsistence, they usually are out of the house, which gives parents newfound feelings of freedom to do things they might not have done when the kids were at home. About one-fourth of the luxury consumers reported this as a life-changing event in the past two years, with 28 percent expecting it to occur over the next two years.

Except for buying a new car, about an equal percentage of luxury consumers expect various life stage or lifestyle changes to occur in the next two years. From these data we can assume that these triggers of luxury purchases tend to occur at an equal level year in

In essence, the luxury market is renewing and reinventing itself year after year as it undergoes predictable life stage and lifestyle changes.

and year out except for buying a new car, which, based on this survey, would seem to occur in a cycle longer than every two to four years. In essence, then, the luxury market is renewing and reinventing itself year after year as it undergoes predictable life stage and lifestyle changes.

THE PRODUCT PERSPECTIVE OF LUXURY

This chapter provides top-line findings about luxury consumer purchases in three major product categories. More detailed discussion of these luxury product categories are contained in Chapter 6: Luxury Home Products; Chapter 7: Personal Luxury Products; and Chapter 8: Luxury Services and Experiences.

The three major product categories described in this chapter are:

1. **Home luxuries.** Art and antiques; electronics and photography equipment; fabrics, wall and window converings, furniture, and floor coverings; garden, lawn, and patio products; kitchenware, cookware, and kitchen appliances; bath and building products; linens and bedding; and tabletop products, dinnerware, and stemware. (Details on home luxuries are contained in Chapter 6.)
2. **Personal luxuries.** Luxury automobiles; beauty, cosmetic, and fragrance products; luxury apparel and fashion accessories; and jewelry and/or watches.
3. **Experiential luxuries.** Experiences such as luxury travel, fine dining, and such entertainment as theatre; luxury services, such as spas, beauty treatments, and/or cosmetic surgery; housekeeping and house cleaning; gardening and landscaping services; and home decorators.

In terms of overall purchase incidence—that is, the percentage of households making any home luxury purchase in the past year—82 percent of luxury consumers with incomes of $75,000

FIGURE 4.2

The Frequency of Home, Personal, and Experiential Luxury Purchasing, 2002 and 2003

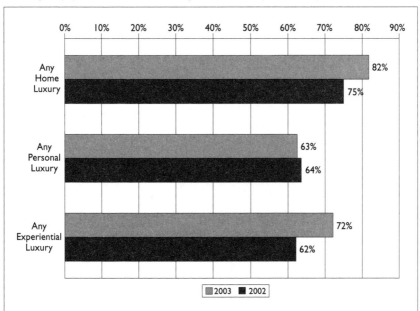

and above purchased home luxuries in 2003, up from 75 percent in 2002. See Figure 4.2. Purchase incidence of personal luxuries was flat from 2002 to 2003 at just under two-thirds of households. Experiential luxuries got the biggest boost in purchase incidence in 2003, rising from 62 percent to 72 percent of all luxury households. By comparison, experiential luxuries are the fastest growing category of luxury, rising from a purchase incidence of 62 percent in 2002 to 72 percent in 2003.

LUXURY ELECTRONICS AND EXPERIENTIAL LUXURIES SHOW BIGGEST PURCHASE GROWTH

Luxury electronics and photography equipment and experiential luxuries, including luxury travel, dining, and entertainment, were the big winners in increased purchase incidence in the 2003 survey as compared with the previous year. See Figure 4.3.

FIGURE 4.3

The Frequency of Purchases of Specific Luxury Items and Services, 2002 and 2003

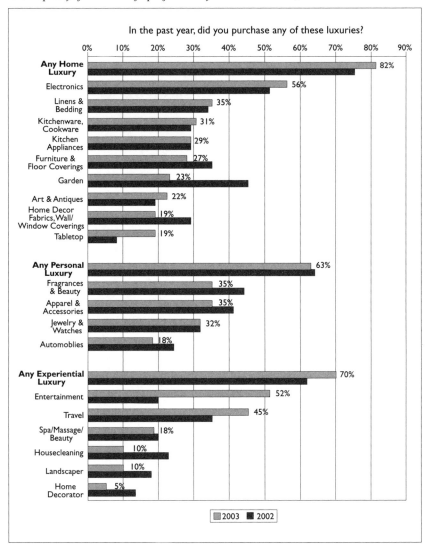

For the second year in a row, luxury electronics and photography equipment are the most purchased luxury product among luxury consumers. With so many new technology options, such as plasma televisions still priced out of reach of the mass-market consumer, personal data assistants with expanded capabilities, home entertainment systems, digital photography, and all the rest, luxury consumers are still propelled in buying mode in this category. Purchase incidence of luxury electronics rose from 51 percent in 2002 to 56 percent in 2003. For the past two consecutive years, luxury electronics has been the number one most purchased luxury.

Purchase incidence of luxury dining and entertainment, defined as "dining and entertainment including restaurants, cultural events, theatre, and so on," more than doubled in 2003 to reach 52 percent. In the previous year, the category of fine dining was not included in the description, which accounts for some of the growth in purchase incidence. However, indications are strong that luxury consumers are bringing new energy to fine dining.

Travel, defined as hotels, luxury transportation, and the like, picked up in 2003 too, rising to a 45 percent purchase incidence among luxury consumers in 2003. This increase is likely due to renewed confidence in travel safety after travel took a hit in the post 9/11 period. However, the present unsettled world situation remains a damper on international travel, keeping luxury consumers closer to home and feeling more protected in their adventures.

LESS EMPHASIS ON LUXURY HOME DECOR IN 2003

While luxury consumers continued to direct their purchase spending to home entertainment and electronics, home decorating at the luxury level took a hit. Purchase incidence for home luxury—including gardens, furniture and floor coverings, decorating fabrics, wall coverings, and window decorations—all dropped in 2003. This indicates that for the luxury consumers, the cocooning and nesting trend is waning in favor of more spending directed outside the home toward social pursuits.

The biggest decline in home purchasing was for luxury garden and garden products (such as lawn furniture, patio accessories, plants, grills, etc.), which dropped from the second most widely purchased luxury product in the previous year to a purchase incidence of 23 percent. The timing of the survey may be one of the primary reasons for the decline. The 2002 survey was conducted in August, a prime time for garden expenditures, whereas the 2003 survey was conducted one week after Thanksgiving in December. Although it is very likely that luxury garden was a declining category in 2003, it may not have dropped as much as this survey indicates simply as a result of the particular time the survey was fielded.

FUTURE VISION OF LUXURY—CONNECTING IS REPLACING COCOONING AS PRIME CONSUMER TREND

One of the most significant changes on the horizon for luxury goods marketers, especially those that sell home goods, is the end of the cocooning trend that has dominated our consumer culture for the past 20 years. The cocooning, or nesting, trend (as it is variously called) was identified in the mid-1980s by trend tracker Faith Popcorn to describe how people were turning their focus inward to hearth and home. The trend was largely driven by demographics, because during that period the baby boomers were in the cocooning phase of life, the period when they were raising young children, and practical necessity kept them grounded at home. So they turned their focus toward home decorating and home entertainment.

It goes without saying that the cocooning trend was very good for home marketers and retailers. But since 1998, the share of household expenditures accounted for by home furnishings, which includes household textiles, furniture, floor coverings, major and small appliances, and other miscellaneous household equipment and decorative accessories, has been in decline. In 1998, home furnishings expenditures accounted for 4.5 percent of the average

FIGURE 4.4

Home Furnishings Expenditures, 1996–2002

HOME FURNISHINGS EXPENDITURES	AVG. EXP.	% SPENDING	AVG. TOTAL HOUSEHOLD EXPENDITURES
2002	$1,518	3.7	$40,677
2000	1,652	4.1	40,238
1998	1,601	4.5	35,535
1996	1,350	4.0	33,797

Source: Bureau of Labor Statistics, Consumer Expenditure Survey

household's budget, as shown in Figure 4.4, whereas in 2002 it made up only 3.7 percent of household spending. Even in real dollars, spending dropped from $1,652 on average in 1998 to $1,518 in 2002.

As cocooning wanes, consumers are emerging like butterflies from their cocoons, driven by a passion to reconnect with the external world. This new connectedness is all about linking up with the world through the media, travel, and electronic networks. It's about becoming a part of something bigger than one's own narrowly defined inner landscape. In other words, luxury cocooners are disconnected; today's luxury consumers are connected.

What does the end of the cocooning trend mean for manufacturers and marketers of home goods, both luxury and mass? What it doesn't mean is the end of consumer spending on the home. All signs point to the continued interest, desire, and passion for making the home a wonderful and beautiful place to be. Home buying and consumer spending on home goods and services will continue to grow. But the end of cocooning does mean that home companies and retailers can no longer expect nesting to be the sole driver for consumers to buy their brand and their products or to shop in their stores.

In the realm of purely decorative home accents, it is going to become harder and harder for marketers to convince consumers to invite these decorative accents into their home. Rather, consumers are looking for more functionality, more meaning and purpose, more style, more specialness, more uniqueness—more of these features in their homes. The simple fact is the home business will no longer be as easy as it was.

But as the luxury consumers emerge from their cocoons, they will look for new products and new experiences on which they can spend their money. With the return of formal business dress, we expect more luxury consumer spending on fashion and accessories and jewelry and watches. As consumers turn their attention to the external environment, spending on the exterior of their home—especially the garden, landscaping, patio, and pool—will increase. Front porches, side porches, and wraparound porches will become key selling features in the housing market.

Consumers are empowered with a new design sensibility. Today's luxury consumers are looking for ways to scale down, throw out, and otherwise eliminate clutter from their home. Influenced by the eastern *feng shui* movement and the growing popularity of home-organizing shows like HGTV's *Mission: Organization* and TLC's *Clean Sweep,* people are embracing the idea of clearing away the clutter they accumulated during their cocooning phase as a way to regain control over their life and their surroundings.

Even the popular home-decorating shows on the cable networks, like TLC's *While You Were Out* or *Trading Spaces,* are not presenting a materialistic cocooning approach to home decor. Rather, they reflect a new do-it-yourself approach to home decorating that is about doing more with less, not about gathering more stuff, collecting more things, or filling up the empty spaces. Architect Sarah Susanka's sleeper best-seller *The Not-So-Big House* (Taunton Press, 1998) has given rise to an entire franchise of books and building plans based on the original concept of living big in smaller spaces.

> Today's luxury consumers are looking for ways to scale down, throw out, and otherwise eliminate clutter from their home.

The new Time Inc. magazine *Real Simple* has become the guidebook for the anticlutter movement, as it perfectly expresses the experiential dimension of luxury. *Real Simple* exemplifies a new point of view in the consumer culture that emphasizes getting rid of the excess baggage we have accumulated, organizing it, and ultimately simplifying one's life. Its less-is-more philosophy strives for a new equilibrium in all aspects of its readers' life.

> The new connecting trend also means that ideas, as well as people, products, and services, move faster and faster.

The subtitle, "life/home/body/soul" encompasses its editorial focus to help readers do more with less in order to achieve the ultimate goal: enriching the soul. But it is hardly antimaterialistic in outlook, as many luxury and near-luxury advertisers throng to the book. *Real Simple* presents information, answers, and solutions to readers so they will "spend less time doing the things you *have* to do and more time doing what you *want* to do."

The new connecting trend also means that ideas, as well as people, products, and services, move faster and faster. Therefore, luxury marketers must develop corporate cultures that are predisposed for action. They must be able to instantly spot shifts, turns, and leaps within the luxury markets they serve. They must respond immediately to new needs, new desires, new opportunities with lightning speed and accurate targeting.

As connecting takes hold, consumers will demand that their shopping experiences support them by more than simply satisfying their acquisition and consumption needs. They will look for their shopping centers and malls to become centers for connecting, linking up, and getting in touch with like-minded people. Today, Barnes & Noble and Starbucks are doing this on a smaller, more narrowly focused scale, but the retail experience is ready for a complete overhaul, as retailers begin to realize the tremendous potential of becoming more than purveyors of goods but places where people want to go to socialize and connect.

On the luxury product horizon, garden and gardening products are going to continue to grow as consumers emerge from their cocoons and venture into the external world. After all, they have spent the past 20 years feathering their indoor nests, so the next target of their decorating drives will be expressed in the garden. The garden boom will be expressed through the acquisition of finer garden decor, plants, decorative items, and the like; the installation of major garden improvements, such as pools, hot tubs, walls, walks, ponds, and even the building of outdoor kitchens; upgrading garden tools and equipment, including new lawn mowers, grills, and other outdoor cooking equipment; and the purchase of new animals, fish, birds, and even pest-eating insects to populate new outside rooms.

Automobiles will continue to be one of the luxury consumers' favorite luxurious necessities. Manufacturers very smartly are continuing to broaden the luxury market with new lower-priced, but still luxurious, cars, luxury SUVs, and even luxury pickup trucks to expand the total market. And luxury automobiles will be defined in new ways as the very affordably priced hybrid vehicles from Toyota and Honda become the new status symbol for the environmentally conscious consumer.

More spending on luxury travel and entertainment is also in the forecast. The demand for adventure travel will grow as consumers seek to create experiences as they venture into remote regions of the world. New demand for personal and home services will flourish as these services (like housecleaning, lawn care, and travel planning) free the luxury consumers from mundane, everyday tasks so they have more time to spend in society. The range of ways service providers can enhance the quality of the life for luxury consumers by giving them more time to devote to their passions is endless and bodes well for imaginative service providers who think beyond the obvious.

At the same time that consumers are spending less money on major furniture pieces and decorative accessories, they are hungry for more and better tools, equipment, and accessories to enhance

> New demand for personal services will flourish as these services (like housecleaning, lawn care, and travel planning) free the luxury consumers from mundane, everyday tasks so they have more time to spend in society.

their living experiences in the home. For example, gourmet cooking and dining is an experience that more and more Americans desire to pursue in their home kitchens. So they spend $50,000 or $100,000 remodeling their kitchens with all new gourmet appliances, countertops, and cabinets. After that, what is an extra $5,000 or so added to the budget to replace the pots and pans, coffee maker, food processor, and everyday tableware to complete a full 360° inside and outside redo of the whole kitchen? As a result, luxury consumers are willing to buy all kinds of things they don't strictly need but that will enhance the cooking and dining experience. This characterizes consumer psychology for so many discretionary and luxury products. That is, consumers buy things, whether it is a new All-Clad sauté pan, Reidel wine glasses, Viking stove, or Waterford candlestick, to achieve a feeling, an experience. Therefore, the thing that people buy becomes the means to an end, and the end is a feeling.

P *e r s o n a l* **P** *e r s p e c t i v e   o n* **L** *u x u r y*

Real Simple Magazine's Robin Domeniconi
Luxury Is Simplicity: The New Mantra for Luxury Living

The concept behind *Real Simple* magazine is "about simplifying your life." The goal for its readers is to help them "lead a balanced, fulfilling life no matter what they're juggling. Whether working or working out, tending to children or decorating a home, these women find the information and inspiration they need to achieve their dreams in *Real Simple*." Although it's a title that is often displayed along with the "shelter" books on the magazine racks, Robin Domeniconi, president and publisher of *Real Simple*, explains it is far more than just another home title. "It's a lifestyle book. It covers every aspect of a woman's busy life."

"Lifestyle is built on personal satisfaction. It's not about saving up for status items or impressing your friends," says Robin Domeniconi, *Real Simple* magazine.

With regular features devoted to beauty, home, style, body, food, and organization, *Real Simple* helps its readers achieve a lifestyle that is at once easier and better. "Lifestyle is built on personal satisfaction. It's not about saving up for status items or impressing your friends. *Real Simple* is a way of life, and it is all about personal satisfaction—not about perfection. We are all about living life and finding the time to do the things [we] want to do. Anything that offers an experience or delivers a strong emotional connection makes you feel great. It's what our readers are all about. But the magazine and the lifestyle that our readers live is all personal. Mine may be totally different than yours. But this magazine offers solutions for all mindsets."

Firmly grounded in reality, *Real Simple* presents a philosophy of life that is also profound. According to Domeniconi:

> We give our readers practical solutions to make their lives easier and better. We give people solutions so they have more time to do what they really want to. Time is the ultimate luxury. We could have a story on the Swiffer mop or salad-in-a-bag, because these are not just products anymore. People are buying solutions to their problems and they are willing to pay a lot of money for that. Any kind of product that offers to give you back time is going to do really well.

Unlike other titles that present an idealized, perfected view of life (think *Architectural Digest* or Martha's books), *Real Simple* presents the practical, with tips and solutions for how to do it better, not how to do it perfectly. With its substance-over-style approach, *Real Simple* devoted its May 2004 cover to a display of household cleaning products. Domeniconi explains:

We have broken every rule. Our readers have the highest average income of any other women's consumer magazine and on our May 2004 cover we are showing cleaning products. We're selling over 400,000 copies on the newsstand every month, and we are doing it in a way that has broken every rule. The editorial architecture makes it easy for you to pull out this information in a very calming, beautiful way and, ultimately, gives you time to do what you want to do.

For the future, Domeniconi sees the role of *Real Simple* as continuing to help its readers simplify and streamline their life:

Cocooning was going back to your place to get away from it all. Today we're decluttering and we're cleaning, but we also want to connect with friends and family. The concept behind *Real Simple* was as relevant 20 years ago as it will be 20 years down the line. We stay relevant by talking to our readers—finding out the things in their lives that they want to simplify. And everyone on our staff *is* the *Real Simple* reader—we know the complexities we feel in our daily lives are a problem for women across the country.

Our job is to make it all simple, which is actually very complex. That is the luxury that *Real Simple* offers. Our readers are getting an edited-down version of all this work that we've gone and done. We edit their lives for them. We cull it all down to the essentials.

The new luxury consumer, according to Domeniconi, is not interested in luxury for luxury's sake but because luxury is simply part of her life:

The new luxury consumer is better educated, has a lot of money, and is very discerning and goes beyond just the fluff. [She demands] a functional rationale to support [her] emotional luxury purchase. [She] will spend $400 on that Dyson vacuum cleaner because, not only is it beautiful and [she falls] in love with it, but also because it offers a functionality of having a retractable hose and being bagless. The [new luxury consumers] reason for purchasing luxury is that higher brands give the highest quality and value.

LUXURY CONSUMERS STILL IMPROVING THEIR DINING AND COOKING EXPERIENCES

Even though purchases of home furnishings dropped slighty in the past year, luxury home expenditures for the kitchen, including cookware and housewares; kitchen appliances; and tabletop items, dinnerware, flatware, and other items for dining and entertainment, were about even or rose in 2003. Not all home expenditures are equal, as spending on upgrading kitchen appliances is viewed as an investment, not an expense; and because the kitchen is an investment, it justifies more generous spending on all things related to it and the dining room, including dinnerware on which to serve the gourmet meals whipped up in the new kitchen.

Personal Perspective on Luxury

Martin's Herend Imports' Lise Behe
Luxury Is Handcrafted Perfection

With a heritage dating back nearly 200 years, Herend Porcelain, located in the village of Herend, Hungary, started out as a manufactory of reproduction Chinese porcelain. At first offering custom-made replacements for antique Chinese porcelain to 19th-century buyers, Herend expanded to introduce its own dinnerware styles, as well as figurines with their trademark handpainted fishnet design favored by the company's most famous collector, the late Princess Diana. The brand gained international attention when, in 1860, Queen Victoria ordered a set of dinnerware at the World Exposition. The pattern was re-named "Queen Victoria" in her honor and was used at Windsor Castle. Today, that pattern is a Herend classic and consistently ranks among its top two designs in the U.S. market. Representing Herend Porcelain in the states is Martin's Herend Imports, the brand's exclusive distributor since the 1950s.

In explaining what makes Herend Porcelain special today, the company's Director of Marketing Lisa Behe says that although the world of porcelain manufacturing advanced from the industry's 18th- and 19th-century roots, Herend never embraced modern manufacturing techniques. What some might view as an anachronism, others see as the epitome of luxury: perfectly handcrafted porcelain. As Behe explains:

> Today, some things are called "handmade" because some-one's hand touched it. But not Herend. This is a factory where the people are doing everything. It's not created on a big assembly line with machines doing everything. If we use molds for an item, it's a hand process with someone filling the mold and checking it for consistency. All the finishing is done by hand. If there is piercing or flowers or leaves to be applied, that is all handmade. And all the painting is done by hand, not with decals. So when you look at a piece of Herend, you might notice one has a lit-tle more brush stroke than another. That's not a flaw; it's uniqueness. Every piece is a unique art object.

The commitment to quality carries over into the materials the company uses. The clay comes from the Limoges area of France, which is the purest and highest quality. "Ours is hard-paste porcelain. It is a very strong and durable substance made with kaolin. With a hard-paste porcelain such as Herend's, you can literally stand on a tea cup and it won't break. It's the most durable of ceramics," Behe says.

The company goes to great pains to eliminate any flaws or imperfections from its final pieces through relentless inspections and quality control checks. "Herend never sells any irregulars or seconds. They have a very stringent quality control process at each step, so after they make the shapes, it is inspected; when it's fired, it is inspected; when it's painted, it is inspected. And at any point the people at Herend can and will say, 'This isn't good enough,' and pull it out of production," Behe says.

So how much does such handcrafted perfection cost? Not as much as one would imagine, with the company's smallest bunny figurine, bunnies being their most popular animal overall, costing under $40 for a miniature one inch high. But the range extends to $1,130 for their largest bunny in the fishnet pattern. "Our dinnerware goes from $165 to $2,000 per place setting with the Queen Victoria pattern under $500 for a five-piece place setting. Even though we are always designing new patterns, our designs are timeless," Behe says.

The essential brand value for Herend, as Behe describes it, is this: "Everything is made by hand to the absolutely highest-quality standards. It's as near perfect as a handmade thing can be." That is why Herend is an aspirational brand for many younger and older customers who want to add this exquisite quality to their home. But its reputation also adds value to a Herend gift in the $60 to $120 price point. Behe concludes, "We are committed to developing more products in the gift price ranges so that our retailers, many of whom are specialty gift and

> "Everything is made by hand to the absolutely highest-quality standards. It's as near perfect as a handmade thing can be," says Lisa Behe, Martin's Herend Imports.

tabletop stores, can offer their customers a wonderful Herend piece for $100 that is the absolutely finest porcelain in the world."

Jewelry and Watches Are Strong Personal Luxury Performers in 2003

Although purchase incidence of both luxury apparel and accessories and luxury fragrances and beauty products dropped in 2003, purchase incidence of jewelry and watches was about even with purchase incidence in 2002. Purchases of luxury automobiles also dropped in 2003, from 24 percent in 2002 to 18 percent in 2003.

Part of the downward shift in purchase incidence of personal luxuries, notably apparel, fashion accessories, and beauty and fragrance products is due to a shift in Unity's survey sample in the 2003 sales year. In the latest year, our aim was to increase luxury male consumer participation, so our 2003 sample is 49 percent male and 51 percent female, as compared with the 2002 survey in which women made up 68 percent of the sample and men only 32 percent. Because luxury apparel, accessories, and beauty and fragrance products are female-skewing categories, their inclusion is the main factor behind an apparent drop in purchase incidence of personal luxuries.

EXPERIENTIAL LUXURIES GET A BOOST IN 2003

The luxury consumers were more active in purchasing experiential luxuries in 2003, with purchase incidence of luxury entertainment and fine dining more than doubling to reach 52 percent and luxury travel up from 35 percent in 2002 to 45 percent. Spa, beauty, and massage and other cosmetic treatments remained about the same, with a purchase incidence of roughly one-fifth of luxury consumers. In 2003, luxury consumers purchased fewer house cleaning, landscaping, and decorating services than were reported in 2002.

P *e r s o n a l* **P** *e r s p e c t i v e   o n* **L** *u x u r y*

Starwood's Douglas McKenzie
Luxury Is Delivering an Experience That
Transcends Ordinary Luxury Hotel Services

Starwood's luxury group, consisting of 77 hotels in 26 countries, strives to deliver the highest levels of luxury to customers, while still delivering outstanding value for guests. Starwood's luxury hotel brands include the Gritti Palace in Venice, the Phoenician in Scottsdale, Arizona, Bora Bora Nui Resort in French Polynesia, and the St. Regis in New York; the brands target the traveler with an income of $250,000 and beyond. With typical prices ranging from $800 to $1,000 per night, the Starwood luxury hotels take ordinary, everyday luxury to new heights. Douglas McKenzie, vice president of sales and marketing, explains: "We focus on how our clients experience luxury in our hotels. It goes way beyond satisfaction to a personal experience. Part of that experience is imparting a feeling of exclusivity. Our guests want to feel like the one and only guest we are dealing with. They expect everything to be done for them on a very exclusive basis."

"We focus on how our clients experience luxury in our hotels. It goes way beyond satisfaction to a personal experience," says Douglas McKenzie, Starwood.

Accustomed to serving royalty, Hollywood celebrities, and United Nations' delegates, the hotel staff recognizes that these guests place a premium on their privacy. Guests also expect personalized services, and they are sure to get it. According to McKenzie:

> When you are spending that kind of money for a hotel room, you want more and more done for you. Our concierge service has increased enormously over the last few years. Today in New York, people are in the habit of going shopping and telling the store to "just send it back to the hotel." You can imagine in December at the St. Regis what a challenge it is to have dozens and dozens of shopping bags coming in. We make it easy for our guests, more enjoyable, and it's all part of a wonderful experience that you take away with you and remember. We are building experiences that people go back and talk about. We are building memories for people, and that is a luxury.

But even in the lofty regions the Starwood luxury hotels target, their customers are still concerned with value. "People are paying for that wonderful experience, the feeling of exclusivity, and it is not a matter of extravagance or buying the most expensive thing. These moneyed people who are used to luxury still look at the value of what they are buying. They want to get their $800 worth of hotel staying. They know the value of money. There is still a lot of good common sense in the spending patterns of wealthy people; otherwise, they wouldn't be wealthy," McKenzie says.

Connecting with suitable business partners that attract the same type of highly affluent clientele has proven Starwood's best marketing ploy. McKenzie concludes:

> After 9/11, a lot of New York hotels were empty, and so they started dumping their prices. We can't do that, so we've become more aggressive with our partnerships to attract more of the right kind of client. For example, we partner with cruise lines and do some joint database marketing

with them. And we work with Christie's, whose clients come to New York for its auctions. We work with Bentley and some department stores that have a similar customer profile to ours. Our approach, rather than to move down the income scale, is to move horizontally . . . to find other similar people. Marketing to our level of the luxury market is fragile. It is all about how to keep your existing clientele happy while expanding and then bringing new people in to taste your product.

PURCHASE INCIDENCE INCREASES WITH INCOME

Purchase incidence rises with income, and in many cases the super-affluents' purchase incidence is twice that found among the near-affluents. See Figure 4.5. The uptick in purchase incidence is far less apparent from near-affluent levels to the affluents. In many cases the affluents have about the same, or just slightly elevated, purchase incidence as compared with the near-affluents. Consumers at the $150,000 and above income level exhibit vastly increased luxury consumption, whereas those in the $75,000 to $149,999 level tend to purchase at about the same rate. Therefore, the income cutoff of $150,000 marks the key separation between the ordinary luxury consumer and the extraordinary one.

Consumers at the $150,000 and above income level exhibit vastly increased luxury consumption, whereas those in the $75,000 to $149,999 level tend to purchase at about the same rate. Therefore, the income cutoff of $150,000 marks the key separation between the ordinary luxury consumer and the extraordinary one.

FIGURE 4.5
Purchase Incidence by Income

PURCHASE INCIDENCE BY INCOME SEGMENT	TOTAL % 2003	TOTAL % 2002	2003 % NEAR-AFFLUENTS	2003 % AFFLUENTS	2003 % SUPER-AFFLUENTS
Any Home Luxury	82%	75%	79%	80%	85%
Electronics	57	51	53	52	64
Linens & Bedding	35	34	25	32	48
Kitchenware, Cookware	31	29	25	22	43
Kitchen Appliances	29	29	15	24	45
Furniture & Floor Coverings	27	35	18	20	41
Garden	23	45	22	21	25
Art & Antiques	22	19	14	18	33
Tabletop	20	8	16	22	28
Home Decor Fabrics, Wall/Window Coverings	19	29	13	17	25
Any Personal Luxury	63%	64%	54%	56%	56%
Fragrances & Beauty	34	44	33	28	41
Apparel & Accessories	35	41	30	29	45
Jewelry & Watches	32	32	27	32	36
Automobiles	18	24	15	13	25
Any Experiential Luxury	70%	62%	65%	71%	78%
Entertainment	52	20	48	55	53
Travel	45	35	39	48	47
Spa/Massage/Beauty	18	20	13	21	24
Housecleaning	10	23	4	12	16
Landscaper	10	18	4	9	15
Home Decorator	5	13	1	6	8

LUXURY SPENDING INCREASED IN 2003

Total spending on luxuries, based on the survey median, was $9,375 in 2003, a 5 percent increase over total luxury spending in 2002. Total spending on home luxuries declined some 12 percent, whereas spending on experiential luxuries rose 29 percent from the previous year. Let's look more closely at the typical luxury consumer's spending in each luxury category, shown in Figure 4.6.

SUPER-AFFLUENTS SPEND ALMOST FIVE TIMES MORE ON LUXURY THAN DO NEAR-AFFLUENTS

Predictably, spending on luxuries rises with income. See Figure 4.7. The near-affluents spent on average $4,825 for luxuries in

FIGURE 4.6
Luxury Spending, 2002 and 2003

	2003	2002	% CHANGE
Total Luxury Spending	$ 9,375	$ 8,900	5%
Home Luxury	$ 4,125	$ 4,700	−12%
Electronics	1,750	2,000	−13
Linens & Bedding	750	500	50
Kitchenware, Cookware	750	500	50
Kitchen Appliances	1,750	2,000	−13
Furniture & Floor Coverings	3,750	3,000	25
Garden	750	1,000	−25
Art & Antiques	3,750	4,000	−6
Tabletop	750	500	50
Home Decor Fabrics, Wall/Window Coverings	1,750	1,200	46
Personal Luxury	$ 2,500	$ n.a.	
Fragrances & Beauty	380	300	27
Apparel & Accessories	1,750	2,000	−13
Jewelry & Watches	1,750	1,200	46
Automobiles	37,500	35,000	7
Experiential Luxury	$ 9,020	$ 7,000	29%
Entertainment	3,570	1,500	138
Travel	8,230	5,000	65
Spa/Massage/Beauty	750	550	36
Housecleaning	1,750	2,000	−13
Landscaper	3,750	2,500	50
Home Decorator	7,500	5,000	50

FIGURE 4.7
Luxury Spending by Income Category, 2002 and 2003

	2003	2002	2003 NEAR-AFFLUENTS	2003 AFFLUENTS	2003 SUPER-AFFLUENTS
Total Home Luxury	**$ 4,125**	**$ 4,700**	**$ 2,500**	**$ 3,083**	**$ 8,875**
Electronics	1,750	2,000	1,750	1,750	3,750
Linens & Bedding	750	500	380	380	750
Kitchenware, Cookware	750	500	380	750	750
Kitchen Appliances	1,750	2,000	1,750	1,750	3,750
Furniture & Floor Coverings	3,750	3,000	2,750	3,750	7,500
Garden	750	1,000	380	750	750
Art & Antiques	3,750	4,000	1,750	1,750	7,500
Tabletop	750	1,200	750	750	750
Home Decor Fabrics, Wall/Window Coverings	1,750	500	750	750	3,750
Total Personal Luxury	**$ 2,500**	**n.a.**	**$ 1,750**	**$ 2,000**	**$ 7,500**
Fragrances & Beauty	380	300	120	380	380
Apparel & Accessories	1,750	2,000	750	750	1,750
Jewelry & Watches	1,750	1,200	750	1,750	1,750
Automobiles	37,500	35,000	37,500	37,500	37,500
Total Experiential Luxury	**$ 9,020**	**$ 7,000**	**$ 4,418**	**$ 7,231**	**$14,007**
Entertainment	3,570	1,500	2,020	2,220	6,120
Travel	8,230	5,000	4,090	5,580	13,770
Spa/Massage/Beauty	750	550	380	380	1,750
Housecleaning	1,750	2,000	750	1,750	1,750
Landscaper*	3,750	2,500			
Home Decorator*	7,500	5,000			
Total Luxury	**$ 9,375**	**$ 8,900**	**$ 4,825**	**$ 9,000**	**$22,500**

*Too few respondents to average spending

The serious jump in luxury spending, as in luxury purchase incidence, is found at the $150,000 and above income level. The super-affluents spend 2.5 times more than do affluents, and nearly 5.0 times more than do near-affluents.

2003, as compared with $9,000 tallied by the affluents. That means consumers in the next highest income range, $100,000–$150,000, spend nearly twice as much buying luxuries as the near-affluents. Because these two segments have about an equal purchase incidence (i.e., percentage of households that buy), the affluents' greater annual spending indicates that they spend more when they buy luxury than do the near-affluents, though both segments are about equally likely to buy specific luxuries.

In total spending, the biggest jump is found among the super-affluents. They spent, on average, $22,500 on luxuries in 2003. That is 2.5 times more than the affluents spent and 4.7 times more than the near-affluents spent on luxury.

In conclusion, although the near-affluents and affluents tend to purchase luxuries at just about the same incidence, the affluents tend to outspend the near-affluents on the luxuries they buy. But the serious jump in luxury spending, as in luxury purchase incidence, is found at the $150,000 and above income level.

WHY PEOPLE BUY LUXURY: THE EMOTIONAL UNDERPINNINGS OF LUXURY CONSUMERS

As we move toward a deeper understanding of luxury consumers, it is interesting to see how remarkably similar in overall attitudes and motivations they are, regardless of gender, age, generation, or even income levels. Even though subtle differences exist among luxury consumers, enough so that we have segmented the luxury market into four distinct psychographic segments—X-Fluents (extreme affluents), Luxury Cocooners, Luxury Aspirers, and the iconoclastic Butterflies, all of whom are profiled in depth in the following chapter—we generally find only differences of degree but not of kind when we look at how the luxury consumer approaches planning, shopping, and buying luxuries.

No matter whether they are just slightly affluent or extremely wealthy, luxury consumers tend to rate attributes and motivators toward luxury in the same rank or order. Thus, for example, at every income level they most strongly agree with this attitude statement: "Luxury doesn't always have to be the most expensive thing or the most exclusive brand." See Figure 4.8 for other attitudes of luxury consumers. They also tend to buy the same luxury goods in the same overall order, even though the more affluent buy more and spend more when they do. For example, luxury electronics and photography equipment are the most purchased luxury goods at all income levels.

Luxury marketers therefore need to understand that their more affluent consumers are far more similar to each other than they are different, despite whether their household income is $80,000 or $180,000 or even $280,000. Clearly, the $280,000 luxury consumer has a lot more money to shop with and can dig deeper when shopping than can the $80,000 near-affluent consumer. Yet each one of these shoppers is motivated and driven by the same basic motivations and desires. The more affluent may dress a little finer, drive more expensive cars, and live in fancier houses (or they may not!), but when it comes down to the passion and motivation for consuming luxury, more or less affluent makes virtually no difference.

FIGURE 4.8
Attitudes about Luxury

	STRONGLY AGREE	AGREE	NEUTRAL	DISAGREE	STRONGLY DISAGREE
Luxury doesn't always have to be the most expensive or the most exclusive brand.	49%	39%	8%	3%	1%
When you buy a luxury item, you expect it to be noticeably a cut above the average.	45	41	10	3	1
Luxury isn't how much something costs but how much it means to me.	43	40	14	2	1
I enjoy the feeling of buying luxuries on sale and usually search out the lowest price or the best value.	43	37	15	2	1
Luxury is not about conspicuous consumption or buying things to impress.	43	34	15	7	2
Luxury is having the feeling that I can do what I want when I want to.	40	45	12	3	1
Luxury is being able to pursue my passions and interests.	38	45	13	3	5
Luxury is for everyone and different for everyone.	38	39	18	3	1
For me life's luxuries are about my feelings and making memories with my family and friends.	35	40	20	4	2
Luxury is buying those extras in life that make it more comfortable and meaningful.	33	54	10	2	1
Luxury is being free to express my personality and individuality in the things I wear, in the car I drive, in the way I decorate my home.	31	45	19	4	2

(continued)

FIGURE 4.8
Attitudes about Luxury Continued

	STRONGLY AGREE	AGREE	NEUTRAL	DISAGREE	STRONGLY DISAGREE
I feel privileged to have a luxury lifestyle.	31%	38%	24%	4%	2%
Buying luxury items is a way to pamper my loved ones and myself.	30	41	15	3	1
Luxury is about feeling pampered, such as having a massage or a soak in a hot tub.	30	47	17	4	2
When quality is equal between two products, I buy based on the luxury brand's reputation.	27	38	24	8	3
At my stage of life, I am less interested in buying more things and more interested in spending my money on special experiences that I will remember the rest of my life.	24	36	28	9	4
Once you experience luxury in your life, you never want to go back to the ordinary.	23	38	24	11	4
Although luxury experiences are nice, they are fleeting, so I prefer to buy luxury items I can keep and cherish.	21	42	24	11	3
Buying luxury items seems less important to me today than it did in the past.	15	33	36	12	4
I have cut back on buying more luxury things for my home than I used to in the past.	12	30	32	20	7
Luxury is defined by the brand of the product, so it isn't a luxury if it isn't a luxury brand.	8	16	24	32	20

5

THE INNER LIFE OF LUXURY CONSUMERS—FIELD GUIDE TO THE NEW LUXURY CONSUMERS

THE DRIVES AND MOTIVATIONS PROPELLING THE LUXURY CONSUMER IN THE MARKETPLACE

There are basically three ways to study any market like the luxury market. You can conduct a demographic analysis by comparing and contrasting those quantifiable facts and figures that describe the market, such as income, marital status, household composition, and the like. Or you can conduct a behavioral study of the market's purchasing behavior, what consumers buy and how much they spend. Another way to study a market is through psychographics. A psychographic study of the luxury market provides insights into the inner life of consumers, what drives them, motivates them, and moves them in the marketplace. By taking the results of the attitude statements presented in the last chapter and using a special computer program that groups or clusters respondents based on their overall similarities and differences in response to a battery of statements, four unique types of luxury consumers emerge. These luxury consumers are Luxury Cocooners, Butterflies, Luxury Aspirers, and X-Fluents (extreme affluents), as depicted in Figure 5.1.

What distinguishes one type of luxury consumer from another is largely a difference in degree, not of kind. In other words, luxury consumers are far more like each other than they are different from each other. They all, to a greater or lesser extent, favor experiences over material goods. Their demographics are virtually identical and their basic perceptions and attitudes about luxury are quite similar, although there are enough differences attitudinally to make a study of their distinctive attitudes productive for marketing and brand strategists. Even though the differences in attitudes are slight, each segment displays different luxury buying and spending patterns, which confirm the distinctiveness of each as a market segment to target through branding and marketing communications messages.

Here is the battery of attitudinal statements and the average value for each segment based on a five-point scale where 1 equals strongly agree, 2 equals agree, 3 is neutral, 4 is disagree, and 5 equals strongly disagree. See Figure 5.2.

FIGURE 5.1
Luxury Consumer Segments

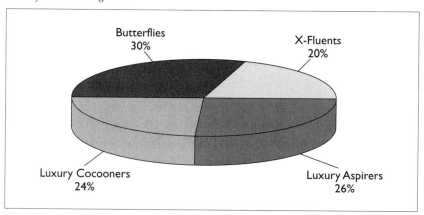

FIGURE 5.2
Luxury Segmentation Analysis

	LUXURY COCOONERS (24%)	BUTTERFLIES (30%)	LUXURY ASPIRERS (26%)	X-FLUENTS (EXTREMELY AFFLUENTS) (20%)
Luxury doesn't always have to be the most expensive or the most exclusive brand.	2.3%	1.5%	1.2%	1.7%
When you buy a luxury item, you expect it to be noticeably a cut above the average.	2.1	1.4	1.9	1.3
Luxury isn't how much something costs but how much it means to me.	2.3	1.5	1.5	1.9
I enjoy the feeling of buying luxuries on sale and usually search out the lowest price or the best value.	2.3	1.5	1.6	1.7
Luxury is not about conspicuous consumption or buying things to impress.	2.6	1.8	1.4	1.9
Luxury is having the feeling that I can do what I want when I want to.	2.5	1.5	1.8	1.5
Luxury is being able to pursue my passions and interests.	2.5	1.6	1.7	1.5
Luxury is for everyone and different for everyone.	2.5	1.6	1.7	1.8
For me life's luxuries are about my feelings and making memories with my family and friends.	2.7	1.5	1.6	2.2
Luxury is buying those extras in life that make it more comfortable and meaningful.	2.3	1.5	2.0	1.5

(continued)

FIGURE 5.2
Luxury Segmentation Analysis Continued

	LUXURY COCOONERS (24%)	BUTTERFLIES (30%)	LUXURY ASPIRERS (26%)	X-FLUENTS (EXTREMELY AFFLUENTS) (20%)
Luxury is being free to express my personality and individuality in the things I wear, in the car I drive, in the way I decorate my home.	2.6%	1.6%	2.3%	1.6%
I feel privileged to have a luxury lifestyle.	2.4	1.7	2.4	1.7
Buying luxury items is a way to pamper my loved ones and myself.	2.3	1.6	2.4	1.5
Luxury is about feeling pampered, such as having a massage or a soak in a hot tub.	2.3	1.5	2.5	1.7
When quality is equal between two products, I buy based on the luxury brand's reputation.	2.6	1.7	2.8	1.8
At my stage of life, I am less interested in buying more things, and more interested in spending my money on special experiences that I will remember the rest of my life.	2.7	1.8	2.0	3.1
Once you experience luxury in your life, you never want to go back to the ordinary.	2.9	1.8	3.1	1.6
Although luxury experiences are nice, they are fleeting, so I prefer to buy luxury items I can keep and cherish.	2.7	1.9	2.6	2.1
Buying luxury items seems less important to me today than it did in the past.	2.7	2.0	2.4	3.6
I have cut back on buying more luxury things for my home than I used to in the past.	2.8	2.0	2.8	3.9
Luxury is defined by the brand of the product, so it isn't a luxury if it isn't a luxury brand.	3.3	2.7	4.2	3.4

FIGURE 5.3
Field Guide to Luxury Consumer Segments

LUXURY MARKET SEGMENTS—SUMMARY	LUXURY COCOONERS	BUTTERFLIES	LUXURY ASPIRERS	X-FLUENTS (EXTREME AFFLUENTS)
Market Penetration	24%	30%	26%	20%
Consumer Psychology	The Luxury Cocooners are still wrapped up in their luxury cocoons and continue to devote time and attention to making their "nests" more luxurious. They express their identity through luxury purchases and participate fully in their luxury lifestyle.	The most highly evolved luxury consumers, the Butterflies know things won't make them happy. Yet even though they are less materialistic in outlook, they are highly involved in luxury purchases. Their focus is on personal and experiential luxuries, and so they have emerged from their cocoons to seek connection with the outside world. They gain the least satisfaction of any segment in home luxuries. They are looking for balance between their inner emotional life and the external world in the pursuit of luxury.	The Luxury Aspirers have not yet achieved the level of luxury to which they aspire. They view luxury as an expression of what they have and what they own. For these consumers, luxury is best expressed in the things and brands they buy and display.	The X-Fluents are the most highly indulgent luxury consumers, buying most frequently and spending more. Although they share a yearning for the experiences that luxury affords, unlike the Butterflies they are firmly grounded in the material world. They seek out luxury things and experiences, spending freely on their luxury passions. They are highly invested in luxury living and are dedicated to maintaining their luxury lifestyle.

(continued)

FIGURE 5.3
Field Guide to Luxury Consumer Segments Continued

LUXURY MARKET SEGMENTS— SUMMARY	LUXURY COCOONERS	BUTTERFLIES	LUXURY ASPIRERS	X-FLUENTS (EXTREME AFFLUENTS)
Purchase Incidence	• Any Home Luxuries: 75% • Any Personal Luxuries: 57% • Any Experiential Luxuries: 63%	• Any Home Luxuries: 85% • Any Personal Luxuries: 64% • Any Experiential Luxuries: 75%	• Any Home Luxuries: 78% • Any Personal Luxuries: 55% • Any Experiential Luxuries: 69%	• Any Home Luxuries: 91% • Any Personal Luxuries: 71% • Any Experiential Luxuries: 82%
Luxury Home Spending	$4,000	$3,875	$3,750	$4,750
Personal Luxury Spending	$2,250	$4,313	$1,125	$4,250
Experiential Spending	$4,750 (Low overall purchase incidence; extremely high spending on home decorating boosts average.)	$3,750 (Very low spending on home decorating draws down average.)	$4,500 (High spending on home decorating boosts average.)	$5,375
Total Luxury Spending	**$7,500**	**$10,250**	**$7,500**	**$15,250**

BUTTERFLIES HAVE EMERGED FROM THEIR LUXURIOUS COCOONS

Representing the largest segment in the luxury market, the Butterflies are the most evolved luxury consumers. These are consumers who have emerged from the cocoon of luxury comfort they have enveloped themselves in for the past decade. They are turning away from their self-indulgent ways and becoming reconnected with the outside world. As they turn their backs on the cocoon, they are assuming their position in the social, political, and cultural landscapes that define their identity in relation to society. Luxury remains important to them as a means of self-expression, but they are more likely to think twice before buying luxury. The Butterflies are looking for a new meaning in their life, and they recognize that a conspicuous consumption lifestyle is not the way to achieve their personal goals. They have an iconoclastic point of view, challenging conventional wisdom and rejecting status symbols as meaningless. Feeling somewhat conflicted by having so much and yet being nonmaterialistic in orientation, the Butterflies are looking for a new equilibrium between the roles they play in their inner and their external worlds.

Even though distinctions between the luxury segments are subtle, the Butterflies stand out as the most evolved luxury consumers. They have the most mature perspective on their role and responsibilities as luxury consumers, because, for the Butterflies, having wealth carries with it social responsibilities. They don't necessarily feel guilty about having so much; they are not focused solely on their own inner life and personal identity but instead are equally concerned with their position in society. As they seek to find a new equilibrium between their interior and exterior worlds, they embody the expression "With great wealth comes great responsibility." Just look at Bill Gates,

> The Butterflies are looking for a new meaning in their life, and they recognize that a conspicuous consumption lifestyle is not the way to achieve their personal goals.

Oprah Winfrey, and Ted Turner, all prototypical Butterflies. For these people, their great wealth is being directed toward charities and endowments that they believe will improve the state of all humanity. They seek to leave the world a better place once they are gone and even before.

As luxury consumers, the Butterflies spend lots on luxury, despite the fact that they are the least materialistic of all the segments. Their total luxury spending is second only to the X-Fluents. When buying luxury products, they are more highly influenced by word-of-mouth advice from their friends and social circle. They look for and expect outstanding service from store personnel and demand an extraordinary buying experience. Butterflies value luxury products for their overall superior quality, craftsmanship, and performance in addition to the way the product enhances the quality of their life. Of all the segments, they are least motivated by status or exclusivity of the product. The egalitarian Butterflies are democratic in the way they view luxuries—that is, everyone is entitled to luxury.

As they seek balance in their life, the Butterflies are likely to employ luxury services, such as home cleaning, landscaping, and gardening, to save time for other, more valuable personal pursuits.

Butterflies Spend Freely on Luxury

For many luxury marketers, the Butterflies represent their ultimate target market, especially for personal and experiential luxury marketers. Second only to the X-Fluents in total luxury spending and overall purchase incidence, the Butterflies purchase home, personal, and experiential luxuries at a higher rate than the Cocooners or Aspirers do. Their average spending on all luxuries in the past year was $10,250—37 percent higher than spending by Cocooners or Aspirers. Their spending is directed away from home luxuries, though they still spend more than Aspirers on average for luxury home products and toward more personal and experiential luxuries. (Note: Their average spending total on experiential luxuries is lower than that of Cocooners or Aspirers because Cocooners and Aspirers had extremely high average spending on home decorating, which is not a priority category for Butterflies. Although the Butterflies averaged only $750 on home decorating spending, the Aspirers and Cocooners averaged in excess of $9,000 on this category, thus exerting a strong upward influence in the survey averages.) See Figure 5.3.

LUXURY COCOONERS ARE STILL ENVELOPED IN THEIR LUXURY COCOONS

Because the nature of the luxury market is to be constantly in motion, evolving, transforming itself from one level of luxury to another, an apt name for the segment of the luxury market that is most home focused is Luxury Cocooners. They have yet to undergo the metamorphosis that will transform them into a Butterfly, yet I expect that many Luxury Cocooners will ultimately evolve into Butterflies as they mature and reach the empty nest life stage. But for now, the Luxury Cocooners remain wrapped in their luxury cocoons. In their purchases of luxury, especially luxury home products, they buy luxurious things to fill up their emotional empty spaces. Unlike the Butterflies, who know that things won't make them happy, the Cocooners tend to view what they have, what they own, the houses they live in, and the way their houses are decorated as most important to maintaining their sense of self and personal identity.

They are bound to hearth and home and are less philosophical about their social and societal responsibilities as affluent, luxury consumers. The changes in

> Unlike the Butterflies, who know that things won't make them happy, Cocooners tend to view what they have, what they own, the houses they live in, and the way their houses are decorated as most important to maintaining their sense of self and personal identity.

the world around them, including the ups and downs of the stock market and 9/11, have less impact on them as luxury consumers than that felt by the Butterflies. Prototypical Cocooners include Donald Trump and Martha Stewart, both of whom have focused on building, enhancing, and perfecting their home surroundings.

Cocooners Spend More on Home and Home-Focused Experiential Luxuries

Because the Cocooners are focused on their home, their spending is also directed toward home and home-related experiential purchases, such as home decorating. Even though their purchase incidence of home luxuries is behind the Butterflies (85 percent among Butterflies as compared with 75 percent among Cocooners), they spend a shade more on average on home luxuries ($4,000 in the past year) than do the butterflies ($3,875). Their experiential spending is driven by home-related service purchases, notably home decorating, landscaping, and house cleaning/maid service. With their dominant interest being the home, their spending on personal luxuries ($2,250 on average) is far less than that of the Butterflies ($4,313). Overall, their total average spending on luxuries was $7,500 in 2003. See Figure 5.3.

LUXURY ASPIRERS HAVE NOT YET REACHED THE LEVEL OF LUXURY TO WHICH THEY ASPIRE

With about one-fourth of the sample falling within this segment, aspiring luxury consumers have not yet achieved the level of luxury to which they aspire in their life. They view luxury as an expression of what they have, what they own, and what they want to achieve in the future. These consumers do not embrace luxury as a feeling or an experience; rather, for them luxury is best expressed by the things they buy and for which they shop. This segment is more materialistic in its orientation toward luxury and is more brand conscious as well. Luxury Aspirers seek badge value in the luxury goods they buy and at the same time look for discounts and sales on those brands that they aspire to buy. They most strongly agree with this statement: "Luxury is defined by the brand of the product, so it isn't a luxury product if it isn't a luxury brand." Aspirers spent $7,500 on luxuries on average in 2003, about the same as Cocooners. See Figure 5.3.

> Aspirers do not embrace luxury as a feeling or an experience; rather, for them luxury is best expressed by the things they buy and for which they shop.

X-FLUENTS LIVE THE LIFESTYLE OF THE RICH AND FAMOUS

Representing the smallest segment in the luxury market, the X-Fluents are the extreme affluents, though their average income is on a par with the rest of the survey sample. They are the most highly indulgent luxury consumers as they direct their considerable energy and wealth toward buying and spending on luxuries. These consumers love the luxury lifestyle they have achieved. They differ from the Butterflies in not bringing such a philosophical bent to the consumer experience. They enjoy all the goods and privileges of their luxury lifestyle and don't feel the kind of responsibility to the rest of society that the Butterflies do. Of all the segments, they are the most positive about their current financial well-being and, in turn, are the most optimistic about their spending on luxury in the coming year. Just over half of the X-Fluents said they spent more on luxuries in the past year; and over one-third, the largest percentage among the segments, expect to spend more on luxuries in the coming year. Prototypical X-Fluents include such cultural icons as the Hilton sisters, Ivana Trump,

> X-Fluents are the most highly indulgent luxury consumers as they direct their considerable energy and wealth toward buying and spending on luxuries.

and many of the rich and famous who Robin Leach profiles on his show "The Lifestyles of the Rich and Famous." Interestingly, even though the X-Fluents spend more on luxury, their income levels don't differ that sharply from typical luxury consumers with a range of incomes from highest to lowest and everything in between.

X-Fluents Spend More on Luxury

Although they value and appreciate experiential luxuries as the Butterflies do, X-Fluents are decidedly more materialistic than the Butterflies when it comes to other luxury purchases. They have the highest overall purchase incidence in all luxury categories (91 percent bought luxury home products, 71 percent personal luxuries, and 82 percent experiential luxuries in 2003), and they spend the most in all categories of luxuries ($4,750 on home luxuries, $4,250 on personal luxuries, and $5,375 on experiential luxuries). Being the highest-spending segment overall with an average of $15,250, they spend about 50 percent more than the Butterflies do on luxury. See Figure 5.3.

X-Fluents Are the Most Active Luxury Purchasers, Followed Closely by Butterflies

Figure 5.4 lists the purchase incidence of each of the four luxury consumer market segments. In most categories, the X-Fluents take the lead in overall purchase incidence with the Butterflies close behind.

FUTURE VISION OF LUXURY— LUXURY CONSUMERS ARE SEEKING EQUILIBRIUM TO REDUCE STRESS

It's an oft repeated phrase since 9/11, but it is surely true— everything has changed. Maybe not as a result solely of 9/11, but

FIGURE 5.4
Luxury Purchase Incidence by Segment

SEGMENT LUXURY PURCHASE INCIDENCE	% TOTAL	% COCOONERS	% BUTTERFLIES	% ASPIRERS	% X-FLUENTS
Any Home Luxury	**82%**	**75%**	**85%**	**78%**	**91%**
Electronics	56	51	58	54	64
Linens & Bedding	35	32	41	25	43
Kitchenware, Cookware	31	25	33	24	41
Kitchen Appliances	29	25	31	26	32
Furniture & Floor Coverings	27	23	30	20	37
Garden	23	15	26	25	23
Art & Antiques	22	15	12	14	26
Home Decor Fabrics, Wall/Window Coverings	19	19	23	9	23
Tabletop	19	17	20	15	30
Any Personal Luxury	**63%**	**57%**	**64%**	**55%**	**71%**
Fragrances & Beauty	35	24	44	24	45
Apparel & Accessories	35	24	38	35	46
Jewelry & Watches	32	31	33	28	37
Automobiles	18	13	22	10	28
Any Experiential Luxury	**70%**	**63%**	**75%**	**69%**	**82%**
Entertainment	52	43	47	55	62
Travel	45	41	39	52	45
Spa/Massage/Beauty	18	19	20	10	26
Housecleaning	10	7	10	10	9
Landscaper	10	8	9	8	15
Home Decorator	5	2	5	4	7

that fateful day in September 2001 could be said to have started a new chapter in the world's history. How different the world was back in 1999 before the entrance into the new millennium. We were enjoying a decade of phenomenal growth in the luxury market when the leading luxury companies posted 10 to 20 percent revenue growth on average throughout the 1990s. For luxury marketers, prospects looked bright for the next decade. Although there was conflict in the Middle East, there always has been trouble in that region, and, after all, the Middle East is halfway around the world. Here in our homeland, we were enveloped in a national cocoon of safety and security. But after September 11 and the start of the war on terror and our military's involvement in Iraq, we discovered we were asleep at the wheel. We weren't safe at all . . . the oceans and our borders couldn't protect us . . . our economy is giving mixed signals about its health as oil prices are skyrocketing . . . the stock market is stalled . . . our world, our expectations, our plans, our goals are not as sure as before.

Buffeted by the changes occurring all around them, luxury consumers today are searching for a new equilibrium and balance between their inner emotional landscape and their position in the social, political, and professional milieu. Just as we have discovered on a national level, the luxury consumers cannot continue to wrap themselves in a luxurious cocoon, insulating themselves, feathering their nests, and feeding themselves a steady diet of comfort foods. Today, that way of life looks too self-indulgent, too self-centered, too self-involved. The luxury consumers, as the most affluent members of our society, are challenged to take their rightful position of leadership in society. The luxury consumer today is undergoing a metamorphosis that is transforming him or her into a Butterfly.

Expressed through this metamorphosis is a striving for a new equilibrium. Luxury consumers are changing, shifting, moving in response to the changes in the world. They are trying to find a balance between their interior emotional world and the external world. They express new dichotomies, conflicts, and challenges:

- Enhancing *interior* environments and navigating the *exterior* world
- Interest in *electronics* and passion for the *garden*
- *Reactive* impulses and *empowered* by information
- Desire for *uniqueness* and recognizing that *luxury is for everyone*
- Need for *self-expression* through luxury and identification with *social markers* of affluence
- Means to achieve *affluent lifestyle* and the thrill of *getting a bargain*
- Acquiring luxury *things* and craving luxury *experiences*

Today's luxury consumers don't necessarily want to give up anything they already have in pursuit of a new equilibrium. In other words, they still want it *all!* For some, equilibrium is achieved by shuffling the existing order of things, changing priorities, and devoting more or less time, more or less money, more or less resources to achieve a new balance. But for others, especially as the luxury consumers age and their children leave the nest, they may well begin to look at their luxurious empty house as more of a burden than a pleasure. When that happens, we can expect these luxury consumers to sell off and scale down their living quarters. But they won't scale down their overall lifestyle luxury quotient. Their new digs might be smaller but no less luxurious. The best-selling book *The Not So Big House* (Taunton Press, 1998) reflects this reordering of priorities: giving up square footage and "McMansions" for better and finer-quality appointments in a more livable home design.

> For some, equilibrium is achieved by shuffling the existing order of things, changing priorities, and devoting more or less time, more or less money, more or less resources to achieve a new balance.

6

LUXURY HOME PRODUCTS— THE PRODUCTS THAT DELIVER TO PEOPLE'S PASSION

OVERVIEW

Having probed the history and definition of luxury and the different types and dominant characteristics of the luxury consumer market, including both overall purchase behavior and the motivations and drives for luxury, I now turn attention more closely to specific luxury product categories, starting with home luxuries in Chapter 6, personal luxuries in Chapter 7, and experiential luxuries in Chapter 8.

PRODUCTS MUST DELIVER LUXURY PERFORMANCE

The new luxury paradigm—the shift from things to experience—demands a new way of thinking about and talking about luxuries. The intrinsic qualities of luxury goods—superior quality, exclusivity, fine materials, attention to detail—that have traditionally described a "thing" convey little meaning when viewed through the experiential lens. From the new luxury experiential point of view, superior quality in and of itself carries little value; rather, the value of superior quality is derived from the experience or feeling it delivers to the consumer. Because it is no longer the thing but the experience, when talking about luxury, the way we think of luxury goods, their attributes and features, we must use action verbs and active descriptors to describe the feeling conveyed or delivered to the consumer. That is where the true value lies and why luxury goods command a price premium. Therefore, we need to introduce a new word into the luxury marketing discussion: the concept of *performance.*

Performance is a key word against which to judge our luxury products and brands—for example, how well does this luxury handbag, shoe, ring, sheet set, or table setting deliver a luxury feeling to the customer? Defined as the "fulfilling of a function," the concept of performance bridges the gap between the thing and the experience of the thing from the consumer's point of view. Although *performance* is a natural descriptor for luxuries that have a mechanical component and involve nuts and bolts, gears, and wheels, such as cars, watches, and electronics, it's not a term that comes immediately to mind when talking about other static luxury goods. Yet performance is the very best term to describe how a product delivers or performs its luxury functions experientially for the consumer. The concept of luxury brand performance must be freed from a narrow mechanistic view to be seen in the more expansive light of experiential marketing.

> Defined as the "fulfilling of a function," the concept of performance bridges the gap between the thing and the experience of the thing from the consumer's point of view.

For example, luxury jewelry performs in the feeling one gets from wearing an exquisite bauble: you feel more beautiful, more sophisticated, more stylish. Luxury fashion performs in a similar emotional way to enhance one's beauty, making you feel "marvelous," as Billy Crystal would say. So, too, home fashion (rugs, furniture, art, decorative accents) performs as an expression of one's good taste in one's personal environment and delivers feelings of serenity, security, and peace through careful placement and design.

> The concept of luxury brand performance must be freed from a narrow mechanistic view to be seen in the more expansive light of experiential marketing.

The concept of luxury performance connects both the intrinsic definition of luxury (i.e., quality performance, design performance, uniqueness performance) with the experiential about how the luxury makes consumers feel and the way they experience luxury. It is through performance that old luxury (the noun or *thing*) becomes transformed into the new luxury that delivers an experience, a feeling, or an emotion to the consumer.

Sub-Zero's Paul Leuthe
Delivering Luxury Kitchen Performance

When Sub-Zero Freezer Company acquired Wolf Gourmet in March 2000, it was considered a "marriage of fire and ice," as the Sub-Zero Web site describes it. It just made sense for Sub-Zero, the leading brand of luxury refrigeration products, to team up with Wolf, a brand known for professional-quality cooking, to deliver superior design and performance in the home kitchen. Paul Leuthe, corporate marketing manager, explains: "Both brands target the same affluent clientele, mostly women aged 45 and above who have the discretionary dollars for this kind of expense. While our target is mostly female, it is usually a joint decision, with the wife driving the product selection."

Yet there are subtle but meaningful differences in how consumers view their refrigeration and cooking purchases. Leuthe says:

We target the same consumer, but there is a whole different set of considerations and emotions that become involved. Refrigeration is more passive; it sits there and just works. Cooking equipment, we quickly learned, is more involving and participatory. You can't just sit there and watch it do its thing. That's why we find that guys get more involved in the cooking decisions. It's one of those BTU, horse-power kinds of things. Men really get into the cooking performance. We describe the two brands—Sub-Zero and Wolf—as "corporate companions and kitchen soul mates."

Sub-Zero was founded in 1945, and Wolf has been around for more than 70 years, so both brands have witnessed the evolution of the modern home kitchen to meet the ever-increasing demands of the home cook. Leuthe explains:

There has been a transformation in the kitchen and the way we cook since the 50s, when it was still the housewife's exclusive domain. Just since the 90s, we see a difference with more men involved in the kitchen and a desire for families to work together to rediscover themselves. The kitchen represents a core family value that we grew up with, so people are focusing more on it as a place to share good times and gather together.

People's perspective on luxury has changed. It is not about conspicuous consumption or buying a brand because it's a brand. Our brands really deliver performance, where two professionals can work together in the kitchen and prepare wonderful food for the family. What could be more meaningful?

> "People's perspective on luxury has changed. It is not about conspicuous consumption or buying a brand because it's a brand. Our brands really deliver performance," says Paul Leuthe, Sub-Zero.

The key to the success of Sub-Zero and Wolf is that their customers do their homework to find the best solution. "It is not uncommon for our customers to spend upward of $20,000 to $30,000 on our appliance packages, and that is just for appliances. When you add the cost of cabinets and construction, kitchen remodels are very expensive. So people really do their research. They want substance, products that perform. They look at our Web sites, they visit our dealers, they talk to their friends. They need to make the most informed decision, and they value that Sub-Zero is the specialist in refrigeration," Leuthe says.

The key word that Leuthe uses to best describe their customer is *passionate:* "Our customers have a passion for the kitchen. They value the passion that we bring to refrigeration through Sub-Zero and the passion we bring to cooking with Wolf. Our customers are passionate and won't settle for anything less than the best. It's this passion that stands out."

As a company, Sub-Zero is dedicated to staying close to its customers and their needs. Leuthe says, "We do a lot of research to uncover needs that people have but can't really articulate. In defining luxury, it's about staying close to your clients and your market and making sure that you are developing product to meet their needs even before they are anticipated. That keeps our product lines fresh and our company always evolving."

HOME LUXURIES—NOT ALL HOME SPENDING IS CREATED EQUAL; SOME IS AN INVESTMENT, THE REST IS AN EXPENSE

Although fewer than one-third of luxury consumers (31 percent) get their greatest luxury "kicks" from home luxury purchases, they still buy a prodigious amount of luxuries for their home. In the past two years, luxury electronics and photography equipment have been their favorite luxury home indulgence. This would include purchases of computers, televisions, home entertainment centers, cameras, personal data assistants (PDAs) and other luxury electronics. Some 57 percent of luxury consumers bought this category in 2003. As a product category, the entire realm of electronics, which most often delivers entertainment programming, is highly experiential, so it is no surprise how high on the luxury consumers' purchase scale it appears.

Best Buy's Barry Judge
Luxury Is a Sanctuary within Chaos

As recently as seven years ago, Best Buy, the nation's big-box retailer of record for everything entertainment, was strictly a mass-market retailer, competing primarily on price for the entertainment and technology products it sold. Since then, however, Best Buy has been evolving a mass-to-class strategy that continues to be refined today as it assumes a new leadership position as retailer of choice for the affluent technoenthusiasts that make up a meaningful market segment.

In the role of vice president of consumer and brand marketing, Barry Judge is the executive chiefly responsible for giving consumers reason to shop at a Best Buy store. Judge explains the company's mass-to-class shift:

> We used to be strictly mass, but as we evolved about four years ago, we started looking much more closely at a subset of the market that we call "tech-entertainment enthusiasts," who are early adopters of new technology, TVs, computers, technology, and the software you play with them, like movies, music, games. We focused on what they wanted and found what differentiated us was "merchan-

dise authority," whereby we could be a one-stop shop for all the products, services, connections, cords, and batteries that make [them all] work.

Then we found four segments underneath the tech-entertainment enthusiasts that exhibit very different psyches within the enthusiast marketplace. These include a high-end consumer who has more wealth, a young enthusiast consumer, a married "soccer-mom" consumer, and a business consumer. What ties these people together is enthusiasm for the products, but selling to them and getting them to buy from you varies based on their unique need or mindset. So we have been a mass concept, but now we are trying to understand how we can tailor our mass concept to a more upscale audience.

Key elements of Best Buy's mass-to-class strategy are to first bring in an assortment of higher-end brands, which may include brands Best Buy has not had access to before. The second key is to focus on enhancing the knowledge of the salespeople to represent a higher caliber of technology training as well as more personal skills. The third element integral to Best Buy's evolution in luxury is providing customized solutions in terms of products, services, and installation. This is an extension of their "Geek Squad" concept, which sends out computer technicians to solve those pesky computer problem snafus.

But the hallmark of Best Buy's new luxury focus is to create *luxury spaces* [my words, not the company's] within the big-box store, where the upscale consumer can feel more comfortable. These new luxury spaces are boutiques within the Best Buy store that are modeled after Best Buy's own Magnolia brand, a West Coast–based chain of upscale entertainment technology stores that they acquired. Judge says, "Through Magnolia we are trying to create a sanctuary environment within the chaos of Best Buy. We are setting off an area of the store that is more consistent with the lifestyle of the upscale consumer in terms of solitude and dis-

playing the products in a more home-like environment. We are trying to push the brand up a bit from its mass roots."

Today, the prospects are bright for Best Buy as it moves to target a more affluent, upscale audience, especially as these shoppers' needs for adopting new technology are fairly predictable.
According to Judge:

> Better technology is coming all the time, like LCD or DLP,
> which is a digital light processor. Today, they [this tech-
> nology] are in only 2 percent of households, so there will
> be a much higher adoption rate over the next five years.
> With these flat TVs, because they look really good, people
> will start wanting them for the kitchen and bedroom, in
> addition to the living room or home theatre room.
>
> Although we have major challenges in the luxury mar-
> ket given the mass stamp of our brand in the past, we also
> see the opportunity far beyond a customer acquisition
> strategy. We already have a lot of these high-end customers
> shopping in our stores but for more commodity items and
> entertainment software. Now we have to leverage the traffic
> to showcase what we can do from a service side and higher-
> end brand standpoint.

Linens and Bedding Are the Second Most Widely Purchased Home Luxury

Luxury linens and bedding rank number two as the most purchased home luxury in 2003, bought by about one-third of luxury
consumers (35 percent). All linens are consumable in the sense
that they eventually wear out (I have an entire closet full of bath
towels that desperately need replacing), so that may stimulate
purchases. But they also, like electronics, are highly experiential

products tied up with the bed and bath, the most intimate and sensual aspects of our life.

SFERRA Fine Linens's Paul Hooker
Luxury Is the European Tradition of Fine Linen

A leading arbiter of luxury taste, the *Robb Report,* advises its readership that "if a man spends $2,000 or more on a suit, he should spend $2,000 on a sheet set that will make his nights more pleasurable." The message: Dress your bed as you would dress your body. Good rule of thumb, even if the more frugal luxury consumers surveyed spent only one-fourth that amount annually. Helping to improve the quality of luxury American's sleep is SFERRA Fine Linens, a company that provides the linens and furnishings for society homes, heads of state, and the Vatican.

Today SFERRA Fine Linens's president, Paul Hooker, explains how the company keeps its roots in the past according to the tradition of 19th-century European quality, at the same time addressing 21st century business challenges:

> We keep refining our concept of luxury to reflect how our customers define it. Today, luxury is about pampering oneself with a nonessential, whether it is a Heineken beer or a Lamborghini. Luxury works along an entire spectrum. For SFERRA, we look at luxury from five vantage points.
>
> First, luxury is about quality. When we sell our product to our customer, the quality has to be the best. Because if it isn't, nothing else matters. In the linen category, it's about the quality of the yarns, the construction techniques, the

finish, and the details [that] all go into making the product the very best it can be.

Second is tradition. Our company was founded in 1891 and we are established. We are not going away tomorrow. We know what we are doing and our tradition embodies that.

Third for SFERRA is pricing. Our products are at a price point that embodies luxury. If we had the quality and the tradition but at a very low price, we wouldn't be believable or honest with our customers. Luxury is a total experience.

The fourth perspective of luxury is our retail environment and where the products are sold. It's very important that the retail environment reflect luxury. For example, we just teamed with ABC Carpet to stock a leased fine linens department in their New York City flagship store. This is a good partner, since ABC is a microcosm of our customer, who ranges in age from 35 to 54.

And fifth is our brand image, our packaging, design, and the whole presentation. We just completed a major study to update our logo. We used to be "Sferra Brothers, Purveyors of Fine Linens since 1891." But out went "Purveyors" and "Brothers." Now it is very defined, simple, and elegant: "SFERRA Fine Linens, Italy, 1891."

> "Our products are at a price point that embodies luxury. If we had the quality and the tradition, but at a very low price, we wouldn't be believable or honest with our customers. Luxury is a total experience," says Paul Hooker, SFERRA Fine Linens.

Although SFERRA has a clear standard of luxury, it is fluid in how it interprets luxury within different categories and classes of goods. Hooker defines: "We aim to be best of class in each class where we sell. It's like Ralph Lauren selling to the masses through Marshall's, which is one of [Lauren's] biggest customers, and also selling $400 shirts in Saks. All luxury companies are trying to figure out how to cross the divide and sell to the classes and the masses. We are trying to reduce some prices and create items in collections to reach a wider audience but still have the best product possible at the price point."

For Hooker and SFERRA Fine Linens, the challenge is to keep enhancing the luxury value of their products. "We are always pushing the bar up. We offer an everyday line that is better than most people's luxury line. We use technology and know-how to keep refining our products, so the customers don't have to even think about thread count; they just need to touch it and hold it. When they feel it, they are sold," Hooker concludes.

The Category of Luxury Kitchenware and Housewares Is the Third-Ranked Home Luxury

The third most widely purchased luxury home products were luxury kitchenware, cookware, and housewares, with a total purchase incidence of 31 percent. And do I need to say that cooking equipment and our kitchen supplies are an incredibly important source of eating and dining experiences? As we look more closely in the coming sections on home product purchases, we continue to return again and again to the experiential equation that these product purchases encompass.

LUXURY CONSUMERS SPENT SLIGHTLY LESS ON HOME PRODUCTS IN 2003

Total spending on luxury home products averaged $4,125 in 2003, an overall drop of about 12 percent from spending in 2002 of $4,700. Whereas average spending on certain home luxuries, including linens and bedding; kitchenware, cookware, and house-

wares; furniture and floor coverings; and home decor fabrics, wall
and window coverings, and tabletop, increased in 2003, the overall spending trend declined.

Super-Affluents Spend Nearly Four Times More Than Near-Affluents on Home Luxuries

The luxury consumers' household income is linked directly to
purchase incidence and spending in all categories of luxury, including home. Although the average spending on home luxuries
is $4,125, the near-affluent and the affluent segments spend less
than the average, whereas the super-affluents spend more than
double the average. See Figure 6.1.

FIGURE 6.1
Home Luxury Spending by Segment: 2002 and 2003

	2003	2002	2003 NEAR-AFFLUENTS	2003 AFFLUENTS	2003 SUPER-AFFLUENTS
Total Home Luxury	**$4,125**	**$4,700**	**$2,500**	**$3,083**	**$8,875**
Art & Antiques	$3,750	$4,000	$1,750	$1,750	$7,500
Electronics	1,750	2,000	1,750	1,750	3,750
Furniture & Floor Coverings	3,750	3,000	2,750	3,750	7,500
Garden	750	1,000	380	750	750
Home Decor Fabrics, Wall/Window Coverings	1,750	500	750	750	3,750
Kitchen Appliances	1,750	2,000	1,750	1,750	3,750
Kitchenware, Cookware	750	500	380	750	750
Linens & Bedding	750	500	380	380	750
Tabletop	750	1,200	750	750	750

Super-affluents average $8,875 in total spending on home luxuries, which is 3.6 times more than the near-affluents, who average $2,500, and nearly 3.0 times more than the affluents, who spend on average $3,083.

LUXURY HOME MARKET POTENTIAL IS $126 BILLION

By projecting the luxury segments' purchase incidence and average spending on all home luxuries across the total number of households within each market segment, the total market potential for home luxuries is about $126 billion. See Figure 6.2. The super-affluents (incomes of $150,000 and above) have the largest share of total home luxury market potential with $65.3 billion, or 52 percent. Near-affluents, with a total home luxuries market potential of $29.5 billion, or 24 percent of the total, and affluents, market potential of $31.2 billion, or 25 percent, are of about equal size in terms of total market potential.

Home Luxuries Are Bought on Sale

Luxury consumers who can afford to pay full price in just about any category they choose to shop in are also vehement bargain shoppers. The majority of all luxury consumers made their last luxury home purchases on sale or at a discount off the full price in *all* home categories. The most heavily discounted categories in luxury home purchases include electronics (only 16 percent paid full price); kitchenware, cookware, and housewares (24 percent paid full price); and tabletop (26 percent paid list price).

FIGURE 6.2
Home Market Potential

	(IN MILLIONS)	% SHARE OF MARKET (SOM)	NEAR-AFFLUENTS	AFFLUENTS	SUPER-AFFLUENTS
Art Market	$ 20,030.5	15.9%	$ 2,989	$ 3,182	$ 13,860
Electronics	33,946.5	26.9	11,316	9,191	13,440
Home Fabrics, Window/Wall Coverings	7,727.3	6.1	1,190	1,288	5,250
Furniture & Floor Coverings	31,036.0	24.6	6,039	7,777	17,220
Garden & Patio	3,660.7	2.9	1,020	1,591	1,050
Kitchen Appliances	16,894.5	13.4	3,203	4,242	9,450
Kitchenware, Housewares, Cookware	4,631.5	3.7	1,159	1,667	1,806
Linens & Bedding	4,403.2	3.5	1,159	1,228	2,016
Tabletop, Dinnerware, Stemware, Flatware	3,700.5	2.9	1,464	1,061	1,176
Total	**$126,030.6**	**100.0%**	**$ 29,537**	**$ 31,225**	**$ 65,268**
% SOM			**23.4%**	**24.8%**	**51.8%**

DEPARTMENT STORES: FIRST CHOICE FOR LUXURY HOME SHOPPERS

For luxury shoppers, department stores are one of their favorite choices when shopping for their home. In four of the nine luxury home product categories—linens and bedding, kitchenware and cookware, fabrics and wall and window coverings, and tabletop—department stores are rated number one for luxury home shoppers. See Figure 6.3.

Specialty luxury retailers are either number one or number two in six of the nine home categories. They are tops in furniture, lamps, and floor coverings, and kitchen appliances and building and bath products. They are the second most popular choice in garden and outdoor; home decorating fabrics and wall and window coverings; linens and bedding; and kitchenware and housewares.

Rounding out the most widely used shopping source for luxury home products are discount stores (which include mass merchants, outlet and discount stores, and warehouse clubs), the number one choice for garden and outdoor and number two in furniture, lamps, and floor coverings. The Internet and other nonstore outlets are strong channels for home luxuries, ranking among the top three retail choices in five of the nine home luxury categories.

BRAND'S ROLE IN HOME LUXURY PURCHASES IS MOST IMPORTANT IN ELECTRONICS

Luxury brand plays the most significant role when consumers purchase luxury electronics and photography. The luxury brand is rated very important (44 percent) or somewhat important (42 percent) among over 80 percent of luxury electronics buyers. In no other home luxury product category does the brand impact the purchase decision so strongly.

The next most important home category for brand is kitchen appliances, where 35 percent rate the brand as very important

FIGURE 6.3

Where Luxury Home Consumers Shop

	#1 CHOICE	#2 CHOICE	# 3 CHOICE
Art & Antiques	Other Stores/Art Galleries (27%)	Internet/Mail Order/TV (26%)	Spec. Home Furnishings/ Furniture Store (18%)
Electronics	Electonics Spec./ Computer (59%)	Internet/Mail Order/TV (40%)	Warehouse Club/ Discount (15%)
Home Decorating Fabrics, Window/Wall Coverings	Department Store (27%)	Spec. Home Furnishings/ Furniture Store (22%)	Other Stores (14%)
Furniture & Floor Coverings	Spec. Home Furnishings/ Furniture Store (50%)	Warehouse Club/ Discount (17%)	Department Store (16%)
Garden	Warehouse Club/ Discount Store (38%)	Spec. Home Furnishings/ Furniture Store (28%)	Department Store (26%)
Kitchenware, Cookware, Housewares	Department Store (40%)	Spec. Home Furnishings/ Furniture Store (25%)	Internet /Mail Order/TV (23%)
Kitchen Appliances	Spec. Home Furnishings/ Furniture Store (29%)	Other Stores/ Hardware Stores (29%)	Department Store (25%)
Linens & Bedding	Department Store (40%)	Spec. Home Furnishings/ Furniture Store (25%)	Internet /Mail Order/TV (16%)
Tabletop	Department Store (47%)	Internet /Mail Order/TV (27%)	Spec. Home Furnishings/ Furniture Store (24%)

and 44 percent rate it somewhat important in their last purchase decision. Following kitchen appliances, brand is very (40 percent) or somewhat (38 percent) important for kitchenware, cookware, and housewares purchases.

FIGURE 6.4

Brand's Role in Home Luxury Purchases

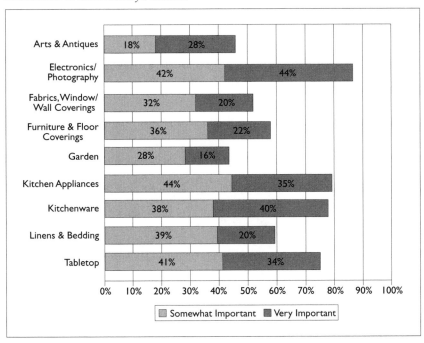

Rounding out the home categories, where brand is most influential in the purchase decision, is tabletop, dinnerware, and flatware with some 34 percent rating the brand very important and 41 percent rating it somewhat important in making their last purchase decision. For all other luxury home categories the brand is important for less than 60 percent of consumers. (Note: Chapter 10 is devoted to a discussion of luxury branding)

FUTURE VISION OF LUXURY— HOME LUXURY PROSPECTS ARE MIXED

As the Butterflies' influence on the luxury market continues to grow with their distinctive turn away from home toward reconnecting with the outside world, the forecast for marketers and retailers in the home luxury space is mixed. Generation X consumers are the logical target for home goods, as they remain grounded at home caring for the kids, whereas the empty nest boomers have emerged from their cocoons. We have seen how the Gen Xers, being much smaller in size, will never fill the gap left by the huge baby boom generation in the luxury home market. Therefore, home marketers will have to work harder than they have before to remain relevant to the home desires and passions of luxury consumers at all stages of their life. It is likely with the aging of the boomers that more home spending will be motivated by major life stage changes, such as trading down from the big family home to a smaller, more convenient luxury living space for two or the purchase of a second home. For the future, the following points seem to be the most critical for luxury home marketers and retailers to consider in developing their strategies:

- **It will be harder to get luxury consumers to "invite" purely decorative items into their home.** With the new anticlutter home trend taking hold, consumers are looking to clear off the tabletops and give only a select few pieces display space on shelves, mantels, and cupboards. As a result, luxury consumers are becoming increasingly discriminating about the decorative objects they bring home. Where they once felt compelled to fill up every empty space with something, today they want clean lines, space, and harmony. In today's connecting world, it simply will no longer be as easy for home marketers, especially those that sell things of a primarily decorative nature, to sell their wares.

- **Price-value is critical.** In the luxury business, there is a tendency to think that a company's investment in building and sustaining a reputation as a luxury brand gives the company the privilege, if not the right, to charge a premium for its goods and to never discount. But that strategy is just not in line with today's new economic reality. With Costco taking aim at the $100,000 and above consumers and home stores working deals with consumers to make the sale, luxury home marketers need to develop strategies that enhance the price-value relationship in the buyers' favor, at the same time using superior product performance values to craft a luxury brand image.

- **Turn decorative values into luxury performance attributes.** What about those home product categories that are linked less to performance and more to fashion, such as decorative fabrics? This may well be the big luxury-branding opportunity for the home: to turn decorative values into performance attributes. At their core, decoration and decorative values are all about communication . . . communicating beauty and esthetics to the individual. It's art, and art must connect in order to communicate. The secret is the power of the designer or artist to express a vision that connects and communicates with his or her audience. Some decorative messages (I think of the ubiquitous roosters we see everywhere now) lose their power through overexposure and misuse. Other decorative messages just don't connect to one's taste and feelings; for example, some people prefer blue, whereas others go for red. But the secret of success in decoration and decor is connecting with the consumer through an expression of beauty, peace, comfort, good feelings, and taste. In other words, transform the experiential qualities of the home brand into product-specific attributes.

Personal Perspective on Luxury

Hunter Douglas's Kim Kiner
Luxury Combines Style and Function

As vice president of product design at Hunter Douglas, the Netherlands-based company that is the world's leading manufacturer of window fashions, Kim Kiner knows lots about the emotional performance of luxury window coverings: "Luxury is a way to trade up from ordinary window coverings to Hunter Douglas. Our products provide pleasure; they satisfy a passion; they add comfort, exhibit the ultimate functionality, and are desired; all the while they also add value to the consumers' homes."

Its window fashions have become so well known in the home market that Hunter Douglas is one of the few luxury brand names featured in real estate listings. Its presence in the home sends important signals of the home's value, its luxury appointments, and how it was cared for by previous owners. "All of our products are custom-made to the size of the windows. So it is very difficult to take those window coverings [with them], and most people leave them with their homes. As people sell their homes, those upgrades make a difference to the new buyers," she says.

For Hunter Douglas, luxury window fashions go way beyond good looks. For Hunter Douglas, form follows function, as Kiner explains:

> Hunter Douglas started as a manufacturer of metal blinds. Then everything changed in 1985 with the innovation of the Duette® honeycomb shades. Hunter Douglas had the vision to take a honeycomb material developed for energy efficiency and turn it into a window fashion with style but that also conserves energy. That is how Hunter Douglas came to be known as a window fashion leader, because before that, window coverings were pure function. That is what the Hunter Douglas brand name is known for today: highly functional products that deliver with exceptional style through proprietary innovations.

Hunter Douglas's combination of high fashion and design along with superior quality and functionality encourages consumers to trade up to the Hunter Douglas brand rather than trading down to a no-name. Word of mouth plays a critical role in getting the Hunter Douglas brand message out. As Kiner says, "Consumers pass along our name. People visiting [someone's] home see them [the brand] and talk about the wonderful functioning of our products. It is getting to the point where once people have owned Hunter Douglas, they don't want anything else. And if you couldn't afford Hunter Douglas the first time around, you make sure you can the second time you decorate a home."

"That is what the Hunter Douglas brand name is known for today: highly functional products that deliver with exceptional style through proprietary innovations," says Kim Kiner, Hunter Douglas.

But as a luxury marketer, Hunter Douglas is challenged by discounters and the 1-800 vendors who sell some of the less proprietary Hunter Douglas brands at a discount. As a result, Hunter Douglas encourages its retailers to sell on a services model. Its new Window Fashion Gallery stores are a key tactic in the new retail service model, as Kiner explains: "Our Window Fashion Gallery stores are all independent dealers, but they are destination stores for our full line of products. There are a few hundred Window Fashion Gallery stores today, and they feature all of our products in the best settings. We designed the stores with a signature look, so the selling presentation is similar. All the products are displayed consistently. They [the stores] also offer the best services to the customer, and they don't discount our products in an uncomplimentary way."

Along with focusing retail on gallery stores, Hunter Douglas is also launching a new, even more upscale, enhanced luxury brand called The Alustra Collection under the tag line "Legendary Quality. Visionary Style." Designed to counter the downward gravitational pull toward commoditization experienced in the luxury sector, The Alustra Collection presents a more distinctive and exclusive product line and was scheduled for launch in July 2004 through the Window Fashion Gallery stores. The Alustra Collection takes the luxury Hunter Douglas product to a new plane of luxury. "The Alustra Collection targets a niche market. It isn't for everybody. It's for people that want something a bit more distinctive, a bit more unique, a higher level of style. What's important is that our customers stay within the Hunter Douglas brand, because we think there are probably some customers out there who might think Hunter Douglas is too mass at this point," Kiner concludes.

7

PERSONAL LUXURY PRODUCTS—PERSONAL LUXURY PERFORMANCE PARAMETERS

Personal luxuries, the category of luxury goods that are worn—or in the case of cars that you "wear" as they take you from place to place in style—are a primary passion of about one-fourth of luxury consumers. Some 28 percent claim that personal luxuries, as opposed to home or experiential luxuries, provide them with the most personal satisfaction and happiness. Not surprisingly, the younger luxury consumers, ages 24 to 34, are overly represented in the group that gets its greatest kicks from personal luxuries. Again not surprisingly, unmarried singles are more highly represented in this segment too. The profile of the luxury consumers who find the greatest satisfaction in personal luxuries is the "Sex in the City" role model. This TV show has had a profound influence on the culture, particularly the young adult market, bringing luxury brand awareness to this crowd. But now that the show is on cable reruns, where is the next influencer of leading-edge fashion trends going to come from? Condé Nast's hit magazine devoted to shopping, *Lucky*, and

Lucky's new baby brother, *Cargo,* are two of the few media on the horizon that can even come close to reaching this youthful, but affluent, demographic.

P *e r s o n a l* **P** *e r s p e c t i v e   o n*   **L** *u x u r y*

Cargo's Ariel Foxman
Luxury Is Knowledge That Money Is Well Spent

That women would clamor for a magazine devoted to shopping like *Lucky,* the overnight hit title from Condé Nast, is no surprise. That men would be eager for a similar magazine about their shopping interests is far more of a stretch, but early signs are that *Cargo, the New Buyers' Guide for Men,* which debuted in March/April 2004, is finding its audience among a younger, more sophisticated male reader looking for a hipper alternative to informed shopping.

Ariel Foxman, the founding editor-in-chief of *Cargo,* explains the rationale behind the new book: "We are like *Lucky* in the sense that we cover fashion and grooming for men, but we go further into all the things that interest men, from cars, tech, liquor, and nonfashion gadgets as well as fashion and grooming. The magazine aims to help men reduce the time spent shopping and maximize the time spent enjoying their purchases. We tell you what's out there and what's worthwhile. As a magazine, we sit next to other men's interest titles on newsstands, like *GQ, Details, Men's Health,* and *Esquire.*"

In today's overcrowded media marketplace, the success of a magazine is partly execution, partly luck, but mostly timing; and *Cargo* seems to have hit the mark by tapping a burgeoning cultural trend, the emergence of the "metrosexual," a young cosmopolitan male interested in fashion and grooming along with other traditional male pursuits. Foxman explains:

At Condé Nast we were putting together the magazine, executing the prototype, and deciding the title and cover long before the term *metrosexual* entered the mainstream media. Then all of a sudden metrosexual and *Queer Eye for the Straight Guy* became big, and it allowed for a national conversation saying men are interested in these product categories. They want to know more about great products that can enhance their lives and give them a competitive edge. But that is only a small part of what we are doing. There is nothing metrosexual about a cell phone or an Ipod, also things we focus intently on in our pages.

> "Men have always been interested in the purchase that is going to make them cooler or smarter or faster then the guy next door. It's only now that this is beginning to include grooming and fashion," says Ariel Foxman, *Cargo* magazine.

In my review of its latest issues, *Cargo* surely lives up to its lifestyle goal. Although it carries some of sister *Lucky*'s trademarks, such as the Post-it® stickers to mark the pages of products to buy, *Cargo* is decidedly broader in its coverage and extends into many more aspects of contemporary male life, such as wine, flowers, and entertaining. The luxury of *Cargo* is in providing its readers with the knowledge and know-how to make them savvy shoppers. Foxman explains this way: "From *Cargo*'s perspective, luxury isn't about a price point or an indulgence factor. For our reader real luxury is having the know-how to pick the product that is going to be most valuable to you in the long run. Luxury needs to be put into context, not just of status but one [context] that justifies and explains why something is worth more money. If you can understand it and appreciate it, that becomes luxury for our guys."

Cargo's brand of informed consumerism is particularly important for its male audience, as Foxman explains: "Men put a lot more pressure on themselves to make the right purchase. They want to be the smartest one in the pack, and they want the other guys to notice."

For today's men, *Cargo* aims to help them get beyond shopping paralysis, whereby they simply refuse to make a decision because they don't know enough to make the right one. In the fashion realm, *Cargo* helps men achieve freedom from the fashion police so that they can put together looks with confidence and aplomb. "Our readers are not interested in a head-to-toe luxury look. The real luxury for them is to have the freedom to wear a $3,000 watch with a $100 blazer and $300 pair of jeans and pull it off. It is the casualness of luxury that is so much more appealing than the everything-Gucci, everything-expensive look," Foxman concludes.

INDULGENCE IN PERSONAL LUXURIES APPARENTLY DECLINED SOMEWHAT IN 2003

Although the total of luxury consumers who bought personal luxuries—defined as clothing, apparel, fashion accessories, jewelry and watches, and automobiles—remained stable in 2003 at 63 percent, purchase incidence of specific product categories declined in 2003 compared to 2002. Purchase incidence of fragrances and beauty products, apparel and fashion accessories (including shoes and handbags), and automobiles apparently declined in 2003, whereas purchase incidence of jewelry and watches remained the same.

A shift in the consumer survey sample to include more men probably accounts for most of the decline in purchase incidence of female-skewing personal luxury categories in 2003. The latest survey included a near-equal split between male and female luxury consumers compared with the 2002 survey, when nearly 70 percent of the sample was female. Because fashion and apparel and beauty and fragrance products skew toward a female consumer market, this shift toward more male survey participation may well account for some of the decline. If we compare just the women's purchase incidence in 2003, it is about equal to last year's results.

Aerosoles's Kimberley Grayson
The Ultimate Luxury in Shoes Is Comfortable Style

Although some women, like Dominique Browning, go for the right handbag to feel well dressed, for me the shoes make the essential fashion statement. But nature plays a dirty trick on "shoe women" like me as we age. The soles of our feet lose padding (guess it migrates to our tummies, hips, and thighs), so we can no longer withstand the pressure of suspending all of our weight onto the balls of our feet. As we age, the sexiest, most to-die-for shoes come with a hefty price tag: discomfort.

In our group discussion among affluent women, one shared a story about being at a wedding where one woman drew a lot of attention wearing a pair of $400 black pumps. The "poor" woman in her pricey pumps had to take them off and sit with her feet elevated, while the woman telling the story danced the night away in her $59 equally good looking pumps. She must have been wearing Aerosoles brand, my personal secret weapon for combining style with comfort at a price that is unbelievable.

Kimberly Grayson, senior vice president of marketing at Aerosoles, a privately held firm based in Edison, New Jersey, describes the luxury embodied by the Aerosoles brand: "We so often hear the statement of wanting to have it all. The idea of having it all in shoes is being able to look good, feel good, and afford to do that. Now, if that's not luxury, I don't know what is."

With an average price point under $100, old luxury snobs might choke to call Aerosoles a luxury brand, but a democratically, experientially oriented new luxury woman wouldn't hesitate for a

"You put on a pair of Aerosoles and the combination of looking good and feeling good is luxurious. And we are an affordable, everyday luxury," says Kimberly Grayson, Aerosoles.

moment. "The concept of luxury in a consumer's mind has changed. That is why Aerosoles is a luxury because it is an experience, a feeling. You put on a pair of Aerosoles and the combination of looking good and feeling good is luxurious. And we are an affordable, everyday luxury," Grayson continues.

Eyeing new opportunities to deliver an enhanced style and comfort combination, Aerosoles launched a more upscale line in 2004 called Aerosoles Signatures Collection. Grayson explains:

> It is our ultimate Aerosoles. It is everything that women have come to know and love about Aerosoles, but we have taken it up a step. As a confirmed Aerosoles wearer from even before I came to the company 11 years ago, I didn't believe we could add anything to make them even better. But we have put new technologies and innovations into this line. So you pick up a pair of Aerosoles at $50 to $65 and say, "Wow, what an amazing shoe for the price." Now you pick up a Signature, under $100 for shoes and $100 for boots and say the same thing. We've taken it up a notch, and we've heard they compare to $250 to $300 shoes in the marketplace.

Taking Aerosoles to the next level also means getting the product out into the marketplace. "Our strategy is to do everything we can to get a customer into a pair of shoes as easily as possible, so she can be as happy as possible and come back and buy as many more as possible," Grayson says. In order to do that, the company has a very sophisticated but simple multichannel strategy that combines dedicated stores, retail partners, a catalog, and the Internet. What's even more innovative about Aerosoles's multichannel strategy is that all the parts actually work together. "We don't hesitate if an order comes in through our catalog, but we are out of stock in the warehouse that feeds the catalog; we'll send it to our retailer stores, where our computer systems locate the shoes and send them to the customer. It's seamless to the customer," Grayson concludes.

TOTAL PERSONAL LUXURY SPENDING
REACHED $2,500

The typical luxury consumer spent approximately $2,500 in 2003 on personal luxuries. Interestingly, those consumers who found their greatest luxury satisfaction in personal luxuries spent only $2,250 on average, and they demonstrated a less affluent demographic linked to their younger age and higher incidence of single marital status.

Average spending on fragrances and beauty products rose 27 percent to an average of $380, and spending on jewelry and watches went up 46 percent to $1,750 on average. Average spending on luxury apparel and fashion accessories dropped slightly to $1,750 from $2,000 in 2002.

For those households that purchased a luxury automobile in 2003, the average amount spent was $37,500, representing a 7 percent increase over the average $35,000 in 2002. See Figure 7.1.

Super-Affluents Are Most Extravagant Spenders on Personal Luxuries

Super-affluents are the big spenders on personal luxuries. Their average total spending reached $7,500 in 2003, which is more than 4.0 times the amount spent on personal luxuries among near-affluents ($1,750) and 3.8 times more than spent by the affluents ($2,000). See Figure 7.1.

FIGURE 7.1
Spending on Personal Luxuries, 2002 and 2003

	2003	2002	2003 NEAR-AFFLUENTS	2003 AFFLUENTS	2003 SUPER-AFFLUENTS
Total Personal Luxury	**$ 2,500**	n.a.	**$ 1,750**	**$ 2,000**	**$ 7,500**
Fragrances & Beauty	$ 380	$ 300	$ 120	$ 380	$ 380
Apparel & Accessories	1,750	2,000	750	750	1,750
Jewelry & Watches	1,750	1,200	750	1,750	1,750
Automobiles	37,500	35,000	37,500	37,500	37,500

FIGURE 7.2
Personal Luxuries Market Potential

	IN MILLIONS	% SHARE OF MARKET (SOM)	NEAR-AFFLUENTS	AFFLUENTS	SUPER-AFFLUENTS
Automobiles	$170,362.5	87.9%	$68,625	$49,238	$52,500
Fashion & Fashion Accessories	9,351.8	4.8	2,745	2,197	4,410
Fragrances, Cosmetics, Beauty Products	2,430.2	1.3	483	1,075	872
Jewelry & Watches	1,654.5	6.0	2,471	5,656	3,528
Total	$193,799.0	100.0%	$74,324	$58,165	$61,310
% SOM			38.4%	30.0%	31.6%

PERSONAL LUXURIES MARKET POTENTIAL

The total market potential for personal luxuries is $193.8 billion, but automobile spending accounts for nearly 90 percent of the total. Just given the fact there are so many more near-affluent households (12.2 million) than there are super-affluents (5.6 million), the near-affluent households have the highest overall market potential for personal luxury marketers, accounting for 38 percent, or a $74.3 billion total. See Figure 7.2.

But if we remove automobile spending from the equation, we find the total market potential for personal luxuries (fashion and fashion accessories, fragrances, cosmetics and beauty products, and jewelry and watches) is only $23.4 billion. For this class of goods, the affluent market segment (income $100,000 to less than $150,000) and the super-affluent ($150,000 and above) are about equal in total market potential, or $8.9 billion and $8.8 billion, respectively. Under this calculus, the near-affluents represent a total market of $5.7 billion, or 24 percent, of the total market potential.

With Exception of Fragrances and Beauty Products, Personal Luxuries Are Bought on Sale

There is only one category in which a majority of personal luxury buyers (60 percent) paid full price: fragrances and beauty products. Once you run out of your favorite brand of moisturizer, you can hardly wait for it to go on sale to buy a replacement. Also, industry pioneer Estee Lauder set the standard for the whole industry when she decided to never put her products on sale but instead offer biannual special promotions whereby consumers are given a goodie-bag (i.e., samples) with a certain level of purchase. That strategy worked like a charm as women everywhere hankered after those giveaway packs. But today, Estee Lauder is developing a custom line of cosmetics for discounter Kohl's, suggesting that the Lauder company's hard line against discounting may be giving way to the economic realities of today's value-oriented marketplace.

In every other personal luxury product category, including automobiles, apparel and fashion accessories, and jewelry and watches, buying on sale or at a discount off list price is the norm with the majority making their last purchase on sale or at a discount off the list price.

Guthy-Renker's Michelle Taylor
Luxury Is Skin Science Combined with Beauty Know-How

Established in 1988, Guthy-Renker was an early pioneer of television retailing, using the long form infomercial to sell motivational videos hosted by football legend Fran Tarkenton and featuring Napoleon Hill's *Think and Grow Rich* content. After founders Bill Guthy and Greg Renker realized that 70 percent of the direct-response purchasers were women, they decided to turn their marketing attention toward the feminine audience. So they teamed up with female actresses and celebrities to develop cosmetic and skin care lines that would resonate with the new target. Best-selling product lines like Victoria Principal's Principal Secret, Judith Light's Proactive Solution, Susan Lucci's Youthful Essence, and Kathie Lee Gifford's Natural Advantage were the result.

Today, Guthy-Renker utilizes all direct channels, including television, direct mail, telemarketing, and the Internet to promote its beauty lines, as well as partnering with QVC to further broaden its direct-to-consumer exposure. On television selling, the company's Vice President of Cosmetics Development Michelle Taylor says, "When it comes to beauty products, there is something powerful about being in the privacy of your home and learning about these products and how to use them. You are in the driver's seat as far as you want to learn, not held captive in a department store chair."

The celebrity spokesperson model is a perfect fit for television retailing. Celebrity spokespeople are first and foremost entertainers, and the celebrities Guthy-Renker teams with have a true passion for the product. "Our luxury is represented by our celebrities, like Cindy Crawford or Jane Seymour, who is involved with Natural Advantage. The customer identifies with someone like Cindy Crawford and believes in her expertise in beauty. Our customer understands and can afford the science behind our brands. She is looking for a solution to a beauty problem, and the celebrity is someone she can relate to," Taylor continues. A key marketing distinction for the Guthy-Renker stable of brands is building on and strengthening the trust relationship with the celebrity spokesperson, so there isn't a lot of cross-marketing between Victoria Principal's customers and Susan Lucci's, for example.

> "When it comes to beauty products, there is something powerful about being in the privacy of your home and learning about these products and how to use them," says Michelle Taylor, Guthy-Renker.

Having spent years with Elizabeth Arden, L'Oreal, and most recently Kiehl's as its president, Taylor has expertise firmly grounded in the development of luxury cosmetics and beauty products. And it's in product development, Taylor explains, where Guthy-Renker excels:

We are always developing new products and doing R&D to find new ingredients with special properties. While we develop products, we like to work in parallel to develop a relationship with a particular celebrity. Many times we identify needs and opportunities in the marketplace, like a new beauty problem in search of a solution, and then we try to identify the attributes that we would want in the product, and that gets married with a celebrity [who] has an affinity to that beauty solution. The product line comes to embody the values and beliefs of the particular celebrity that's involved with the line. For example, we are working with

Leeza Gibbons on a line called Sheer Cover, a mineral-based cosmetics line. This product was absolutely customized around her own beauty regime.

But even though the customer may be attracted to a product line through the celebrity endorsement, ultimately the products have to perform to keep the customer coming back again and again. "The relationship with the celebrity is the initial relationship," Taylor explains. "But as people begin to use the product and like the product, that becomes reinforcing . . . a secondary relationship that continues to grow because the customer really likes the product and the results."

For the future, the Guthy-Renker company will continue to push the boundaries of science to find new ingredients that help its customers fight the battle of aging. Taylor concludes: "There are always beauty problems to solve. The more science advances and the more that ingredient research is increased, the better able we are to offer our customers more efficacious products that really make a difference on the skin. So science and technology are really the feeders of new product innovation, and that is where the luxury for our customers comes in."

TOP CHOICES FOR PERSONAL LUXURY SHOPPERS: DEPARTMENT STORES, SPECIALTY LUXURY RETAILERS AND BOUTIQUES, AND INTERNET/MAIL-ORDER/TV SHOPPING

For personal luxury shoppers, the department store is their preferred place to shop. Department stores are the number one pick for shoppers looking for apparel/fashion accessories and fragrances/beauty products. Shoppers for apparel and fashion acces-

FIGURE 7.3

Top Choices for Personal Luxury Shoppers

WHERE LUXURY CONSUMERS SHOP	#1 CHOICE	#2 CHOICE	#3 CHOICE
Clothes & Apparel	Dept. Store (63%)	Spec. Fashion (47%)	Internet/Mail Order/TV (16%)
Fashion Accessories	Dept. Store (57%)	Spec. Fashion (33%)	Other Stores (14%)
Fragrances & Beauty	Dept. Store (58%)	Internet/Mail-Order/TV (25%)	Other Stores (17%)
Jewelry	Jewelry Store (59%)	Internet/Mail-Order/TV (17%)	Dept. Store (16%)
Watches	Jewelry Store (44%)	Internet/Mail-Order/TV (20%)	Dept. Store (18%)

sories turn next to specialty fashion boutiques as their second favorite choice; Internet, mail-order, and TV shopping places is second for fragrances and beauty. See Figure 7.3.

Jewelry stores rank first among jewelry and watch shoppers, whereas Internet, mail-order, and TV shopping is a strong second choice for jewelry and watches. (Note: Shopping choice was not asked for automobiles)

BRAND'S ROLE IN PURCHASE MOST IMPORTANT IN AUTOMOBILES AND BEAUTY PRODUCTS

Luxury brands are considered very important by the majority of luxury consumers in two categories: automobiles, where 76 percent say brand is very important, and fragrances and beauty products, named by 68 percent as very important. For apparel/fashion accessories and jewelry/watches, brand plays a less dominant role in influencing the purchase decision. See Figure 7.4.

FIGURE 7.4
Role of Brand in Purchase

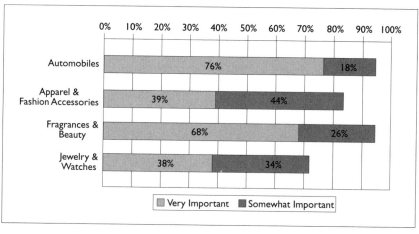

FUTURE VISION OF LUXURY—PERSONAL LUXURIES WILL BECOME MORE IMPORTANT

In comparison with home luxuries, the personal luxuries market is fairly small, yet its categories are likely to get a boost in sales from the Butterflies and their connecting trend. They will use the things they wear and how they dress themselves as social markers that proclaim their values and identity. For Butterflies, fashion isn't likely to be all panache; rather, they are likely to look for brands, styles, and fashions that truly express their personality. Like the "stealth luxury" consumer who wants to wear his fur inside, not outside, of his coat, the Butterflies are value oriented, but they still seek out distinctive styles that proclaim their personal identity. For the future, here are key opportunities in personal luxury:

- **Luxury fashion marketers can't afford to alienate the affluent, but middle-aged, luxury consumer.** Some of the more poignant moments in discussions with luxury consumers centered around fashion. These were frustrated women with a passion to buy fashionable clothes and the budgets to support their passion, but they literally couldn't find a thing to wear. They described themselves as the "forgotten women" when it came to the fashion business. A very affluent former fashion model said, "I used to be a size 8 my whole life. I modeled for years, and I was a stick figure at 5′9″. But after 50 and menopause, all of a sudden I'm turning into my mother! I've gone from an 8 to a 12 or 14, in that range . . . I'm still young enough not to want to look like my mother. Just because your body changed doesn't mean your style has to." The message for the fashion establishment is to design upscale fashions for the women who can truly afford to buy them and wear them—that is, middle-aged women with middle-aged spread but a desire to look sexy, attractive, and their best.

- **Jewelry is a new opportunity.** Jewelry is the least branded of any personal luxury product and thus it is a wide-open opportunity for building a brand. The best jewelry branding benchmark is Tiffany, a company that has combined an outstanding shopping experience with a wide selection of product across all price ranges, from sterling silver's low price to platinum and diamond's high. Tiffany has also taken the simple box in which the product is presented and made it an icon of luxury. The primary lesson in studying Tiffany's success is how it has combined many of the intrinsic luxury-brand qualities (e.g., premium quality, craftsmanship, recognizable style, etc.) with the experiential. Buying and presenting a gift from Tiffany, the most emotionally charged consumer-shopping experience, sends myriad emotional messages. That is the magic of Tiffany, combining new luxury with old luxury. Today, most other jewelers are focused on product, product, product, thus missing the big opportunity in experiential luxury branding of jewelry.

- **Pick your retailing partners carefully.** Certain retailers, notably Saks Fifth Avenue, Neiman Marcus, Nordstrom, Barneys

New York, and Bloomingdale's, have become arbiters of luxury and the authority on luxury brands for their consumers. If the brand is selected to be featured by these stores, then it is suddenly elevated to luxury brand status. That is why luxury marketers must be ever vigilant and careful about distribution. Luxury consumers want the luxury experience to extend throughout the entire buying process, from contemplation of the purchase to shopping and selection and purchase and use, so the store where the brand is shown is of nearly equal importance to what the brand is.

8

LUXURY EXPERIENCES AND SERVICES—IT ALL COMES DOWN TO THE EXPERIENCES

Despite the fact that luxury consumers buy prodigious amounts of luxury goods every year and spend in excess of $300 billion doing so, they still gain the greatest satisfaction and happiness from luxury experiences. Not just affluent luxury consumers, but the economy as a whole is going experiential. For example, in 1984 about half of American consumers' total $2,503.3 billion in personal consumption was spent on material goods, both durables and nondurables. By 2003, the percentage spent on material goods dropped to about 40 percent, whereas the services side of the equation accounted for 59.3 percent of the total $4,606.2 billion personal consumption spending, as reported by the Bureau of Economic Analysis. As a culture, we have such a surfeit of goods, even among lower-income households, that we have a continually growing hunger for more experiences.

This yearning for experiences ultimately is about personal transformation and self-actualization, as described by psychologist Abraham Maslow. Buying a new car or a new plasma-screen television or even a new Sub-Zero refrigerator represents an upgrade in one's standard of living, but it does not fundamentally change the individual. On the other hand, a trip to Japan, a hike along the Appalachian trail, attending a performance of *Hamlet,* or a walk through a beautifully landscaped garden can be life-changing experiences expanding one's insight and exposing one to new ideas, new cultures, and new ways of looking at the world. Through experiences, but not through material goods, our personal identity and sense of self are ultimately transformed. Today, this drive for self-actualization is the ultimate expression of consumerism.

In the following discussion of luxury experiences, I group luxury services, such as housecleaning, landscaping, and home decorating, with experiences, notably travel, dining, entertainment, and spas, beauty treatments, and cosmetic surgery. Services such as housecleaning, landscaping, and the like represent less transformative purchases, though by hiring someone to clean your house, you are free to do other, personally transformative things. So for services and experiences, the basic message is the same: Creating a memory, learning something new, and exploring new ideas all bring about personal change. Transformations, therefore, represent the next evolutionary step in commerce.

P *e r s o n a l* **P** *e r s p e c t i v e* *o n* **L** *u x u r y*

Matterhorn Nursery's Matt Horn
Luxury Is an Escape into Nature

Matterhorn Nursery Inc. is a 38-acre preserve located off Palisades Parkway in Rockland County, New York, that combines exquisite display gardens with a retail center called Matterhorn Gardener's Village, where the aspiring gardener can buy plants, tools, and equipment to re-create Matterhorn's garden lushness. As the entrepreneurial founder of Matterhorn, Matt Horn has won more awards than you can shake a garden hoe at, like the 2003 "Garden Center Innovator of the Year" award from *Garden Center Merchandising and Management* magazine; the 2004 "Retail Sales" Award and "Landscape Design Program Honor Award" from Perennial Plant Association; and the New York State Nurseryman's Association "Environmental Beautification Grand Prize Award."

If you wander into Matterhorn Nursery expecting to find just another garden center, you're in for a surprise. With over 20 separate stores making up Matterhorn Gardener's Village laid out along pathways and around ponds, the nursery is designed to give visitors a refuge from hectic day-to-day life. Horn's business formula is down-to-earth simplicity itself yet innovative in today's business world of spreadsheets, financial plans, and balance sheets. "What makes our nursery so different is that we are different," Horn explains. "It is easy for everybody to be the same, like Home Depot, Wal-Mart, Kmart. We look for more eclectic and odd things that people might enjoy. We are really giving people ideas, which a lot of other places don't."

Providing a wonderful experience together with gardening knowledge and enlightenment is the motivation behind the display gardens at Matterhorn, a fee-based attraction where visitors can see an exclusive David Austin rose garden and a Japanese garden along with other gardens devoted to ferns, hostas, and ornamental grasses, as well as Matt's Folly, where Horn gives his creativity wing. "Even in the greatest gardens I've seen, in all honesty they are very simple gardens. They are immaculately done, creating an ambience and outdoor living areas that people can live in and enjoy. But they are simple," Horn explains.

With a passion for growing things in all aspects of his business, Horn has figured out the secret of getting people to pay $2 for a petunia, when they can get a four-pack for 50¢ at Wal-Mart; and that means delivering an outstanding quality experience. "The word *quality* is so overused, but quality is definitely the keyword of what sells. When you see our petunias growing in the right soil and then take them home and find out how very successful they

"Just because you have money doesn't mean you have taste. Luxury is really about taste. Everyone has luxury in them. It's how you get it out of them. Luxury doesn't need to be expensive," says Matt Horn, Matterhorn Nursery.

are in your garden, people are willing to pay more for quality," Horn says.

Regarding luxury in the garden, for Horn it's not about spending lots of money or buying the most expensive thing. He says, "Just because you have money doesn't mean you have taste. Luxury is really about taste. Everyone has luxury in them. It's how you get it out of them. Luxury doesn't need to be expensive."

With his business about evenly divided between garden retailing and landscape design and services, Horn's clientele is composed of affluent luxury consumers. For the future, Horn sees developments in indoor gardening and greenhouses, as well as in tropical plants introduced as "temporary perennials." "People are going out and paying $150 to $200 for a palm tree, putting it in for the summer, and then throwing it out at the end of the year. Someone coined the term *temperennials,* which are temporary perennials. But you see people who put in tropicals and perennials that are hardy in the South but who don't have the luxury dollars to just throw them away at the end of the season, so they bring them inside over the wintertime. In the future, you are going to see an evolution of more people having greenhouses on their property and more sunrooms."

For Matt Horn and his like-minded customers, the reward of gardening goes beyond just having a beautiful landscape to look at. It is really about the experience of getting your hands dirty to make something beautiful grow. Horn says, "The real reward for me is keeping a garden. Once a garden is created, it takes lots of work to maintain the garden to the expected values of the customer. To me, that is the real experience."

SELF-ACTUALIZATION IS THE ULTIMATE GOAL FOR LUXURY CONSUMERS

It's this desire for transforming experiences to become a fuller, more complete, more self-actualized individual that is so distinctive among today's luxury consumers, in particular the more highly evolved Butterflies. For Butterflies, their luxury consuming—whether buying a couch, a comforter, a coat, cosmetics, or a car—is driven by a desire for the "self-actualization" described by Abra ham Maslow in his hierarchy of needs. Self-actualization is the need that is expressed only after the lesser needs in the heirarchy—physiological, safety, love and affection, and esteem—are satisfied. See Figure 8.1.

For luxury consumers, many of whom have an excess of material goods, a supportive family, and a career that provides status and other emotional rewards, self-actualization is the ultimate goal. This need is described by Maslow as "the desire to become more and more what one is, to become everything that one is capable of becoming." It explains the pursuit of self-fulfillment through spiritual enlightenment, greater knowledge, peace, and the appreciation of beauty, culture, art, and aesthetics.

Luxury consumers express self-actualization needs as they turn from a pursuit of materialism to a yearning for new experiences. Luxury product marketers need to study how the products they sell further an emotional experience for the consumer. This, then, becomes the focus of luxury marketing, giving new meaning to the phrase *experiential marketing.*

Experiential marketing is infusing all product development, marketing, and sales efforts with the feelings and transformative values that the product promises to deliver to the customer. Rather than stressing product features in advertising, such as the exquisite craftsmanship and finest-quality materials, advertising must com-

FIGURE 8.1
Maslow's Hierarchy of Needs

- **Physiological needs:** These are biological needs, such as those for oxygen, food, water, and a relatively constant body temperature.

- **Safety needs:** Safety needs have to do with establishing stability and consistency in a chaotic world. These needs are mostly psychological in nature. We need the security of a home and family together with freedom from physical violence, crime, and the like.

- **Need for love, affection, and belongingness:** Love and belongingness are the next need. Through the expression of this need, people overcome feelings of loneliness and alienation.

- **Need for esteem:** There are two types of esteem need. First is self-esteem, which results from competence or mastery of a task. Second is the attention and recognition that comes from others. This is similar to belongingness, but wanting admiration has to do with the need for power. Desire for status and the aspiration for status symbols, like expensive cars, are an expression of this need for esteem.

- **Need for self-actualization:** This is the ultimate need that is expressed only after the foregoing needs are satisfied. The need for self-actualization is "the desire to become more and more what one is, to become everything that one is capable of becoming." People who have everything can maximize their potential. They can seek knowledge, peace, esthetic experiences, self-fulfillment, oneness with God, and more.

Derived from Abraham Maslow, *Toward Psychology of Being*, 3rd ed. (New York, John Wiley, 1998).

municate the feeling that the product will inspire in consumers. To this end, luxury goods marketers should copy lessons from the service provider's marketing handbook. Luxury goods need to be sold, advertised, and promoted more like luxury services.

WHEN THINGS ARE NOT ENOUGH, LUXURY CONSUMERS EXPRESS DESIRE FOR EXPERIENCES

Hear the words of Butterfly consumers expressing a new, more highly evolved desire for life-changing experiences, as they turn away from materialism and the pursuit of more things:

- "You reach a point where you don't want stuff anymore. Over the years you accumulate stuff, and once you have everything you want, you come to the point where it is enough. There are more important things, like services."
- "It's changed over time. When we were first married, I appreciated the products, but now I appreciate the services. We learn to appreciate the experiences more because those are things that nobody can ever take from you. Personal things that we are doing for ourselves are important to us. It changes over time."
- "Things are less important to me now. The 'things' that I had are now being saved for my grandchildren. Those things are still important but not as important to me personally. I have over 1,000 porcelain dolls, and my granddaughters are going to get them all eventually."
- "You ask yourself how many more years you have when you hear about people who are sick. I say, 'Seize the day.'"

FUTURE VISION OF LUXURY—NEXT LUXURY BOOM WILL BE IN EXPERIENTIAL LUXURIES

For more luxury consumers, experiential luxuries provide greater luxury satisfaction than do home or personal luxuries. Yet experiences and luxury services are fleeting, and once they are experienced, they are used up and gone, but they are remembered and continue to live in one's memory. For a minority of luxury consumers, products provide the greatest satisfactions by being lasting pleasures and enjoyment.

Looking to the future, the next boom in luxury will come in experiential luxuries, including luxury services. The simple fact is that luxury product sales boomed in the 1990s with luxury goods companies growing as much as 10 to 20 percent annually throughout the decade. But every boom market reaches a plateau where the market nears saturation. When a market plateau is reached, an individual company's sales growth comes mostly by taking share from the competition rather than through organic market growth. Today, the market for luxury goods has largely peaked. Now that the luxury goods market has plateaued, future revenue growth will slow to a more normal 2 to 5 percent annually unless marketers can figure out a way to up their ticket prices in today's deflationary economy. As a result, competition among rival companies will become even more intense.

Not so with services. This is where the next boom in the luxury market will arise. Over the past 80 years, the overall U.S. economy has been steadily shifting from a product-based to a service-based economy. That trend will continue and even pick up steam in the experiential luxury arena. Consumers will clamor for new luxury experiences that only experiential and service marketers can provide. Luxury goods marketers are advised to tap into this emerging trend by discovering ways to link their luxury products to luxury services. For example, more luxury marketers are participating in luxury retailing (i.e., a service), which gives marketers two profit-making opportunities: first, by producing the goods and, second, by selling them directly to the luxury customer.

For companies marketing luxury products, they need to continue to evaluate if there are ways to catch the experiential luxury wave. Can they sell services or become more experiential? Can they turn their product into a service or an experience? For example, the luxury goods marketers that operate their own retail stores are right on the experiential trend and so are better positioned for the future than are their competitors that sell only through third-party retailers.

For those product marketers that stay focused on the products, they need to assume a new experiential approach to product development and marketing. That is, the company needs to get inside the heads and hearts of their customers and look at their products the way their customers look at the products. After all, when consumers buy a luxury product, they aren't really buying a "product"; rather, they are buying a feeling, an experience.

The luxury product, therefore, becomes a means to an end, not the end in itself. This way of looking at products is completely at odds with how the traditional luxury goods companies view their products. Much creativity and significant man-hours are invested in designing, manufacturing, and delivering a new product to the retail shelves. For com-

> Experience marketing is infusing all product development, marketing, and sales efforts with the feeling that the product promises to convey to the customer.

panies, the product becomes the focus of their efforts and the center of their world. But to really maximize the sales potential of the product, they need to view the product from the consumer's point of view, which is a feeling that arises from the purchase of the product. Experience marketing is infusing all product development, marketing, and sales efforts with the feeling that the product promises to convey to the customer. It's about how the product performs experientially for the consumer, how it delivers those special feelings and meanings to the consumer.

PURCHASE INCIDENCE OF EXPERIENTIAL LUXURIES BOOM

In total, 72 percent of luxury consumers in 2003 participated in one or more of these experiential luxuries: dining and entertainment (52 percent); travel (45 percent); spa, beauty treatments, cosmetic surgery (18 percent); landscaper, gardeners (10 percent); housecleaning and/or maid services, including party planning and catering (10 percent); and home decorators or design contractor (5 percent). This makes experiential luxuries purchased by more luxury consumers than personal luxuries, though it trails behind home luxuries in overall purchase incidence. Purchase incidence of experiential luxuries rose ten percentage points from 62 percent in 2002.

> "Dollar for dollar, experiences are a much better investment in happiness," says Leaf Van Boven, researcher.

Commenting on why luxury consumers gain the greatest luxury satisfaction from experiences, researcher Leaf Van Boven believes the key is the transformative value of experiences. According to him, "What strikes me about experiences is that they are luxuries available to all. Of course, some experiences are truly luxurious, like world travel. But many experiences are luxuries open to all: hiking, biking, camping, picnics with family, visiting local museums, musical acts, and so on. The same isn't as true of material possessions, where some luxury goods are just plain too expensive for some people to afford. There's no getting around the fact that Prada shoes cost a lot of money. Indeed, in our surveys, experiences tended to cost less than material possessions. Dollar for dollar, experiences are a much better investment in happiness."

Personal transformation through new experiences, whether a luxury vacation at a five-star hotel or a visit to the local museum, are in reality a self-actualizing experience. Whether these experiences cost lots or a little money, they work on the emotional, even spiritual, level in a totally personal and unique way. In other words, we can all enjoy a visit to an art museum, but the way it affects me (i.e., transforms me) is totally different from how it transforms you.

Personal **P**erspective on **L**uxury

Cosmetic Surgeon Dr. Paul Glat
Luxury Is Looking Good

With a curriculum vitae a mile long, including his position as head of the Division of Plastic Surgery, director of the cleft palate and craniofacial programs and director of the burn unit at St. Christopher's Hospital for Children, Dr. Glat, like a lot of his patients, was found by me through an Internet search. I was looking for a board-certified cosmetic surgeon to help me deal with the inevitable results of aging. Dr. Glat was certified by the American Board of Plastic Surgery and voted Philadelphia's top plastic surgeon by *Philadelphia* magazine from 2001 to 2004. I sought his counsel to implement a two-phased cosmetic surgery plan I put into place as my 50th birthday approached.

As a middle-aged woman who has had children, I am a potential candidate for nearly every procedure that Dr. Glat has in his "bag of tricks," but he didn't push a full arsenal of procedures at me. Instead, he wanted to know exactly what my goals and desires were. Commenting on the growth in the business from people like me searching for cosmetic surgery solutions, Dr. Glat explained that "cosmetic surgery has definitely gone from class to mass today. It used to be a taboo subject that you never talked about. People would sneak up to the back door of the office so nobody would know they had anything done. Now it is much more acceptable and everybody is talking about it."

The aging of the baby boom generation is the reason for the phenomenal growth in cosmetic surgery, but so too are new techniques and tools that offer safer but significant improvements. Attesting to the new acceptance of "getting work done," cosmetic surgery procedures were up 7 percent in 2003. But noninvasive treatments, such as botox, chemical peels, and microdermabrasion, are seeing the greatest growth today, rising 43 percent in the number of procedures in 2003, according to statistics compiled by the American Society of Plastic Surgeons.

As Dr. Glat explains: "There are lots of factors behind the growth in cosmetic surgery. One is that advertising is more accepted in medicine today. Another is that we have new technology and techniques that are more effective and more affordable now, like laser, collagen, and botox, that give people a taste of what can be accomplished. It just whets your appetite for more. And people, particularly baby boomers, are starting at a younger age.

Combine all this with the fact that it's become more acceptable and more people are trying it."

My two-phased personal transformation started with my nose and then on to a mini-face-lift to remove my increasingly prominent nasolabial folds (those deep wrinkles you get from your nose down to your chin) and to tighten up my neckline. I blamed a schoolyard injury in fifth grade (I took a soccer ball to the face) for my prominent nose. Although I had never liked my nose, I had lived with it for 40+ years, but if I was going to turn back the clock ten years, it just made no sense to live the second half of my life with my nose as it was. Besides, I always heard that your nose and ears keep growing throughout life, and that was simply too scary to think about.

I wasn't striving for perfection through cosmetic surgery, just a slight adjustment. Dr. Glat has to deal every day with people's unrealistic expectations, as he says: "This focus on appearance unfortunately has become a big part of our society. People watch shows like *The Swan,* which I'm not fond of, and have unrealistic expectations. It is misleading and unrealistic, especially for young girls, to strive for a perfection they can never attain. As surgeons, we have to be careful about the people we choose. We are more aware of body-image disorders that certain patients might have. We have to be a little bit of a psychologist to screen people."

Having become a cosmetic surgery statistic two times over, I am perfectly thrilled with the results. I understand from Dr. Glat that the nose is one of the more delicate and challenging areas to work on. I love what he did for my nose, because he kept it true to my face. And recovery from the nose surgery, though I had unbelievable bruising, was really a breeze.

The face-lift—Dr. Glat called it mini, but it felt maxi to me— was much more of an experience. I thought that compared with the nose, where he actually had to break bone, the face-lift involving only soft tissue would be less of an ordeal. But I was wrong. After he separated the skin from the muscle, pulled and tightened the skin, liposuctioned the fat under my chin, and stitched up around the ears and into the scalp, I was pretty much done in. The fact that I had to stay overnight in the hospital, whereas I went home right after the nose surgery, also should have been a clue to the extent of the procedure.

The hardest part of recovery, after the initial shock of the extensive head bandaging, drains, and swelling, was not being able to sleep comfortably for two weeks. But today, it's like the amnesia you experience after a tough labor. With time, you forget all about the pain and discomfort and just see the results. And I am thrilled with the results. I have been rejuvenated, and Dr. Glat gave me that wonderful gift.

On the magic he works on his patients and the contribution of his profession, Dr. Glat has this to say: "It is nice that people today have access to these things. They make such a significant change in how people perceive themselves and how they interact in public. There is a lot of benefit to cosmetic surgery as long as patient selection is good and the patients pick good surgeons who give good-quality results." As for Dr. Glat and me, we have another date planned sometime in the future when the mirror tells me it is time to do a little work on my eyes and forehead.

LUXURY CONSUMERS SPENT MORE THAN $9,000 ON EXPERIENTIAL LUXURIES

Total spending on experiential luxuries reached $9,020 in 2003, up 29 percent over the $7,000 that was spent in 2002. The spending picture on experiential luxuries was mostly positive, with spending increasing significantly in travel, dining, and entertainment. Only in housecleaning services did the average amount spent decline. See Figure 8.2.

Super-Affluents Spent about Twice the Average on Experiential Luxuries

Total spending on experiential luxuries kept pace with income levels in 2003. See Figure 8.2. Near-affluents spent only $4,418 on experiential luxuries, whereas the affluents spent about 1.6 times more than that amount, or $7,231. Super-affluents, however, are the biggest indulgers in experiential luxuries, spending on average $14,007, or more than three times what the near-affluents spent and about double what affluents spent.

EXPERIENTIAL LUXURY MARKET POTENTIAL

By projecting the luxury segments' purchase incidence and average spending on experiential luxuries across the total number of households within each market segment, we estimate the total market potential for experiential luxuries at $148.7 billion. See Figure 8.3. The super-affluents are the largest share of the market, accounting for nearly half of the total experiential luxury market, or $70.1 billion. Affluents, with a $45.3 billion market potential, represent about one-third of the total market for experiential luxuries; the near-affluents, with a $33.4 billion potential, are less than one-fourth of the total market potential.

Except for Travel, Most Experiential Luxuries Are Full Price

Unlike the purchase of luxury products where the majority of consumers buy on sale in just about every category, the business of experiential luxuries remains largely one based on paying full list price. Luxury travel is the only widely discounted experiential luxury where 64 percent of buyers got a "deal," so a majority of luxury consumers take advantage of discounts when they travel.

FIGURE 8.2
Spending on Experiential Luxuries by Income Segment

	2003	2002	2003 NEAR-AFFLUENTS	2003 AFFLUENTS	2003 SUPER-AFFLUENTS
Total Experiential Luxury	**$9,020**	**$7,000**	**$4,418**	**$7,231**	**$14,007**
Entertainment	$3,570	$1,500	$2,020	$2,220	$ 6,120
Travel	8,230	5,000	4,090	5,580	13,770
Spa/Massage/Beauty	750	550	380	380	1,750
Housecleaning	1,750	2,000	750	1,750	1,750
Landscaper*	3,750	2,500			
Home Decorator*	7,500	5,000			

*Too few respondents available for averaging spending by income segmentation

FIGURE 8.3
Experiential Luxury Market Potential

EXPERIENTIAL LUXURIES	IN MILLIONS	% SOM	NEAR-AFFLUENTS	AFFLUENTS	SUPER-AFFLUENTS
Entertainment & Dining	$ 42,325.4	28.5%	$11,829.1	$12,332.1	$18,164.2
Travel	82,754.7	55.6	19,460.2	27,051.8	36,242.6
Spa/Beauty	12,243.4	8.2	1,046.8	2,581.6	8,615.0
Home Services	11,402.9	7.7	1,022.4	3,307.8	7,072.8
Total	$148,726.4	100.0%	$33,358.5	$45,273.3	$70,094.6
% SOM			22.4%	30.4%	47.1%

Otherwise, when a consumer plans on buying an experiential luxury or service, he or she expects to pay the full asking price.

Fine Dining Is More about the Experience Than about the Food

For the 20th anniversary of the American Express Platinum Card, my company, Unity Marketing, had the opportunity to conduct an in-depth survey among what we termed "experiential affluent consumers" (i.e., consumers with household incomes of $100,000 or more who achieved their greatest luxury satisfaction and happiness through experiential luxuries). With an average household income of $175,000, the American Express Platinum Luxury Survey respondents were even more affluent than those in Unity's typical luxury survey samples, but the findings about these experientially motivated luxury consumers provide insight into the fine dining experiential equation.

The experiential affluent consumers included in the American Express Platinum Luxury Survey are very active luxury restaurant goers, with over three-fourths eating out in luxury once a month or more. Good food isn't the most important factor in the fine dining decision; rather, these highly discerning diners are looking for superior service in addition to a good meal and great wine. Number one on the list of why they choose a restaurant is the reputation of the chef or the restaurant. Receiving special services or a good table is the second most important criterion, followed by good restaurant reviews.

TRAVEL IS PRIORITY FOR LUXURY CONSUMERS

Researching luxury travel was a special emphasis of the American Express Platinum Luxury Survey that Unity Marketing conducted for the 20th anniversary of the American Express Platinum

Luxury Card. Typical experiential affluent consumers in the survey traveled just under six times in 2003. When they travel, they fly with the masses but vacation with the classes. Flying coach predominates among the luxury travelers, but once they get to their ultimate destination, nearly two-thirds regularly stay in a luxury hotel.

These luxury travelers are in search of rest and relaxation. They describe ocean cruises as the ultimate in stressless vacationing, and they value privacy as very important when they travel. When they travel, luxury consumers don't want to compete with other visitors for guest services.

Personal Perspective on Luxury

Crystal Cruises's Gregg Michel
Luxury Is Spaciousness Combined with Choices

Hinging a company's luxury value around empty space is an intriguing concept and one that works beautifully for Crystal Cruises. As an operator of three luxury mid-sized ships, the company aims to be not only the luxury cruise line of choice but the best in the luxury service business. Crystal Cruises's President Gregg Michel explains the commitment to service excellence: "We benchmark our competition not just against other cruise lines but against other leisure experiences you might have had, like land-based hotels or resorts. Our service philosophy at Crystal is to be the best in the luxury service business." Crystal's commitment to excellence is surely reaping rewards as the cruise line was just named number one in *Travel & Leisure* magazine's "World's Best Service" for cruise lines in 2004. In addition, its record score of 96.94 on a 100-point scale means that Crystal Cruises ranks as the sixth highest hotel service in the world.

Crystal Cruises's key point of differentiation in the luxury cruise business is the spaciousness of its ships. That translates into a higher ratio of service personnel to guests. Michel explains:

> Our ships range in size from 50,000 to 68,000 tons for only 940 to 1,080 guests, and that spaciousness really sets us apart from the other cruise lines. Crystal Cruises provides a feeling that you are not in a crowd, and that is a basic tenant of our package.
>
> This means our service staff is not diluted and there is more attention paid to servicing our guests. We find that people want services that are tailored to their desires, so it's our business to anticipate a guest's needs and wants. It means getting to know the guests by name, but also exceeding their expectations.

Extra space also translates into more entertainment offerings for the guests. According to Michel:

> Some of the cruise lines we compete against are smaller vessels, so with our ship's larger size we can offer more to the guest. Having these larger ships with proportionally fewer people on them means we can offer the guest a wider variety of choices. This includes dining options; for example, we have seven evening dining venues on our newest ship, *Serenity*. We also have entertainment, such as our acclaimed production shows and Caesar's Palace at Sea, our large casinos operated by land-based Caesar's Palace.
>
> We also have a strong focus on health and fitness, including spa services, exercise rooms, Pilates, and yoga, as well as beauty salons. Another important aspect of the Crystal experience is our focus on enrichment activities where people can learn while they vacation. It's an area that we feel we do the best.

Hardly the drudgery of a college lecture on board, the Crystal Cruises's Creative Learning Institute is all about personal enrichment and development, or self-actualization, in the words of Maslow. Through partnerships with quality organizations, the cruise line expands its patrons' minds with a high calibre of instruction while they venture from place to place. Michel says, "We have taken our enrichment program up one step higher with partners like Yamaha for keyboard lessons as well as Berlitz for language, Cleveland Clinic and the Tai Chi Cultural Center for wellness programs, the Society of Wine Educators, and BarnesandNoble .com. We build the Creative Learning Institute around four basic pillars: (1) arts and entertainment; (2) business and technology; (3) lifestyle and wellness; and (4) wine and food. This even sets us apart from land-based properties. We provide a real learning experience."

> "You have to express luxury at all levels of your product . . . you have to be luxury at all points in the cycle," says Gregg Michel, Crystal Cruises.

For the future, Michel says Crystal Cruises will continue to raise the bar on the luxury service experience to distinguish its unique qualities from its direct cruise competitors and land-based resorts:

> People always want choices in entertainment, enrichment, dining, health and fitness, and accommodations, as well as quality service. That is what we compete on and what we believe will continue to set us apart. You have to express luxury at all levels of your product. That includes treating people with respect at the beginning of the cycle through presell; taking the reservation; giving people the same kind of service through the middle of the cycle; and in the follow-up after you have provided the service. You have got to be luxury at all points in the cycle. If you are consistent, then you will build your brand.

TRAVELERS WANT TO CREATE MEMORABLE EXPERIENCES

Because relaxation is a travel priority, luxury travelers tend to participate in less strenuous outdoor/nature experiences rather than go in search of skiing, scuba diving, or other more vigorous sports. For them it is more likely to be golf, nature walks, sunbathing, and lazing on the beach. They also consider sightseeing, fine dining, and cultural experiences very important when they travel, according to the American Express Platinum Luxury Survey.

The emphasis of luxury travelers is to create memories that will last a lifetime. In these following statements, which about three-fourths or more of experiential affluent consumers strongly agree or agree with, we can see the transforming values that luxury travel confers:

- "I value my time traveling as a way to break out of the day-to-day routine and have totally new experiences." (90 percent)
- "Travel is made special when I'm with my family and/or friends." (85 percent)
- "I try to reward my hard work with vacation travel." (81 percent)
- "Travel is a luxury that makes my life more meaningful." (80 percent)
- "When I travel, I don't want to stay in accommodations that are less luxurious or comfortable than I have at home." (76 percent)
- "Travel is important to me for personal enrichment and becoming a more complete person." (76 percent)
- "I consider travel a necessity for my life." (73 percent)
- "When I travel, I enjoy getting special treatment and service that make me feel pampered." (73 percent)

9

PRICING LUXURIES—IT HAS VERY LITTLE TO DO WITH THE MONEY

The first and most important thing we need to understand about the pricing of luxury goods and services is that it has next to nothing to do with the money. The affluent luxury consumers can afford to pay full price for just about anything they choose to buy. Sure, there are superluxe things that are affordable to only a select few, but there are plenty of perfectly acceptable substitutes up and down the pricing ladder. The affluent simply don't *have* to shop at Wal-Mart to stretch their dollars like the middle- and lower-income consumers do sometimes.

People at lower income levels live a much more hardscrabble life. Even though the country's population is blessed to live in affluent circumstances relative to the rest of the world, the more moderate-income households have difficult decisions to make on a day-to-day basis related to the family

> "There are people who have money and people who are rich."—Coco Chanel

budget. For example, when the price of gasoline goes to $2 per gallon, can you still afford to get to work? How do you buy the kids school shoes this month when you also have to take them to the dentist?

These pressing budgetary issues are nonissues for the affluent. They have much greater financial resources and can borrow from Peter to pay Paul without ever really feeling the pinch. The *New York Times* describes the luxury trade-offs the new "frugal elite" are embracing in a January 2003 article entitled "How the Well-to-Do Are Making Do." Katherine Rosman writes: "To vie for the precious dollars spent on elite goods in a down economy, marketers are retooling their product lines, creating modest alternatives to traditional luxuries before their customers (immodestly) ask." The article points to Harry Winston's new less expensive Twelve to Twilight jewelry line starting at $6,500; the Hummer H2 line priced at $52,000, less than half the cost of the H1 $116,000 model; the new, more affordable Bentley GT Coupe for $150,000, when the company's basic models start at $200,000; or the $185,000 membership fee for a vacation club compared with a $500,000 time-share apartment. For 98 percent of the population, these are hardly bargain trade-offs.

On the other hand, this is how one of the new-luxury consumers expressed the trade-offs in a group discussion: "It's whether to buy the $100 bottle of wine or the $40 bottle of wine. I didn't get that $250,000 car, which would have been a little nicer, because that would have been ridiculous. But spending $50,000 on a car is OK, because it's within my means. Had I had less money, getting a Toyota might have been the right alternative."

Because the luxury consumers have all the material goods they need, when things get even a little tight, they simply wait it out until the time is right to get back into the shopping game. And simply having to wait and delay one's gratification may well enhance the ultimate buying experience when the flood gates finally open.

For lower-income folks living closer to the edge, money is a concrete thing. It means something real, and having it or losing it has real implications for people's life. For the affluent, money takes on a whole new symbolic meaning. For them, money transcends the concrete and specific; it symbolizes and measures one's power, prestige, importance, and significance. At the level of luxury and affluence, money is ultimately how we keep score, as Donald Trump once said: "Money was never a big motivation for me, except as a way to keep score. The real excitement is playing the game."

> At the level of luxury and affluence, money is ultimately how we keep score, as Donald Trump once said: "Money was never a big motivation for me, except as a way to keep score. The real excitement is playing the game."

THE FRUGAL AFFLUENT SHOPPERS

In previous chapters we have seen how the majority of luxury consumers made their last luxury goods purchase in every single category but one on sale or at a discount—fragrances and beauty products being the lone exception. They are also much more likely to pay full price for their experiential luxury purchases, except travel, where that category too is characterized by off-price buying.

Part of the reason the affluent buy on sale is simply because they can. Hosting sales events and marking products down have become retailers' knee-jerk strategy to give their revenue numbers a boost. *BusinessWeek*'s October 21, 2002, issue reports: "Prices just keep plunging: Fears of deflation are growing as a profit squeeze prompts more cuts." Where storewide sales used to be a once- or twice-a-year event, they have become department stores' favorite response to competition from big-box retailers and mass merchants. By increasing the frequency and depth of store sales, this once highly effective short-term strategy has been completely overused. Consumers are inured to sales and demand deeper and deeper discounts to become excited about shopping again. Where a 10 percent across-the-board discount used to get people into the stores, today they hold out for 50 percent off or more.

The price-cut, discount-promotion strategy simply can't work forever. First, it becomes less and less effective in driving traffic. Customers have become used to sales and stay out of the stores unless they anticipate the opportunity to save significant money. Second, what stores and marketers are giving away through their endless sponsoring of sales is their profits, and without profit any business will eventually fold. Sales have become the Pandora's box of retailing. Now that the "sale demons" and "discount goblins" that inspire consumers to buy only when things are on sale are out of the box, we can't seem to get them back under control.

At the affluent level, sales do have one positive side effect. An attractive sale or discount can tease a shopper to spend incremental dollars on an impulse buy. This puts an extra $50 or $100 that the retailer would never have seen into the till, and that isn't too bad, at least initially. The affluent shopper buys on impulse when she sees something attractively marked down: "I, like everyone, love a good deal, but I have graduated in my older years to where, if I have to pay full price for it, great. If it's something I need, I don't want to waste my time trying to find a good deal. But I love finding something on sale. I have closets full of clothes, and we all are pretty well equipped with shoes and handbags and whatever. You see something, it catches your eye, it's a good deal, you'll buy it."

For many luxury consumers, the time it takes to search out a deal makes it ultimately not worth the trouble, as this consumer who enjoys a bargain but doesn't seek them out says: "I really love to get things on sale, but I don't actively pursue sales, because I just don't like to spend that much time looking and going from store to store."

Among the negative side effects of shoppers' expectations of buying on sale is that when they actually stoop to paying the full list price, they may feel entitled to receive special services that they wouldn't otherwise expect, as this consumer says: "But if I spend that money and I do pay full price, I expect that that retailer is going to treat me well afterwards if I have any problems with the item. Some of the retailers have changed their return policies to where it's just ridiculous."

Up and down the income ladder in Unity's surveys, the affluent regularly and continually seek out a bargain. The simple fact that today's luxury consumers don't necessarily perceive themselves as well-off, affluent, or rich may be an important part of why they are so discount driven. They view their perspective on their financial status in far more modest terms. They describe themselves as "comfortable" or even "middle class" or "upper middle class" rather than inflate their financial position. See Figure 9.1.

Studied cautiousness is the best phrase to describe the affluents' overwhelming personality trait related to money. They are extremely cautious about what they buy and how they spend their money. Lots of luxury marketers walk around with fantasies about super-rich luxury consumers as shopaholics on steroids, but they

FIGURE 9.1
Self-Described Financial Status

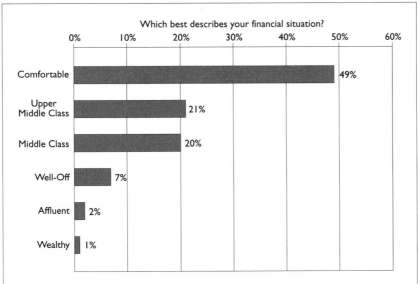

couldn't be more wrong. Luxury consumers have invested a tremendous amount of time and life energy to achieve their current luxury lifestyle, which they deem "comfortable." As human beings, we are programmed to seek comfort. Because these folks have achieved comfort nirvana, they are not about to put their hard-earned luxury lifestyle at risk from extravagant spending or living above and beyond their means. Today's luxury consumers are financially cautious, risk averse in their private life no matter how they behave in business, and highly protective of their financial resources, which is one reason why these luxury consumers who can pay full price hesitate to do so. It makes good financial sense to seek out bargains and the best deal.

P e r s o n a l P e r s p e c t i v e o n L u x u r y

Volkswagen's Karen Marderosian
Luxury Is Adapting the People's Brand for Today's Affluent Marketplace

Volkswagen has taken a lot of heat ever since it introduced the Phaeton, its first venture into the luxury car arena with a $65,000 starting price point. Critics have been brutal, such as J.P. Morgan's European automotive analyst, Himanshu Patel, who declared that "introducing a high-end luxury car under the Volkswagen brand is a clear flop." With the model sporting the VW People's Car hood ornament, the pundits claim Volkswagen has violated its core brand value of affordable transportation vis-à-vis the Golf, the Beetle, and the Jetta.

Even more unthinkable, according to conventional wisdom, is for some driver to pull up to the country club in a Volkswagen instead of a BMW, Mercedes, or Porsche. What will the car valets think? It's by challenging such narrow-minded conventional wisdom where the method in the Phaeton's seeming madness can be found.

The traditional rationales for any automaker to move into the luxury stratosphere hold for Volkswagen. The superpremium models offer more attractive profit margins than do the lower-priced cars. And the affluent target market is less prone to spending fluctuations brought on by economic instability. But for Volkswagen, the issue was even more personal: its lifetime loyal brand buyers were moving into other luxury brands as their incomes rose. Volkswagen USA's Director of Marketing and Advertising Karen Marderosian explains the luxury challenge:

> We view luxury as a migration. Our core customers have always been a little more affluent, a little more educated as auto buyers. They come to Volkswagen not because of low cost but because we offer tangible inherent value, and they appreciate well-made things with European style and design.
>
> But these people have moved up, using Volkswagen as a stepping-stone to go into other luxury brands. While they may move up, they continue to buy Volkswagens and have them in the household. So from a buyer perspective, our kinds of people are the ones that eventually move up to luxury. We don't want these buyers leaving our brand and so wanted to offer an option that would bring them back.

In keeping with Volkswagen's slightly off-center, unconventional brand personality, the automaker identified a target market ready for a nonstatus luxury car: consumers it calls the "transcendent buyers." Marderosian explains:

> We have found a segment of affluent people that generally take their own route. They live their life a little bit differently than everybody else. They want to enjoy their wealth for reasons important only to them. They make their own decisions, don't follow the crowd, and the idea that Volkswagen would come out with a luxury car is intriguing to

> "These are people that can transcend the traditional trappings of luxury and make their own choices on their own terms," says Karen Marderosian, Volkswagen.

them because it isn't the expected luxury decision. These are people that can transcend the traditional trappings of luxury and make their own choices on their own terms.

This description sounds a lot like the iconoclastic, tradition-bending Butterflies.

Although the Phaeton has a starting price point of $65,000, the model stays true to the Volkswagen brand's value-oriented positioning. The Phaeton's features are comparable to a $100,000 Mercedes D-Class. Marderosian continues:

With the Phaeton, you get a lot for what you pay for, so there is a value sensibility to it. For example, we have a 12-cylinder version, but you can't get a 12-cyliner D-Class Mercedes unless you go well over $100,000. So we bring accessibility to luxury. But we don't want to be just another BMW or Mercedes. We want to bring a new sensibility to the luxury buyer who sees things a little bit differently. It's for people who want to treat themselves to the best but don't want to display it to everybody else.

As for luxury, the Phaeton is the car for the person who rejects conspicuous consumption and enjoys "stealth wealth." Luxury used to be about exclusivity, but today it is much more accessible. People who buy Sub-Zero refrigerators shop at Target and Costco. People are breaking down the barriers of traditional luxury and defining luxury on their own terms. The Phaeton is the car for that kind of consumer.

GETTING A BARGAIN IS HOW LUXURY CONSUMERS MEASURE THEIR WINNINGS IN THE SHOPPING GAME

Among affluents money is largely symbolic; it is how you tell the "score." As a result, finding a bargain, hitting a great sale, or getting a $500 jacket for $250 is the scorecard through which the affluent measure their winnings in the shopping game. They don't go for a 50 percent off sale because they need to save that money; they go for it because it is a good, sensible, money-wise thing to do, and it is a heck of a lot of fun.

When you buy on sale, you are the winner in the shopping game and that just plain feels good, as this luxury bargain shopper says: "Whenever I get bargains, I feel so much happier. It's just personal satisfaction. Even if I won the lottery, I would still go for deals. It just makes me feel good." It is at this vicarious emotional level that consumers get their thrill from shopping on sale. "To think you got the best price that you could, that's great."

Sometimes a shopper even feels she got such a good deal that it was more like a steal, as this shopper explains: "I was just at Macy's before I came over here, and I bought my husband three Club Room shirts that were $40, and I paid $12 and some odd cents for all three of them. That makes you feel good. But as I leave the store, I find myself checking behind me, thinking they're going to stop me on the way out because I robbed them."

Costco Wholesale, which operates over 400 warehouse membership clubs, both in the United States and internationally, has mastered the strategy of deep discounting luxury goods. With product selection running the gamut from electronics, office equipment, hardware, and garden equipment to fine jewelry, luxury watches, and art along with luxury vacations through its membership travel service, Costco has succeeded by tightly focusing on its target market: the bargain-hungry luxury shopper.

Jeff Brotman, the company's cofounder and chairman, explained in a recent *Fortune* magazine article entitled "Costco: The Only Company Wal-Mart Fears" (Nov. 10, 2003): "We understood that small-business owners, as a rule, are the wealthiest people in a community." So Costco targets these local affluents, who are eager to spend money when they see both high quality and good value. The company has a widely publicized practice of holding markups to 14 percent, so consumers can find true bargains on name brand luxury goods that Costco picks up as overstocks or discontinued merchandise. Even though selection is limited, the values are there because the company stays true to its luxury shopper who is looking for the best products and best brands at the best prices.

Although luxury shoppers search out discounts and bargains, prices remain a powerful indicator of quality and ultimate value. In a perverse twist of logic, reminiscent of Groucho Marx's famous line "I don't want to belong to any club that will accept me as a member," if the price is too low, then you don't really want to buy it. In other words, you get what you pay for, so a higher price actually signals higher quality. This consumer explains her choice of the more rather than the less expensive option: "Price, first of all, will tell you if it's better quality. And it depends on what you are buying. I purchased a kitchen floor recently, and the kitchen gets a lot of traffic in it, so I would want something better than just plain vanilla flooring. I paid more for something that's going to last." This shopper, too, equates the price with quality and ultimate value: "I pay what I have to because that's where the price falls, and then there is quality to be concerned with. Like the [luxury] brands that they mentioned here, to me they are luxurious items, and that's why they're expensive."

> In a perverse twist of logic, reminiscent of Groucho Marx's famous line "I don't want to belong to any club that will accept me as a member," if the price is too low, then you don't really want to buy it. In other words, you get what you pay for, so a higher price actually signals higher quality.

When it comes to determining what is the "right" price to pay for something rather than the full list or the sale price or the deep discounted price, it ultimately comes down to an issue of trust: Does the consumer trust the store to offer the merchandise at the right price? I heard several people in group discussions express the fact that with prices being so fluid, you absolutely *know* that you are being overcharged every time you pay full price. As one consumer relates: "I went into Marshall Field's a couple of days ago and saw a nice shirt marked at $70 dollars. Then I went back in today and it was half-priced at $35. Now I know that it was $35 overpriced two days ago, and I am so glad I didn't pay $70 then."

So if the price isn't really the price, the consumer turns to negotiating, or haggling, to discover the "real" price, as described in an October 16, 2002, *New York Times* article, "The Latest in Luxury: Haggling." The article reports the trend of shoppers haggling to get a deal, not just in accepted places like jewelry and furniture stores, but also in unexpected places like department stores. The *New York Times* writes: "But now with the economy gone sour and customers holding onto their wallets, many sellers and buyers say that shoppers are haggling more—even at sleek SoHo furniture stores and chain electronics retailers—and getting bigger discounts."

The *Times* article points to a more educated consumer as the reason why shoppers are exerting more pressure on retailers to make a sweeter deal. Luxury consumers, in particular, are very savvy shoppers, well informed, and frequent searchers on the Internet to comparison shop. They have a general idea of the price ranges operating in the categories they are interested in and the prices offered by different stores. They know exactly how to find a bargain and how to get a good price.

But when all is said and done, the question of pricing comes down to what the market will bear. With so many shopping choices and so many discount retailers offering new and innovative twists to traditional pricing paradigms, the luxury shopper is ultimately looking for the *right* price, not necessarily the cheapest price, low-

With so many shopping choices and so many discount retailers offering new and innovative twists to the traditional pricing paradigms, the luxury shopper is ultimately looking for the *right* price, not necessarily the cheapest price, lowest price, or even the highest price.

est price, or even the highest price. The *right* price is the right balance of product features and benefits along with the important luxury values or attributes for which shoppers expect to pay a premium. Remember, it isn't really about the money; the money is the symbol and the score. The value—what the item is worth to me—is where the pricing equation must hinge in order for marketers to calculate the *right* price. This consumer expresses it best: "I'm a shopper. I will shop for the best price. But I'm going to go for the highest quality at the best price. To me, it's to be able to afford the price of quality." Another explains the pricing-value equation in this way: "You can research yourself to death, and you can still end up with something not so good or with a fake. My attitude is, do I like this piece? Is it everything that I want? Do I know what I'm going to do with it? Am I prepared to pay that price for it or whatever I can negotiate it for? I buy it, and I don't think about it anymore."

THE LUXURY-PRICING EQUATION: HOW MUCH DOES A FEELING COST?

In the world of luxury, the price of a product has very little to do with the cost of goods. The traditional pricing methodology, based on some established markup over cost-of-goods, just doesn't apply. Because price sends such a powerful signal of value and luxury, despite the fact that consumers are constantly in search of an even better deal, the luxury-pricing equation plays out mainly in the emotional arena.

Being a shoe freak of the first order, I have been fascinated by the trend to decorate the insoles of women's luxury shoes. Sometimes the insoles match the pattern on the outside of the shoe, such as my recent purchase of a reptilian-skin shoe that came with reptile scales decorating the insoles. In other cases, designers introduce totally new and funky patterns on the inside of the shoe. The startling thing about this trend is, first, it serves absolutely no practical purpose—nobody sees it but the person putting on the shoe. And second: Why did it take so long for somebody to think of this wonderful, innovative idea whose only reason for being is to make the wearer feel wonderful and special? That epitomizes luxury—delivering that feeling of specialness to the consumer. And it adds virtually nothing to the cost of the shoe but immeasurably enhances its value. How much extra am I willing to pay for shoes with decorated insoles? I know I don't buy them only because of the decoration, but if I find a shoe I like and it's comfortable, then I'm willing to pay a premium for that extra special touch that makes me smile every time I put that shoe on. This little touch, which is so straightforward and simple from a manufacturing point of view, helps push the needle to buy when a shopper is in the store.

When it comes to establishing a price for a luxury product, it all boils down to one question: How much is the consumer willing to pay for the special feeling or experience your product delivers? Luxury pricing is all about that subtle interplay between the perceived value and competitive market price.

Pricing one's products is an incredibly complex undertaking that must take into account product costs, overhead and operations expenses, taxes and import duties, exchange rates, competition, and established pricing structures. In the world of luxury, where consumers are seeking an experience or feeling rather than a concrete thing and their medium of exchange—money—is also so highly symbolic, the pricing equation is even more confusing and confounding.

In the luxury market, the right price is the highest one that gets the luxury

> How much is the consumer willing to pay for the special feeling or experience your product delivers? Luxury pricing is all about that subtle interplay between the perceived value and competitive market price.

consumers to buy. In finding that price, we must recognize that our customers want to feel like a winner at the shopping game, so they can't pay too much, but they also want to get a little bit more value, and they know you can't get something for nothing. The perceived value equation always must favor the luxury consumer, but it can't be too far out of balance, just tilted slightly in favor of the consumer. See Figure 9.2.

LUXURY CONSUMERS HAVE A GOOD IDEA WHAT THE *RIGHT* PRICE IS

In our research, we found that typical luxury consumers carry around in their heads a range of prices they believe are "acceptable" for the luxuries they are likely to buy. What are those acceptable price ranges for each product category? Our research, unfortunately, did not get down to that level of detail, but we did ask luxury consumers not just how much they spent in total within the category in the past year, but also how much they spent on the last purchase they made in the category. These data shown in Figure 9.3 help us get closer to understanding what the acceptable price range is for the luxury products they buy. For example, although the typical luxury consumer spent $3,750 in 2003 buying furniture and floor coverings, actual spending on the last item bought within the furniture and floor covering category was $1,700. This suggests that the typical luxury consumer shops just

FIGURE 9.2
The Luxury-Pricing Seesaw

FIGURE 9.3

Spending on Last Luxury Purchase

LUXURY SPENDING PER INCIDENCE	LAST ITEM PURCHASED	TOTAL SPENDING	AVG. SHOPPING TRIPS PER YEAR
Home Luxuries			
Furniture & Floor Coverings	$ 1,700	$ 3,750	2.2
Electronics	1,500	1,750	1.2
Art & Antiques	1,000	3,750	3.8
Kitchen Appliances	825	1,750	2.1
Fabrics, Window/ Wall Coverings	500	1,750	3.5
Garden	200	750	3.8
Kitchenware, Cookware	200	750	3.8
Linens & Bedding	200	750	3.8
Personal Luxuries			
Automobiles	$35,000	$37,500	1.1
Apparel & Accessories	300	1,750	5.8
Jewelry & Watches	600	1,750	2.9
Fragrances, Beauty	80	380	4.8

over two times per year buying furniture and floor coverings. Per item spending on electronics averages $1,500, whereas per item spending on art and antiques averages $1,000. From this per item breakdown, we find the spending on a per item basis is really rather modest for most of the products the typical luxury consumer buys.

Through research, we also know that the majority of luxury consumers made their last luxury purchase on sale or at a discount off the list price, with the exception of their last cosmetic or beauty product purchase. But some product categories have a higher percentage of customers buying on sale than do others. By comparing and contrasting the percentages of consumers who bought their last item on sale, we can calculate an index that measures the relative price competitiveness of one category of luxury goods as compared with another.

For example, the electronics and photography equipment category has the highest percentage of consumers who made their last purchase on sale (83 percent) and so provides the highest price competitive index value (126). That means the electronics and photography equipment category is the most highly price competitive in the luxury goods business, or 26 percent more competitive than the average, which indexes at 100. Figure 9.4 ranks the price competitiveness for each of the luxury goods categories, including both home and personal luxuries.

Compared with electronics and photography equipment, the automobile business is less price competitive. About 60 percent of automobile buyers made their last purchase on sale or at a discount. Because fewer than the average number of buyers bought on sale, the price competitive index for automobiles is 91, or 9 percent less than that for the average luxury good. That doesn't mean there is little or no price competition in automobile pricing but merely that luxury consumers are making their purchase decisions on factors other than price.

These data tell us that price is relatively more important when shoppers are looking at luxury electronics, luxury kitchenware or housewares, tabletop items, apparel and fashion accessories, or

FIGURE 9.4
Price Competitive Index

HIGH PRICE COMPETITION	MODERATE PRICE COMPETITION	LOW PRICE COMPETITION	NO PRICE COMPETITION
Electronics (126)	Jewelry & Watches (103)	Art & Antiques (94)	Fragrances, Beauty, Cosmetics (58)
Kitchenware, Housewares (114)	Garden (102)	Fabrics, Windows/ Wall Coverings (94)	
Tabletop, Dinnerware, Stemware, Flatware (112)	Furniture & Floor Coverings (96)	Kitchen Appliances (91)	
Apparel & Fashion Accessories (112)		Automobiles (91)	
Linens & Bedding (108)			

linens and bedding than when they are shopping for cars, kitchen appliances, fabrics, window and wall coverings, or art and antiques.

LUXURY-PRICING CHALLENGE—TRIPLE THE VALUE BUT ONLY DOUBLE THE PRICE

Success in luxury pricing comes down to a simple concept: You have to stack the value equation in the luxury consumer's favor. In other words, set your price based on the experience, not on the thing itself.

To understand the pricing premium of an experience, take as an example a plain white candle sold in bulk at the hardware store as a backup light source when the power goes out. By adding scent and color to that same candle, you add value, as the candle now interacts on multiple sensory levels and becomes a medium of scent and a home design element. But taking candles to an even higher value level through branding and packaging, custom in-store displays, and marketing communications, a scented candle by Yankee Candle is associated with higher self-actualizing needs, like comfort, relaxation, nurturing, peace, fulfillment, and so on. What then becomes the "price" for those higher-level values offered by a Yankee Candle over a no-name scented version or a plain white taper? That is the luxury factor . . . it is why the enhanced value candle can be sold at a premium over a plain white candle or even just a scented candle. You move the product beyond its simple features and benefits into a whole new value realm.

When you sell to the luxury market, money is not the hard currency. The real currency of the transaction is the value, the luxury value that makes something special and worth paying a premium for but not too high a premium, a just-right kind of premium. The challenge for luxury marketers is to find the range of prices that their target customers are used to thinking about

> Success in luxury pricing comes down to a simple concept: You have to stack the value equation in the luxury consumer's favor.

When you sell to the luxury market, money is not the hard currency. The real currency of the transaction is the value, the luxury value that makes something special and worth paying a premium for but not too high a premium, a just-right kind of premium.

and used to paying. Take that range as a starting point, plot out the specific product features, benefits, and values that those products deliver at each price point range, then find a place to pitch your specific product with a vastly enhanced value proposition. You will want to price the product on the upward end of the competitive set but not necessarily too far out of bounds. The opportunity is to add three times the value but only double the price. That is how you can keep the pricing equation stacked in favor of the consumer but not *too* much in favor of the consumer or else the product loses its specialness.

Adding value doesn't necessarily have to do with adding costs to the product; rather, the value can come from very simple concepts that enhance the specialness to the luxury consumer—think decorated insoles in shoes or the shape of a wine glass. Although I am no expert in glassmaking, it just seems to me it would cost no more to manufacture a wine glass of the exact same size but shaped right for a particular wine as to manufacture one that is shaped wrong. That is the innovative value proposition that Riedel Crystal discovered for its crystal stemware.

P e r s o n a l P e r s p e c t i v e o n L u x u r y

Riedel Crystal's Maximillian Riedel
Luxury Is Delivering a True Wine-Tasting Experience for Different Wines

Having been in the glassmaking business since 1756, Riedel Crystal was the first to introduce wine-specific stemware in 1973. Claus Riedel discovered that different shapes and sizes of glasses could be customized to enhance the specific characteristics of a particular wine and thus enhance the wine drinker's experience. Maximillian Riedel, the company's executive vice president of marketing, explains: "The world of wine and stemware has changed enormously in America and abroad. As more people become interested in fine wine and discover that using the appropriate stemware further enhances their experience of wine, they are buying fine stemware in record numbers."

The Sommelier was the company's flagship line that introduced this brand-new value proposition to the world of wine, as described by the company's Web site: "The delivery of a wine's message—its bouquet and taste—depends on the form of the glass. It is the responsibility of a glass to convey the wine's message in the best manner to the human senses." The company started in 1973 with 10 different sizes and shapes of stemware, and today the line extends to over 30 different shapes for new wines that were not even dreamed of back in 1973.

But even though shape and design are the Sommelier's experiential point of difference and justify the company charging a premium for its glasses over the competition, the line also stacks all kinds of luxury features into the actual item itself. Each glass is handmade from more than 24 percent lead crystal with the upper parts blown into a mold and the stem and base individually handcrafted.

The luxury point of difference for Riedel Crystal is clear, as Maximillian Riedel explains: "Riedel hand-blown full lead crystal Sommelier stems, made in Austria, are not only beautiful to look at, hold, touch, and listen to, but these glasses communicate a wine's maximum harmony and balance, a wondrous sensual experience." Who wouldn't pay a luxury premium, between $60 and $90 a stem, for those values? Frankly, anyone who pays $90 for a bottle of wine ought to invest the same for the right glass to maximize the enjoyment.

But for those who find the Sommelier's price range still a little too luxurious, the company offers an alternative: Vinum. Priced well under the Sommelier level but at a premium compared to standard stemware, the $20 to $30 per stem Vinum line has the same customized shapes for different grape varietels and the same over 24 percent lead crystal content, but it is machinemade rather than handmade. The company positions the Vinum line as "Vitrum-Vinothek" for everyday use.

The impact of Riedel Crystal on the experience of wine tasting and enjoyment cannot be underestimated. The company has built a near-cult following for its wine glasses and encouraged consumers to invest in many different glasses for different wine-tasting experiences, whereas before all you needed was a single glass for white wine and another glass for red. Riedel has also garnered the attention of restaurateurs, who are an important authority for the wine challenged and inexperienced. Maximillian Riedel comments that "based on consumer demand, restaurateurs today pay as much attention to their stemware as to their wine cellars."

MONEY IS LARGELY SYMBOLIC

It's not about the dollars; it's about what the dollars signify. Americans have a very complex relationship with their money. It represents many different deep-seated concepts, and it connects very emotionally with people. This is where businesspeople become confused when talking about the emotional, experiential aspects of marketing. They reason, wrongly, that pricing and spending decisions are played out in the left brain of consumers' minds, in the same way businesspeople make business decisions. But deciding on buying some new piece of office equipment like a postal meter (computers are too sexy and emotion-laden) is just strictly dollars and cents. It's nothing like shopping and buying clothes where emotion is everything.

In conclusion, luxury marketers must remember that the luxury consumer is characterized by a passion for bargains and a high level of proficiency at shopping. Here are the keys to understanding the pricing equation from shoppers' points of view:

- **Luxury consumers always shop for bargains and look for sales.** What is this drive for discounts about when these people can easily afford to pay full price? Higher income brackets exhibit the same frugal shopping behavior. Ultimately, what you pay is a game, and the dollars saved are the scorecard on which consumers measure their winnings and losings.

- **Luxury consumers are very proficient shoppers, and they spend much more time in stores, malls, and online than do any other consumers.** These consumers are well versed in what products are worth, which stores offer the best prices every day, and how specific shops discount and mark down. These affluent consumers have the time, inclination, and passion for shopping like no other type of shopper.

- **More than cheap, they want a value.** Ultimately, it isn't about the money at all but what the money symbolizes. Luxury shoppers, first and foremost, want a good value, and they expect to pay more for that value, just not quite as much as the added value would be expected to cost. So pricing becomes an exercise in discovering what consumers expect to pay for a product of commensurate value and then pricing the product just slightly below, but not too far below, that price. They want a bargain, but they don't expect to get a steal.

- **Price is all part of the experiential equation.** Shoppers get a thrill out of finding a bargain, of getting a $500 skirt for $250, a $1,000 handbag for $575. Searching out and getting a bargain is all part of the fun of shopping. It's not about the price or the money; it is about the experience of getting a good deal.

10

PROMOTING LUXURIES— MYTHS AND MYSTERIES OF LUXURY BRANDING

Many people, both those in and those out of the industry, believe that advertising really makes people desire luxury. The simple fact is that the great bulk of advertising we are exposed to day in, day out doesn't work to drive sales. It might build brand awareness, but even that is questionable with TiVo giving us a technology-based way to skip intrusive television commercials. Of course, the rest of us already use our manual remote controls to bypass commercials once the show we are watching signals us, through a commercial break, that it is time to see what is playing on the other channels.

Although advertisers turning to the print media gain the value of advertising shelf life, as most readers keep magazines on their coffee tables for a time, the fact is that people don't buy *Martha Stewart Living* or *People* or any other publication you want to name for the advertising. They buy publications for the editorials and

> "Half the money I spend on advertising is wasted; the trouble is, I don't know which half."—John Wanamaker (1838–1922), also attributed to Lord Leverhulme (1851–1927).

the stories whereas advertising, unless it is truly arresting, is just passed by.

David Ogilvy, in his classic book *Ogilvy on Advertising* (originally published in 1983 by Crown Publishing Group), points out that six times as many people read the average article as read the average advertisement. He concludes that ads need to be written more like editorials. That may be why savvy marketers are turning more and more to public relations to have their products and brand stories put into real stories—but more on that later. The simple fact is that today the traditional medium of advertising is broken in this multimedia, information-intensive society. Advertisers need to do something vastly different to get their messages through and, it is hoped, drive consumers to action.

INFLUENCERS IN LUXURY BUYING

The finding from Unity Marketing's survey of luxury consumers bears out the conclusion that most advertising doesn't work very well in generating sales or driving purchases. When asked to rank how important eight different influencers were when making their last luxury purchase of home luxuries, personal luxuries, and experiential luxuries, luxury consumers ranked advertisements, including those on television, in magazines, and in newspapers, dead last. See Figure 10.1. Although there were slight variations between the importance of different influencers on specific luxury purchases—for example, recommendations of friends played a significantly more important role in purchasing experiential luxuries than for either home or personal luxuries—the overall ranking is clear when examining index values comparing the relative importance within categories. Three influencers were of the utmost importance in getting luxury consumers to buy: the price-value relationship (with an index value of 125, which means this factor is 25 percent more important than average); brand/company

FIGURE 10.1

How Influencers Rank in Luxury Buying

INFLUENCERS' INDEX	HOME	PERSONAL	EXPERIENTIAL	TOTAL
Price-Value Relationship	131	127	118	125
Brand/Company Reputation	121	133	122	125
Store/Dealer Reputation or Where Purchased	121	124	126	124
Recommendations of Friends	88	86	106	93
Articles & Reviews	90	82	98	90
Internet/Web site	92	82	80	85
Salesperson's Info.	86	90	73	83
Advertisements	71	76	78	75

reputation (also index value of 125); and store/dealer reputation or, in the case of experiential luxuries, the service provider's reputation (index value of 124).

Because branding in the luxury marketing world is both the medium and the message on the promotion side of marketing, the rest of this chapter is devoted to deconstructing the luxury branding myths with which we have been indoctrinated.

LUXURY MARKETING MYTH #1: ADVERTISING IS KEY TO PROMOTING AND SELLING LUXURIES

Reality: The Luxury Marketing "Triple Play" Generates Sales: The Product Brand, Dealer's Brand, and Price-Value Interact to Make Sales

A subtle interplay exists in luxury marketing between three factors that most strongly influence the luxury consumer to buy: (1) product brand, (2) dealer's or store's brand or service pro-

> A subtle interplay exists in luxury marketing between three factors that most strongly influence the luxury consumer to buy: (1) product brand, (2) dealer's or store's brand or service provider's reputation, and (3) price-value relationship.

vider's reputation, and (3) price-value relationship. See Figure 10.2. I call this the luxury marketing "triple play." Depending on whether the shopper is buying a home luxury—such as linens, furniture, an appliance—or a personal luxury—such as a car, apparel, fashion accessories, beauty products—or an experiential luxury—such as travel, spa, a dinner out—the relative importance of each of these three factors may shift, but in all categories of the luxury market these three factors interact synergistically to encourage the consumer to buy.

FIGURE 10.2

Influencers of Luxury Purchases

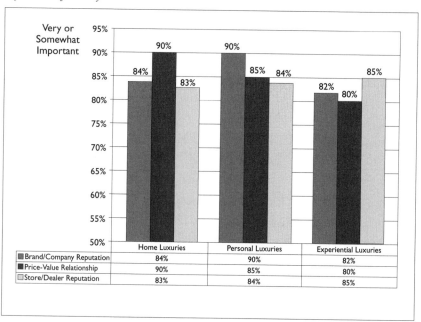

	Home Luxuries	Personal Luxuries	Experiential Luxuries
■ Brand/Company Reputation	84%	90%	82%
■ Price-Value Relationship	90%	85%	80%
▢ Store/Dealer Reputation	83%	84%	85%

Polo Ralph Lauren's Jeffrey Morgan
Luxury Is Telling a Story through Different Retail Worlds

Ever since Ralph Lauren designed and started selling wide neckties back in 1967, and in the process created a cultural phenomenon, Ralph Lauren has crafted a life-style brand that personifies his vision of luxury. Jeffrey Morgan, formerly the head of marketing for Polo Ralph Lauren (and today the president for product licensing), explains how Ralph's vision is transformed into a luxury brand: "Ralph's genius is creating beautiful products that tell a story—a story that depicts romantic and luxurious worlds that consumers can dream of and aspire to."

The worlds for the Polo Ralph Lauren brand are the medium and the message, to borrow Marshall McLuhan's famous expression. Morgan continues: "As marketers, our job is to understand, create, and communicate these worlds. Ralph is not just creating products, he is evoking a way of living. Luxury is always about context, the story of the brand."

The brand worlds of Polo Ralph Lauren are expansive and include many different and distinct lifestyle stories. "We create many worlds, from the modern and sleek to the classic old English. Our company embodies many aesthetics and many worlds that are all expressions of Ralph's taste," Morgan says.

"We are different from other fashion companies. Ralph is famous for saying 'It's not about fashion, it's about living.' Fashion often implies 'of the moment,' that it won't last. Our sensibility is about living, and living is fundamental. Living is also about change, but the changes are

> "Our company embodies many aesthetics, and many worlds that are all expressions of Ralph's taste," says Jeffrey Morgan, Polo Ralph Lauren.

subtle and pleasing. People know they can trust Ralph's taste to stand the test of time," Morgan continues.

The secret of the brand's success is that the customer can buy into one of Ralph's worlds or the entire multiplicity of his world visions. In other words, one person goes for the safari story, another for the western story, and another the old English story, and someone else incorporates all three stories into his or her personal world. Explains Morgan: "We are not afraid to say we are a design-driven company. Ralph is clear in his vision and the customer responds. The brand is a promise for people who trust Ralph's judgment in quality, taste, and beauty. They continue to buy because they love the experience of owning the product."

Key to presenting those Ralph Lauren worlds to the consumer are the Ralph Lauren stores, which Morgan describes as the "purest expression of our brand." When shopping in a Ralph Lauren store, the customer becomes an integral part of Ralph's multidimensional worldview. Morgan explains:

> We are experiential marketers, from the country store in East Hampton to the mansion on Madison Ave and 72nd Street. The store is where we give the three-dimensional experience of the brand. We create different stores for different worlds. For example, you find in our New York City stores the uptown posh world of the mansion on Madison Avenue and the downtown world of our stores in Soho and Bleeker Street. You will find even more different worlds in our stores in New Canaan, Connecticut, and Nantucket, Massachusetts. The Ralph Lauren customer can find us in all their various lifestyles from city to country. The same is true internationally, where our customer finds us in London, Paris, Milan, or Tokyo. All of these stores reflect the Ralph Lauren sensibility in the context of the world where they are located. We have a Ralph Lauren look for you in all of your worlds.

The Polo Ralph Lauren brand is expansive in vision, but firmly grounded in the reality of luxury. "Our brand is all about the lifestyles of our worlds. We define luxury through these concepts. Each Ralph Lauren world is unique and different, but unified by a singular vision of taste," Morgan concludes.

LUXURY MARKETING CATCH-22: HOW DO YOU BUILD A LUXURY BRAND IF ADVERTISING DOESN'T WORK ANYMORE?

Just because most advertising doesn't work to generate sales doesn't mean that luxury companies should necessarily stop advertising. Rather, they need to create ads that resonate and are relevant to the passions, desires, and fantasies of the consumer. The brand's ads must tell a story that will be so involving that the consumer becomes part of the brand story. But the brand story needs to be revised, refined, reinvented as the values of the consumer change, as they inevitably will. Brands must be expansive so that they can become part of many people's life and can change with the times.

The lesson here is to look at brands that have longevity and have sustained themselves over time, like Polo Ralph Lauren as well as many other luxury brands that have a history spanning decades, even centuries, and you find brands that continue to reinvent themselves to stay relevant. The key word is *relevance* . . . delivering meaning to the consumer's life today and having an expansive vision in order to continue to deliver meaning to the consumer in the future as the consumer's life changes. Look at failed or failing brands—Polaroid, Schwinn, Miller High Life, Singer

> The key word is *relevance* . . . delivering meaning to the consumer's life today and having an expansive vision in order to continue to deliver meaning to the consumer in the future as the consumer's life changes.

(have you noticed that interest in home sewing is going through the roof, but the Singer brand isn't around anymore to take advantage of it?)—and you find companies that failed to keep their brand relevant. They didn't have an expansive vision of what their brand could deliver.

Defining your brand expansively can go far to keep your brand, your company, your story relevant. A new avenue of psychological research is opening up that explores the use and application of storytelling, not so much kids' bedtime stories but storytelling in the age-old tradition of medieval bards and troubadours telling stories of warriors like King Arthur around open fire pits in the great halls of stone castles. These stories touch deep places in the human psyche and brand-building marketers are turning their powerful communications capabilities to tapping these ancient roots through corporate stories and branding tales.

Adjunct Professor at Columbia University and Penn State Jo Tyler, EdD, and also founder of a consultancy called Humanizing Business, is at the forefront of the movement to apply storytelling techniques and principles in for-profit settings. Her recently completed doctoral dissertation is on strategic storytelling or as she describes it: "The use of storytelling by business practitioners in human resources and knowledge management as an element of learning and knowledge-transfer strategies."

Translating that into plain English, Tyler says the fundamental power of storytelling is that it is likely programmed right into the human DNA. So its power in a business or marketing context is its innate ability to put listeners right into the story and get them involved. In this transformative way, the story becomes personally and intimately relevant to the listener. "Storytelling brings relevance in two ways," Tyler relates. "One is a personal connection to me. I can situate myself in this story; I can imagine myself being in this story. The second is the connection back to the business goals or objectives, so I can understand how this story is important to what I have to do." In other words, stories yield both relevance and a call to action, two of the most fundamental qualities missing in most advertising today.

In terms of marketing luxury, communicating the brand values and creating relevancy lead to purchase. Tyler says, "In marketing luxury products or services then, I want to be able to tell stories in the marketplace [i.e., story-based advertising], where the stories are so context rich that it is easy for people to imagine themselves in those contexts, to see themselves as characters in the story. That then dimensionalizes the experience of ownership. The stories become so real that I can make the leap to 'I am doing that' or 'I am spending my time this way.' It makes a connection that is sort of salivary in nature, because now I can imagine myself there, and now I'm closer to wanting myself to be there." That is just the function of Polo Ralph Lauren's worlds; they tell a story so that the consumer is transformed into being part of the story.

> "In marketing luxury products or services then, I want to be able to tell stories in the marketplace [i.e., story-based advertising], where the stories are so context rich that it is easy for people to imagine themselves in those contexts, to see themselves as characters in the story," says Jo Tyler, Humanizing Business.

Tyler goes on to explain that stories have been very common in sales circles—for example, the salesman who personalizes why you should buy by telling you about your smart neighbor down the street who just bought. But stories, Tyler explains, are very infrequently used in marketing environments. So what makes a marketing story effective for brand building and luxury brand selling?

Tyler identifies these criteria: "Stories have an inherent conflict, and the plot of the story is driven by the conflict. A story is a series of actions that come to a climax followed by some kind of denouement or resolution." Although stories usually follow a chronological or linear pattern, in business, Tyler says, listeners like the end to come at the beginning or they like a series of flashbacks. They demand a different internal coherency in the story than moving from start to finish.

Another key to successful business storytelling is adding an invitation to the listener to participate in the story and follow it through the beginning, the middle, and the end. "People are busy and they need to know why they should listen to your story. That is the role of the invitation—in a kid's story the invitation is 'Once upon a time.' It is the contract that says 'I am inviting you along on this little journey. I am going to tell you a story.' And the most important part of the invitation is telling why it is going to matter to the listener. What you don't want to do is make the listener spend time wondering *why* they should be listening to the story instead of listening to the story," she says.

Tyler points to companies like Nike and Lexus that have mastered storytelling in their corporate cultures and extended that capability into their advertisements. But for these great storytelling brands, Tyler warns that it isn't only about a brand having a story behind it:

> The brands *are* the story. When they talk about their brands, it is always in a larger context with lots of detail, be it a backdrop or a situation. These rich details make the brand story like painting a picture. So when the director of marketing for women's athletic shoes at Nike talks about the brand, it isn't Nike hanging out there in isolation. It's always against the backdrop of the story of the consumer who wears these shoes and what happens to her when she wears the brand. The story is how the brand affects who the customer is, how she defines herself, how other people think about her. The story may be about athleticism or about performance or about style. Sometimes the story marries two of those ideas together, so they can take the same shoe into the marketplace through a couple of different stories. By adding deeper and deeper layers of content, or more story threads, the Nike brand is transformed into an expansive brand with more relevance to more people now and in the future by continually telling new stories in new ways.

The lesson of storytelling in the context of luxury brands is clear. It is through stories or, as Polo Ralph Lauren's Jeffery Morgan explains, creation of different worlds that the brand comes alive, connects with the emotions and feelings of the consumer, and strives to make the consumer part of the brand story. It's this personal connection, making the listener (i.e., the target consumer) part of the story where the real transcendent power of storytelling in brand marketing comes into play.

"There is an interesting phenomenon storytellers will tell you that happens whenever a story gets told to a listener," Tyler says. "There isn't just one story, but three stories. The first story is the one the teller tells. The second story is the story the listener hears, and it's not the same story because the listener is situating himself or herself into the story and blending it into his or her own experience. And third is the co-created story, where the meaning is extracted. It's writing a new ending, co-creating the ending, and making it theirs." She points to the way serial ads capture our attention, noting the Nescafe instant coffee ads several years ago with the single man and woman who become romantically involved as they kept meeting around different coffee situations.

Right now I am fascinated by the Captain Kirk-Mr. Spock/William Shatner-Leonard Nimoy serial ads for Priceline. Will William Shatner keep his job as Priceline spokesperson and get the hotel room for free? I have to keep watching to find out. And in another stroke of brilliance, they make me part of the story because nowhere in the Priceline story does anyone ever tell you who Leonard is and how he knows Bill. You, the listener, have to fill in that gap and what a wonderfully expansive storytelling gap that is for Star Trek fans, so you actually become the co-creator of the story and its final ending. But for a marketer the real ending is whether more people use Priceline to book their hotels and travel. Frankly, it hasn't been

> It's this personal connection, making the listener (i.e., the target consumer) part of the story where the real transcendent power of storytelling in brand marketing comes into play.

worth it to me to trade from my current online travel services, but I surely do know the Priceline brand name.

M&C Saatchi's Kate Bristow and Adam Leavitt
Luxury Is Advertising That Spins a Feeling of Specialness through a Story

Even though they subscribe to a couple of Unity Marketing's luxury subscription services, I was altogether unfamiliar with the luxury travel company Crystal Cruises's latest ad campaign, until I happened on its new cable ad quite by accident. Being a sucker for BBC-style costume dramas, I halted my channel surfing on a program with a woman in a 17th-century carriage returning home to her country chateau, where her errant maid is trying on one of the lady's dresses. When the lady catches her chambermaid in her own getup, and you fully expect heads to literally roll, the lady walks over to her dresser and places a diamond-crusted tiara on the maid's head. Flash forward and we see a new vignette in which the maid is getting married in her lady's dress, and the lady smiles as she participates in the wedding. Flash forward again and we see the same elegant woman on a cruise ship, sitting on her private veranda alone, with a server pouring a cocktail. Voice-over says: "You must have done something good in a past life to deserve luxury like this." Then cut to the image of a Crystal Cruises ship at sea.

The production values were so high that it actually looked like a real BBC movie, thus conforming to David Ogilvy's rule to make your advertisement not look like an advertisement. That meant I didn't click right through. Further, the story was involving, so it was fun to catch up with Kate Bristow, director of strategic planning, and Adam Leavitt, vice president of client services, for the

M&C Saatchi agency in Los Angeles that created the Crystal Cruises ad campaign.

Regarding the M&C Saatchi role in luxury advertising, Bristow explains:

> For a personal perspective of the consumer, luxury is whatever makes that person feel special. It's different from person to person, and it isn't something that you would have on a day-to-day basis because it would be taken for granted. It has to be special in some way. And in terms of advertising, we spin that specialness. We weave a story or a fantasy about a product or service that makes you feel special. An advertising agency is selling those dreams, whether it is something fairly accessible like perfume or something more expensive. The story we tell about the perfume, for example, has to make the consumer believe in some way it changes her and makes her special if she wears that perfume.

Luxury advertising has become a harder proposition today because of the growing individualism in the consumer market; what is luxury to one person is very different from what is luxury to another. Further, one person's idea of luxury might turn off another. Bristow says, "It isn't as simple as it used to be 10 or 20 years ago when people had certain symbols that they used as a standard way to suggest luxury, like fur, diamonds, champagne. Put a man in a tuxedo or shoot champagne in a crystal glass and that would symbolize luxury." Leavitt continues, "But the problem is that as time goes by, those symbols of luxury become clichés. The challenge of luxury marketing is now that it has become such a broad category, it is really reaching the masses. How do you give the appearance of exclusivity without turning people off?"

> "In terms of advertising, we spin that specialness. We weave a story or a fantasy about a product or service that makes you feel special," says Kate Bristow, M&C Saatchi.

In the Crystal Cruises ad, the story of luxury is told not in traditional status symbols associated with cruises, such as a couple dressing for dinner in a tux and a formal gown and where they eat and party with other people in a ballroom setting. Bristow adds:

> The image that people in our research really responded to in the ad was our heroine on the balcony by herself as she looked out over the horizon. It was important that she was alone, without a companion, on an area of the ship where she really had space. All that triggers a feeling of a luxurious experience. She was relaxed, had time to enjoy herself, had the freedom of space, and could enjoy it alone. Not having to share her time with other people was crucial to the experience. And she was dressed very simply, but elegantly, in casual clothes. That broke another cliché of cruising that "I don't want to have to bring evening clothes on a cruise. I want to relax and wear my own clothes and don't want to conform with an image of what formal used to be."

By foregoing the clichés of luxury, the Crystal Cruises ad was able to send a message that cruising is an experience that everyday, real people can participate in, not just the rich. Bristow continues:

> Today, luxury isn't reserved just for the very rich. Normal people are saying, "I deserve some luxury in my life." And normal people are choosing experiences over objects. They are not spending their money on diamonds and fur coats and tuxedos. They are adjusting their spending in other areas so they can afford a luxury experience. They say, "This is going to matter more to me than the object I would have previously bought." It strikes me as rather sad and old-fashioned to imagine that buying a fur coat can somehow propel you into a different league. Whereas

being able to travel on a luxury cruise and look back at the photographs over the next year and talk about it with people and remember that experience—that is much more in line with what people want today.

Implicit in this desire for luxury experiences is a personal maturity indicating that the experiences have more meaning. Bristow says, "The crucial thing that people connected with the Crystal Cruise ad was this sense of deserving. People felt that they had earned [the right] to be treated in a special way on vacation. They felt they worked hard all their life, and they had all kinds of stress, so now they deserved some space, some freedom, some level of service. Not in an arrogant way, but just in a 'Hey, we've reached a stage in our lives where this is how we want to live.'"

LUXURY MARKETING MYTH #2: LUXURY CONSUMERS BUY BECAUSE OF THE BRAND

Reality: Brands Justify Purchase; They Are Not the Reason Why People Buy

We all know that some consumers out there are buying luxury brands solely because they *are* luxury brands. Be it status, "badge" value, or just the desire to show that one is part of a special in crowd that knows and values the brand, some people buy Burberry just for the plaid, Mercedes for the hood ornament, or Chanel for the CC. But that definitely is not the case with the typical luxury consumer.

Only in a handful of luxury categories—automobiles, cosmetics and beauty products, watches, and electronics and photography equipment—do a majority of affluent consumers rate the brand as very important in their purchase decision. This perspective on

FIGURE 10.3

Assessment of Brand Importance in Luxury Consumers' Purchase Decisions

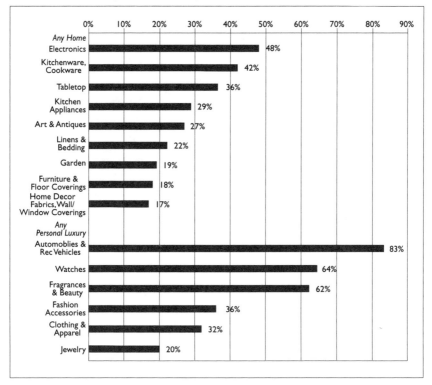

the role of branding is slightly different from the branding index we looked at previously. In Figure 10.3 we find the percentage of luxury consumers who say that the brand was "very important" in making their last purchase decision. What we learn is that in most categories the brand plays a supporting (i.e., rated by most as somewhat important or unimportant) rather than a starring role (i.e., rated by most as very important). By comparison, the influencers' index looked at the role of different attributes that may have influenced the last purchase decision. What floated to the top as relatively more important than other influencers was the luxury triple play: price-value; dealer or store reputation; and product brand. But still on a product basis, the brand is not very important for most consumers in most product categories. In other words, although product brand is more important than media advertising in influencing the last luxury purchase, product brands are rated by fewer than half of the luxury consumers as very important in their most recent purchase decision, except in a few categories such as automobiles, watches, fragrance and beauty, and electronics and photography equipment.

Despite the widely held belief that brands are the big draw in the luxury market and even though brands send quality messages or convey special qualities that the consumer desires, our research didn't find that luxury consumers walk around with a definitive list of luxury brand names in their heads, as they do with definitive price lists. They are much more fluid in their brand reference points and lack die-hard convictions that one brand necessarily is better than, more luxurious than, or somehow superior to another.

The simple fact is that luxury brands are not all that focal on why luxury consumers buy. In other words, you rarely find a luxury consumer saying, "I am going to buy this bag because it is by Louis Vuitton." Rather, you are much more likely to hear, "I am going to buy this bag because I really love it, and it is by Louis Vuitton so it costs more, but it is worth it." In other words, the brand plays a supporting, not a starring, role in the purchase decision. This finding goes against much that luxury marketers hold most dear, but it is the absolute truth.

Among luxury consumers—that is, the top 25 percent of affluent U.S. households with incomes of $75,000 and above who buy luxury—the brand is *not* the reason why these people buy. Only in a handful of product categories is the product brand "very important" in driving the purchase decision. Those product categories—automobiles, cosmetics and beauty products, watches, and electronics and photography equipment—tend to be mechanical

> They are much more fluid in their brand reference points and lack die-hard convictions that one brand necessarily is better than, more luxurious than, or somehow superior to another.

in nature (e.g., gears, movements, wheels, and motion) or so highly personal that they are almost taken into the body (e.g., cosmetics and beauty products). For all the other luxury product categories, the brand is rated by more consumers as "somewhat important" or "unimportant" to the purchase decision than as "very important."

In general, then, luxury consumers do not buy because of the luxury's brand. Further, they don't use the brand as a criterion to define what luxury is. Fewer than one-fourth of the luxury consumers agree with this statement: "Luxury is defined by the brand of the product, so if it isn't a luxury brand, it isn't a luxury." In other words, a product doesn't have to be Chanel, Louis Vuitton, Tiffany, Gucci, or Cartier to be defined as a luxury. What makes a product luxury goes far beyond the name plate or the company's or designer's name.

So if the luxury brand isn't the primal cause why luxury consumers buy, and it doesn't define what luxury is, what role does the luxury brand play in the purchase decision? The luxury brand's role in the luxury marketplace is as a justifier that supports or gives the consumer "permission" to buy. Luxury consumers buy luxuries because they have a desire to, and this desire is emotionally driven and right-brain controlled. The shopper falls in love with a Chanel handbag and is at the cash register paying for it before her rational mind kicks in to remind the shopper that she surely doesn't need another handbag in that color and that costs so much! That is where justifiers come into play. Justifiers are left-brained reasons that give consumers permission to buy luxuries. The more extravagant the purchase or the more cautious and careful the shopper, the more justifiers are needed to stack the buying equation in favor of the purchase. A shopper can justify paying so much more for that handbag simply because it is a well-recognized luxury brand.

The luxury brand, therefore, justifies the purchase. It confirms that the product is of outstanding quality . . . will last a long time . . . will be in style for years to come . . . is worth the price tag . . .

will be admired and noticed by people who matter in one's social circle. The role of a purchase justifier is hardly an insignificant one, but it clearly isn't the reason why people buy. People buy because they love the item, and they use the brand as a justification, a reason, an excuse to buy. The brand and its reputation encourage consumers to dig a little deeper into their pocketbooks to buy. At the luxury level, the luxury brand is like the "Good Housekeeping Seal of Approval," confirming the product is worth the investment. Justifying the luxury

> The luxury brand, therefore, justifies the purchase. It confirms that the product is of outstanding quality . . . will last a long time . . . will be in style for years to come . . . is worth the price tag . . . will be admired and noticed by people who matter in one's social circle.

purchase then is the essential role of the luxury brand and why companies must continue to invest in building stronger and stronger branding relationships with their consumers. The brand may not be the reason why people buy, but it plays a critical supporting role in getting people to buy.

LUXURY MARKETING MYTH #3: EXCLUSIVITY IS CRITICAL TO MAINTAINING THE LURE OF LUXURY BRANDS

Reality: Individuality and Uniqueness Are Luxurious; Exclusivity—It's Better Because Only I Can Have It and You Can't—Is Definitely Not the Appeal

Today's American luxury consumers, coming of age in the egalitarian 1950s and 1960s during the time of civil rights and social unrest, bring a decidedly democratic ideal to their participation in the luxury market. They truly believe that everyone is entitled to luxury. Over three-fourths of luxury consumers agree with this statement: "Luxury is for everyone and different for everyone."

Exclusivity, in and of itself, brings very little luxury value to today's democratically minded luxury consumer. That said, the luxury consumer also yearns for more specialness in his or her experience of luxuries.

The democratic ideal of luxury means that if you and I both have the same luxury, it doesn't make your luxury or my luxury any less luxurious or enjoyable. This puts the lie to the more traditional concept of luxury that is derived from European aristocratic ideals of luxury. From the European aristocratic perspective, luxury is made even more luxurious because it is unavailable to everybody else. This reflects old-luxury thinking that is defined from an external perspective.

Exclusivity, in and of itself, brings very little luxury value to today's democratically minded luxury consumer. That said, the luxury consumer also yearns for more specialness in his or her experience of luxuries. For new luxury consumers, luxury isn't necessarily better because they can do it or have it and others can't, but they don't necessarily want to be doing it when everyone else is doing it too. Although Americans are uniquely classless in their philosophical outlook, they are still driven by an underlying desire for personal expression and individuality. They don't necessarily mind being in a crowd, but they always want to stand out and never get lost in the crowd. So luxury consumers are perfectly happy driving their new Jaguar coupe down the crowded freeway next to a Toyota, Mercedes, Lexus, and Ford Focus, but it would be decidedly uncomfortable if everyone were driving the same Jaguar coupe, because it would take away their privilege of personal expression and individuality. Exclusivity for the sake of exclusivity, as expressed by the European luxury ideal, is not what American luxury consumers value; rather, it's an exclusivity derived from one's ability to express a personal point of view, an attitude, and one's uniqueness.

So the challenge for luxury marketers in the American luxury market is to deliver greater exclusivity by making the luxury consumer feel special and unique but never let the effort morph into class snobbishness or arrogance. It is a delicate balance that is very hard to pull off successfully, but those marketers that do it will achieve great rewards.

LUXURY MARKETING MYTH #4: LUXURY BRANDS ARE SOMETHING YOU OWN AND HAVE

Reality: Brands Must Perform—Luxury Brands Must Satisfy Luxury Consumers' Performance Expectations

In Chapter 6 I discussed the dimension of performance of the brand as critical for transforming old luxury, which was about having and owning the object, into new luxury, which encompasses the experience and feeling the brand conveys. *Performance* is the key word that we should use today when talking about luxury brands. It's performance not only in the sense of mechanical execution (e.g., cars, watches, electronics) but also performance as it relates to how the product delivers or performs experientially.

The concept of luxury brand performance connects the intrinsic definitions of luxury (i.e., quality performance, design performance, uniqueness performance) with the experiential—how the luxury brand makes the consumer feel and the way the consumer experiences luxury. It is through performance that old luxury, encompassing the noun or the thing, is transformed into new luxury, which delivers the experience, the feeling, the emotion to the consumer.

> The concept of luxury brand performance connects the intrinsic definitions of luxury (i.e., quality performance, design performance, uniqueness performance) with the experiential—how the luxury brand makes the consumer feel and the way the consumer experiences luxury.

What luxury brand marketers must do is measure and validate the performance values of their brands against the desires and wishes of their consumer. They need to make sure the brand has all the superior intrinsic features that the brand promises and that it also delivers the experiential values that touch the consumer emotionally. It is in the dimension of performance in all its many aspects that luxury branding must focus.

LUXURY MARKETING MYTH #5: LUXURY BRAND AWARENESS MEANS MARKETING SUCCESS

Reality: Brand Loyalty, Not Brand Awareness, Measures Meaningful Consumer Connection with the Brand

Brand awareness, whereby the consumer recognizes the name of a particular brand, measures only one thing: brand awareness, not marketing success or branding success. Just to be aware of a brand—and this applies especially in the luxury arena where many brands have upward of 80 percent brand awareness in the general population—does not mean that you will buy a brand or even consider buying a brand.

We have already looked at how luxury marketers must connect consumers with their brands through stimulating fantasy and desire. This is best accomplished by using storytelling techniques to involve consumers in the fantasy and make them an integral part of the brand story. How then do you measure the effectiveness of those efforts, if brand awareness won't do it? Brand loyalty is the metric that Robert Passikoff, founder of Brand Keys, a marketing and branding consultancy, proposes as the way the success or failure of corporate strategy to connect with the luxury consumer is measured.

By taking the percentage of luxury consumers who rate brand very or somewhat important in their purchase decision and doing a few more calculations, we can stack up the key luxury product

FIGURE 10.4

Luxury Category Brand Loyalty Index

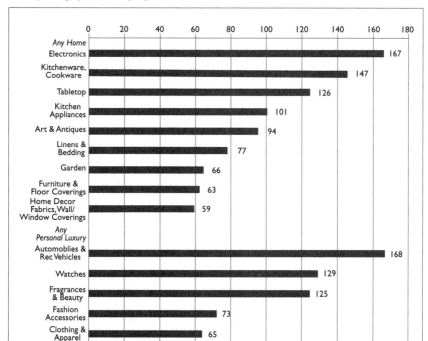

categories to show how consumer brand loyalty operates within and between luxury product categories based on an index average of 100.

The index of brand loyalty, as seen in Figure 10.4, reveals that in home luxuries, the brand is 67 percent more important to consumers in the purchase of electronics and photography equipment (167 index) than it is for the average home luxury. In kitchenware, cookware, and housewares (index 147), brand is 47 percent more important to the luxury consumer than is typical; and when buying tabletop, dinnerware, crystal stemware, and flatware (index 126), brand is 26 percent more important than the norm in home luxuries.

In the personal luxuries categories, luxury consumers rate brand 68 percent more important when buying automobiles (index 168) than the norm. Watches (index 129) and fragrances and beauty products (125) also have a fairly high index rating relative to the other personal luxuries categories.

As we have seen, brand loyalty is highest in categories that are mechanical in nature (e.g., gears, movements, wheels, and motion) or highly personal (e.g., cosmetics and beauty products). High brand loyalty categories are characterized by intense competition among marketers with the top brands—those that forge the strongest connection with the luxury consumer.

Low brand loyalty categories, such as jewelry (index of 40) or home decorating fabrics, window or wall coverings (59 index), signify luxury categories where opportunities abound for new luxury branding strategies because the competitive playing field is virtually open.

P *e r s o n a l* **P** *e r s p e c t i v e   o n* **L** *u x u r y*

Brand Keys's Robert Passikoff
Luxury Brands Are Like Other Brands, Only More So

Robert Passikoff, founder of Brand Keys (http://www.brandkeys.com), a brand and consumer loyalty research consultant, gives a simple answer to the question, "What is a luxury brand?" He answers, that "it's something beyond the necessary, beyond the usual, beyond the commonplace." In essence, luxury means better than ordinary brands. But what makes Passikoff's approach distinctive, even revolutionary, is that the consumer, not the industry or marketer, defines what *better* is. In other words, those intrinsic attributes of a luxury brand, such as craftsmanship, limited production, quality, and so on, may not necessarily translate into better in the consumer's view and so may not necessarily warrant consumers paying a premium for them. Passikoff's business is to discover what makes certain brands better than others, and he does that by measuring how people express loyalty to those brands.

For Passikoff, measuring consumer loyalty boils down to understanding consumers' expectations, first for the product category and then for the brand. He explains this way: "We start first with the product category. We study the value components that consumers bring to the category—the attributes, benefits, values (including both rational and emotional components)—and that define the category from the consumer's perspective." Then the magic occurs when the consultants analyze these components using a sophisticated computer modeling program that identifies the four key drivers that define the category from the point of view of the consumer.

"The drivers may be rational, emotional, self-expression, whatever, depending on the category. These drivers define how the consumers look at the category and how they compare brand offerings within the category. The measure of the specific brand in relationship to the four category drivers becomes the yardstick against which the brands are compared," Passikoff says.

But the four key drivers are different and distinct for each product category. As he explains: "People don't buy watches the way they buy cars, the way they buy shoes, or the way they buy books. Each category has a unique set of drivers against which brand loyalty is measured." For luxury brands, the category drivers are the same as for more mass brands. The key distinction is that consumers bring higher expectations when they buy the luxury brand.

The value of studying brand loyalty is its help in predicting consumer behavior. Brand Keys provides measures that show where the brand's equity lies, what the brand's customers will be thinking about and buying 18 to 24 months down the line, and what needs to be fixed when brand equity starts to slip. "We are able on an ongoing basis to provide leading indicator measures regarding the direction and velocity of change to customer values," he continues.

In the realm of luxury, where brand purchases may be a once-in-a-lifetime event, Passikoff explains that customer loyalty doesn't connote only repeat purchase but also the brands one considers for any purchase. Passikoff explains:

> We use the term *customer loyalty metrics* as a leading indicator of what people will do in the marketplace. So it's not just are they going to buy it ten more times. Rather, it is are they going to buy it at all. In the case of Tiffany, where you buy a diamond engagement ring once in a lifetime, the question is how far can the brand extend into other categories and other future purchases.
>
> The loyalty metric that we measure ultimately flows right to the bottom line to increased profitability. Where the loyalty bond is high, say for a Tiffany, where I bought my diamond engagement ring, it is cheaper to bring me back again as a customer to buy other things than if the bond is weak. So a 5 percent increase in loyalty can mean a savings of as much as 20 percent in marketing costs.

Customer loyalty then becomes the leading predictor of sales performance, because loyal customers purchase those products and services again and again. Loyal customers also refer others to the brand, which helps make the brand immune to the pull of the competition. Passikoff says, "It translates into more cost-effective marketing, and that money goes right to the bottom line."

The place for luxury brands to start is understanding the real consumer drivers that apply within the category. Recognizing that each product and service category is different, luxury brand com-

"In building a luxury brand, you still need to understand what drives the consumer and what people expect," says Robert Passikoff, Brand Keys.

panies can measure accurately what drives people to buy within the category and then make sure the brand measures up to consumers' expectations for those key drivers. Passikoff explains: "In building a luxury brand, you still need to understand what drives the consumer and what people expect. You need to understand what the values are that the category holds and that make people feel valued, that they value, and what their expectations are; then you can build on that.

"Ultimately, you want to make sure the brand can sustain the demands and expectations and the drivers placed upon it. Most of the time consumer expectations are higher than what brands deliver. But that's good because it represents the capability for the brand to change, to move upscale, to differentiate itself even further."

So the place to start in building a brand is first and foremost with the consumer and understanding consumer values. "It's really a function of understanding expectations and then marketing to them," Passikoff declares.

LUXURY MARKETING MYTH #6: LUXURY BRAND IS ABOUT THE PRODUCT

Reality: Luxury Brands Connect Corporate Strategy with Consumer Psychology

The role of the luxury brand is to connect corporate strategy, which controls the design and manufacture of the object and develops the branding messages, with consumer psychology, which persuades people to buy. It's through the performance of the brand, both in tangible and intangible emotional ways, that the company delivers luxury satisfaction to the consumer. Luxury mar-

> Brands are the embodiment of corporate strategy, designed, created, and directed by the company. The brands connect with consumers' psychology and encourage consumers to buy.

keters, although they must design and manufacture the ultimate "best-of-the-best" products, also need to realize that the product, the thing itself, is secondary to the experience of the thing by the consumer.

It is on this experiential plane where luxury brands perform their magic and it's magic indeed. David Yurman, CEO of David Yurman, luxury jewelry and watch marketer, describes the experience of luxury brands connecting with the consumer at the experiential level: "We have a consumer religion. We're out there buying. It's sort of our God-given right. We think we can buy, and we can get things for ourselves. But that experience is really almost a religious experience. It's like 'Don't bother me. I'm at the counter. Don't put that perfume on me. I'm here to search out *that!*' And when they hit 'that,' that is their connection. So we've made a connection. These are very personal moments, these connections with consumers."

The essential role of brands and branding in the luxury market is to influence consumers in their purchase decision, which ultimately is the only thing that really matters. Our luxury brands become the medium through which we influence the consumer to buy. Brands are the embodiment of corporate strategy, designed, created, and directed by the company. The brands connect with consumers' psychology and encourage consumers to buy. The luxury brands don't work alone, but they are a critical aspect of justifying the consumer's luxury purchase. A luxury marketer that focuses *solely* on the product or the thing and designs the ultimate best-of-the-best product is missing a huge opportunity to deepen its connection with the consumer in the emotional realm. Fine-quality things are nice, but they don't necessarily motivate the consumer at the experiential or emotional level. Luxuries that perform only at the intrinsic level are missing the most important dimension of luxury and that is the emotional, experiential realm. That is why it is imperative for every single luxury marketer selling things to fully and completely embrace the experiential dimension of luxury. Luxury marketers not only need to design and produce the best-of-the-best thing, but they need to make sure that their best-of-the-best product also performs and delivers the emotional, experiential satisfactions that the luxury consumer most desires and craves.

Personal Perspective on Luxury

Ten Thousand Villages's Doug Dirks
Luxury Is Doing Good

Just down the road from Unity Marketing's offices is an interesting little company with a different and unique brand value proposition: to make the world a better place. And the company seems to be doing it, as it has expanded to nearly 200 retail stores throughout the country that sell unique handcrafted products imported from 32 countries around the world.

Working as an arm of the Mennonite Central Committee—the relief, peace, and service agency of the Mennonite and Brethren in Christ churches in North America, a Protestant denomination that makes peacemaking a central core of its doctrine—Ten Thousand Villages scours the world looking for unusual and interesting arts and crafts it can sell in its stores and pays the artisans from Third-World countries a fair income in the process. Dirks explains: "We focus on developing or Third-World countries where artisans are either underemployed or unemployed. They are also not normally connected with the so-called commercial trading world. We try to find ways to sell their products so they can earn a decent living and support their families."

A visit to a Ten Thousand Villages store is like a trip to a tribal village in Africa in one corner or a walk through a marketplace in Vietnam in another. Although some of the products are very affordable, luxury is the proper definition of what is sold, as most items are decorative with an aesthetic appeal:

> We work with artisans, so our products tend to be decorative and many of them are art pieces. We recognize that people spend money on things that make them feel good. We just take it up a notch and ask our customers to think about where the products came from, if the artisans are working in decent conditions, if they get a fair deal in the price. Our value proposition then is that Ten Thousand Villages is a place that thinks about these issues. We assure our customers that their money is well used and that the people who are making the product are being treated well and feel good about the transaction.

As a nonprofit organization, its goal is to make money for the people or artisans they buy from, definitely a unique value proposition. A central tenet in the Ten Thousand Villages brand is telling the stories about the products it sells, where they came from, and the people who actually made them by hand. Because the company isn't "robbing" its suppliers to get the lowest possible price, the cost in the store may well be slightly higher than that found in competing stores. The authenticity and the story then help differentiate the product and make it more special. As Dirks explains:

> People are attracted to our product line because it is unusual and different. We try to tell the stories about our products so people can actually see and feel the person behind the product. That way it becomes not just a basket from the Philippines but something that was crafted in the hands of this particular artisan. By buying the basket, the

customer actually partakes in the life of the basketmaker, and people really respond to that. They feel it is OK to pay a little bit more because the basket is special enough and the story goes along with that.

The typical Ten Thousand Villages customer shares many distinctive luxury demographic characteristics, including a keen interest in international affairs and international travel. Dirks says, "They are concerned about how our economy impacts people in other economies. They tend to be folks that listen to NPR and watch PBS, read magazines like *Real Simple* or *Utne Reader.* They are college educated and upper middle class." Most important, the Ten Thousand Villages customer is interested in doing good and giving back to the less fortunate, as well as wanting to bring home some new pot or African mask to hang on the wall.

If you suspected there was a little bit of the United Nations in a Ten Thousand Villages store, then you are absolutely right. By building connections with people in remote lands, sharing their stories, and encouraging fair trade, the company is truly making the world a better place in these troubled times. A focus of its flagship store in Ephrata, Pennsylvania, is an incredibly wide selection of handmade rugs from Pakistan, with prices ranging from $4,000 to $7,000 depending on the thread count for an 8' by 10' rug. Dirks continues:

> We actually have two people from Pakistan working in the store. Yousaf and Amir represent the folks in Pakistan and talk personally to our customers about how the rugs are made, how long it took to make them, and even show them

> "We recognize that people spend money on things that make them feel good. We just take it up a notch and ask our customers to think about where the products came from, if the artisans are working in decent conditions, if they get a fair deal in the price," says Doug Dirks, Ten Thousand Villages.

pictures of where each rug was made. They provide a very personal connection, and people come to our stores and pay $10,000 to $20,000 buying rugs for their new homes with confidence.

Many of the artisans we work with come from predominately Muslim countries, like Pakistan, India, Bangladesh, and Indonesia. We try to tell stories about these folks and how their concerns are the same as ours—to make their family life better, to give their children a good education. We think in the long haul that if we could foster more of this kind of connecting of people and being concerned about each other's welfare that it would improve the situation worldwide. That's a fairly idealistic view, but when we look at the individuals that we know living in some of these places, we find that it makes a lot of sense, and it works.

Ten **T**housand **V**illages: **O**perating **P**rinciples

- We work with disadvantaged artisans.
- We purchase from craft groups that are concerned for their members and that promote member participation.
- We pay fair prices for handicrafts. We pay promptly.
- We pay up to half the value of a handicraft order when it is placed; the balance when the items are shipped to North America. This provides operating capital for artisans to purchase raw materials and for craft groups to pay workers.
- We offer handicrafts that reflect and reinforce rich cultural traditions.
- We promote fair trade.
- We use marketing strategies and messages consistent with our mission and ideals.
- Our ideals include responsible lifestyle choices, efficiency, and Christian ethics. We seek integrity in all our actions and relationships.
- Whenever possible, we work with volunteers in North American operations.

NEW LUXURY BRANDING PARADIGM

In conclusion, the new luxury branding paradigm boils down to a few key ideas:

- **A luxury brand must be expansive.** It must be a big idea that gives the marketer new places to venture and new opportunities to meet in the consumer's personal life.
- **A luxury brand must tell a story.** Storytelling is a fundamental way humans transmit and process information. Brand recognition is no substitute for brand connection, and it's through brand stories that consumers can connect. It's through brand storytelling that corporate strategy connects with the consumer.
- **A luxury brand must be relevant to consumers' needs.** A luxury brand must be relevant to consumers' needs, meeting their passions and desires emotionally and physically. And a luxury brand must stay relevant as luxury consumers' needs change, thus the necessity to have an expansive brand that gives marketers room to grow.
- **A luxury brand must align with consumers' values.** Consumers are bringing a new sensibility into the marketplace that is about more than having and getting. They want their consumerism to provide a greater meaning, and they are looking to "do good" when they shop.
- **A luxury brand must perform for the consumer.** The experience of a luxury brand all comes down to how well the brand performs its experiential duties for the customer. If it makes him or her feel wonderful, special, and unique, as well as performing its specific material role or purpose wonderfully—whether the product is a cooking pan, an evening dress, a set of sheets, or a new PDA—then it meets the consumer's performance expectations. It is luxury.

11

RETAILING AND SELLING LUXURIES—EVERYTHING ABOUT SHOPPING HAS CHANGED AND IT'S NEVER GOING BACK TO THE WAY IT WAS

Over the past ten years *everything* about shopping has changed! Where people shop, how they shop, when they shop, how long they shop, and literally everything else has undergone a dramatic shift. Much of the credit for the transformation of 21st-century shopping goes to Wal-Mart and other general merchandisers and discounters as they have expanded from largely regional stores to national chains and, in the case of Wal-Mart, into an international player on a truly grand scale.

Since 1992 the retail market, excluding sales of motor vehicles, gasoline stations, and food service establishments (i.e., restaurants), grew 77 percent in ten years from $1,275 billion to $2,257.1 billion in 2002, as shown in Figure 11.1. With the overall industry increase of 77 percent as a benchmark, an index identifies the retail sectors that grew faster than the industry as a whole (i.e., have an

FIGURE 11.1

Retail Sales by Type of Store, 1992–2002, in Billions

	1992	2002	% CHG '92–'02	INDEX
Home Furnishings & Electronics	$ 97.8	$ 198.6	*103.1%*	134
Building & Garden	160.2	32.3	*101.7*	132
Food & Beverage	371.5	508.5	*36.9*	48
Health & Personal Care	90.8	191.6	*111.0*	144
Clothing & Accessories	120.3	178.6	*48.5*	63
Sporting Goods & Hobby/Books/ Toys	49.3	81.5	*65.3*	85
General Merchandise Total	248.0	476.1	*92.0*	119
Department Stores	177.1	217.9	*23.0*	30
Other General Merchandisers	70.9	258.3	*264.3*	343
Misc. Stores, including gift, stationery, florists, etc.	55.8	105.0	*88.2*	114
Nonstore	81.3	194.0	*138.6*	180
Total Retail	$1,275.0	$2,257.1	*77.0%*	100

*Excludes motor vehicles, gasoline, and food service stores

Source: Census Bureau

index over 100) and those that grew slower than the industry (i.e., an index under 100).

The fastest-growing retail category over the past ten years was other general retailers, including such stores as mass merchandisers, discount department stores, warehouse clubs, dollar stores, and other general merchandisers besides traditional department stores. Their index was 343, which means they grew at a rate 243 times faster than the industry as a whole. Nonstore retailers, including the Internet, mail-order, and television shopping channels, were the second-fastest-growing retail sector, growing 80 percent faster than the average.

Lagging retail sectors include food and beverage stores (index of 48, so growth was 52 percent less than average); clothing and accessories stores, including jewelry stores (63 index); sporting goods, hobby, book, toy stores (85 index); and the worst performer overall—traditional department stores (index of 30, or 70 percent less growth than the average). Unfortunately, there is no definitive list of industry sales among luxury or upscale retailers to measure long-term sales trends and compare those with what is going on in the mass market. However, a rebound in the luxury retail market has been a subject of much media talk since the start of 2003.

> The retail sector is consolidating with fewer individual stores and more larger establishments.

As you drive along the nation's highways, it certainly appears that the number of retail stores is expanding exponentially with big-box stores and strip malls cropping up on just about every corner. But the reality is that the total number of retail stores has actually declined from 1,118.4 million in 1997 to 1,111.6 million in 2002 according to the Economic Census 2002. That means the retail sector is consolidating with fewer individual stores and more larger establishments. Corresponding with this consolidation toward larger stores, the actual number of shopping centers nationwide has grown from 41,235 in 1995 to 46,438 in 2002, a 13 percent increase, according to data compiled by the International Council of Shopping Centers. That means the smaller, individually owned mom-and-pop stores you would find on city and town streets are folding as shoppers congregate at the malls and in the shopping centers.

P e r s o n a l   P e r s p e c t i v e   o n   L u x u r y

The Taubman Company's William Taubman
Luxury Is Thinking Globally but Acting Locally

With a portfolio that encompasses the most upscale regional malls in America, including Cherry Creek in Denver, the Mall at Short Hills in New Jersey, Beverly Center in Los Angeles, the Mall at Millenia in Orlando, and International Plaza in Tampa, The Taubman Company has a unique perspective on the transformation of luxury shopping over the past several decades. Talking about how luxury shopping has changed, William Taubman, executive vice president of The Taubman Company, explains thus: "The company was started by my father, so we go back a long time. But luxury meant something different back then. There wasn't such a thing as accessible luxury in the way there is today."

What's interesting about The Taubman Company is that it has luxury malls in locations you don't often associate with luxury. For example, one of its newest projects is in Richmond, Virginia, with Saks Fifth Avenue, Galyans, and Dillard's. Along with luxury anchors also come many luxury specialty stores, such as Louis Vuitton, Burberry, and Gucci. Taubman comments on how luxury is expanding into the smaller markets: "Now we see luxury concepts opening in more remote locations. And that all reflects the increasing density of higher incomes in these markets, the increased sophistication of people as they travel more, and the creation of international brand names that share certain values and experiences that translate into consumers' desire for those goods. Today, there is more of a common language of style than there used to be."

As far as luxury is concerned, The Taubman Company has a very expansive definition of what luxury is and how to deliver it to its shopping mall customers. Taubman says that "it starts with price, so that goods at a certain price level become luxury. So we consider Burberry luxury, Louis Vuitton luxury, whereas Coach is more accessible and not as expensive as Gucci. Then there is the fashion profile of luxury, which is about the lifestyle of the more upscale customer. It's brands like the Puma store or Diesel Jeans, which are about a certain lifestyle. We look at luxury from both points of view."

In fashion and luxury, the growing internationalism is giving rise to local retailers across America having to interpret those fashion trends for their local audience. Taubman explains:

> We try to match our malls and stores with the consumers'
> expectations related to the shopping environment and

the merchandising by the types of stores. In our upscale properties, like the Mall at Millenia in Orlando or International Plaza in Tampa, it isn't all the ultrahigh end. We have Tiffany, Cartier, Jimmy Choo, and Chanel, but we also have Gap, Victoria's Secret, Zara, Crate & Barrel, and Pottery Barn. People come to the malls for all kinds of experiences, including to see and be seen by their friends. We have got to fulfill the customers' expectations in terms of what they need.

As for the future of the shopping mall, the challenge is to keep the concept relevant to the changing needs of the shopper. For luxury that means bringing an international perspective into a local market and meeting customers' needs. Taubman concludes:

> The malls are the new downtowns where people come to sit and have a cup of coffee as well as to see and meet people. Shopping remains an important validation of who we are and of our desires. Today, people are exposed to so much more fashion, including international trends in *Vogue* magazine. It used to be much more differentiated, but today there is a greater commonality in the brands and fashions that both the luxury and more moderate customer desires, so the same purse from Gucci can be worn by many different people across the country.
>
> When they shop, they are looking to be pampered in a little different way and in a different kind of environment. They are looking for a different experience. We offer a shopping experience and a selection of goods, many of them international brands, that are much more temporal and less basic.
>
> Luxury brings together all of the cultural and social ambitions of the consumer. When a woman wears a

"Shopping remains an important validation of who we are and of our desires," says William Taubman, The Taubman Company.

Chanel or Gucci purse, she identifies her values both to herself and to others. It's not just that she can afford it, but it says something about the kind of person she is, that she is sophisticated enough to understand these brands and the lifestyle they represent.

IN RETAILING: AS BELOW AT MASS, SO ABOVE WITH CLASS

The trends shaping the mass retail market today, notably consolidation among larger stores with greater financial resources, are also operating in retailing to the upper-income luxury market. In fact, with some exceptions like Beverly Hills's Rodeo Drive, New York City's Fifth Avenue, Chicago's Miracle Mile, and Las Vegas's luxury malls, there are few bastions devoted *strictly* to luxury marketing in the country today. Even in these tony retail centers, decidedly middle-market retailers, such as Gap, Banana Republic, Express, Pottery Barn, and Crate & Barrel, find the shopping atmosphere highly conducive to their marketing strategies. The simple fact is the luxury market is so overwhelmingly attractive with so many people with lots of money to spend that even retailers that started out by catering to the mass crowds now are retrofitting, reinventing, and repositioning their businesses to attract the more affluent shopper.

> The simple fact is the luxury market is so overwhelmingly attractive with so many people with lots of money to spend that even retailers that started out by catering to the mass crowds now are retrofitting, reinventing, and repositioning their businesses to attract the more affluent shopper.

This is certainly a strategy that is winning for retailers like Gap and corporate sister Banana Republic. After a couple of years of slipping and sliding in their brand positioning and merchandise strategy, they have hit on a winning formula for each brand. Gap is delivering value in casual attire or mix-and-match pieces that even work with designer duds; Banana Republic delivers a slightly more upscale, but still high-value, product line of business casual and fashion-forward looks. Banana Republic is getting noticed in elite fashion circles because of its recent addition of high-quality costume jewelry collections in its stores. The secret? Designer Thomasine Dolan Dow interprets jewelry designs from luxury houses like Prada and Van Cleef & Arpels for the masses in faux stones. Many of the new jewelry designs have a retro look, but all aim for maximum fashion impact at a minimal price, usually in the $30 to $70 range. Another key factor in the turnaround at Gap and Banana Republic is the in-store shopping experience. Everything—from the lighting, floors, shelves, displays, and racks—looks good and feels good, and the way the merchandise is displayed is decidedly more upmarket than the prices would suggest.

Target has learned this trick too: Affluent shoppers don't want to feel they are slumming when shopping down at the mass market. Target seems to pay more attention to the shopping environment than do its direct competitors by including such shopper-friendly features as signage, displays, clearer sight lines, and easier-to-navigate aisles. Target also has fashion designer Isaac Mizrahi, who has created an exclusive line for Target under the powerful tag line "Luxury for Every Woman, Everywhere." Target carries its "every woman, everywhere" promise in its brand advertising with ads featuring women of many different shapes and sizes (including a size 14 model as well as the more usual 2 to 4 size range) in a variety of age groups (including teenaged girls, their older sisters, their mothers, and their grandmothers). With greater attention to detail and cut in the product line, as well as such enhanced fabrics as leather and suede, Target is encouraging shoppers to dress head to toe in Mizrahi's line and giving consumers "permission" to mix and match separates in more upscale designer fashions.

Saks Fifth Avenue's Kimberly Grabel
Luxury Loses Its Meaning When Everything Is Luxury

Saks Fifth Avenue is one of the three "sisters" of luxury retailing along with Nordstrom and Neiman Marcus. Together, they take in some $12 billion in revenue from the carriage trade. Kimberly Grabel, Saks Fifth Avenue's vice president of marketing, shares Saks's rich history in luxury marketing: "Since 1924, Saks on Fifth Avenue has catered to consumers looking for the best the world has to offer. Ours is a long heritage in luxury—providing the highest-quality items from the top designers and brands."

Today Saks Fifth Avenue is a division of Saks Incorporated, the former Proffitt's department store chain that merged with Saks in 1998 and subsequently changed its name. Saks Fifth Avenue operates over 60 stores in 24 states in addition to its flagship store at 611 Fifth Avenue, New York. It takes an expansive view of luxury that encompasses such old luxury brands as Chanel, Prada, Louis Vuitton, and Gucci along with new luxury experiences, as Grabel comments: "Luxury today is simply anything that makes a consumer feel good. It can be a luxurious fur coat, a break from a hectic day to have coffee at our café overlooking Rockefeller Center, or a massage in our spa. Luxury can be little (that perfect shade of lipstick you just had to have) or large (that hot new look from Gucci you just had to have.)" In other words, Saks is dedicated to providing it all—a 360° luxury experience from what you wear to where you shop.

"Each consumer defines luxury for himself or herself. It's become not a market position but a highly individual decision," says Kimberly Grabel, Saks Fifth Avenue

Providing exemplary luxury service is a hallmark of Saks. Whenever you read about Saks's service, words like *enhanced, legendary,* or *superlative* usually go along for the ride. "The biggest change for us has been anticipating these new luxury consumers within our doors who might initially be intimidated by the Saks heritage. Our mission is to make sure that all customers feel welcome and invited into our environment," Grabel says.

Saks Fifth Avenue is becoming more accessible to more people because the luxury market is in flux with more people yearning for luxury and with plenty of "scratch" in their pockets to pay for it. "It's not new news that the luxury market is more dispersed than it has ever been in the past. The democratization of luxury is not only much talked about but true. Everyone now feels entitled to a little luxury in their lives, as they should," Grabel says. Recognizing that luxury isn't limited to the population centers of both coasts, Saks is opening new stores in such middle-American shopping backwaters as Indianapolis, Indiana, and Richmond, Virginia. It says something about today's luxury market that these traditional flyover cities can support a luxury retailer on the scale of Saks Fifth Avenue.

But there is a dark side to the new expansion of luxury from the classes to the masses, as Grabel explains: "Luxury has changed greatly over the last several years, and it is truly a moving target. With so many brands positioning themselves as a luxury product offering in one way or another, *luxury* has lost some of its meaning. When everything is a luxury, nothing is!"

The call then for traditional luxury marketers like Saks is to maintain that luxury allure while opening their doors wider and wider to draw in a new audience. That strategy isn't as straightforward as it at first appears. Grabel continues:

> The sheen of luxury alone isn't enough anymore. There must be a real consumer benefit/value inherent in the product offering. In the end, consumers will vote on what is a luxury for them. Each consumer defines luxury for himself or herself. It's become not a market position but a highly

individual decision. That's why it's increasingly hard to talk about the "luxury market" anymore. It's moving before our eyes, and it's out of our control [i.e., luxury marketers] and in the hands of consumers across the country.

But with the masses now rubbing shoulders with the classes when shopping for luxury, Grabel foresees a demand for an even more refined luxury aiming for greater and greater levels of exclusivity. She concludes that "it's now all about exclusivity. It used to be about buying from an exclusive luxury product line; now it's about getting to the top of the waiting list for a custom product from these same lines made in very limited qualities. As more and more consumers access luxury products and experiences, a core group of affluent consumers are kicking it up a notch, with the focus not just on luxury but on extreme exclusivity as well."

SHOPPING IS NO LONGER ABOUT THE THING BUT ABOUT THE SHOPPING EXPERIENCE

We keep coming back to the experiential shift in luxury: that it's not about the thing, it's about the experience. So when people go shopping, the question is not what I want to buy and where I am likely to find it; rather, it is what kind of shopping experience I am looking for today and where I am likely to find that experience. The thing, the object, the material good has slipped out of the equation; the focus of the consumer is on the experience of shopping, a fact that Saks Fifth Avenue clearly recognizes today.

The result of this shift is a new focus on the shopping experience. Not just the more obvious merchandise and displays or the architectural appointments, but the less obvious lighting, color, music, scents, and feeling of space. A leading designer of retail spaces, Ken Nisch, chairman of JGA, a Southfield, Michigan, architectural and retail design firm, shares his unique perspective on the importance of luxury retail space in building and promoting the luxury brand.

JGA's Ken Nisch
Luxury Is Turning More Implicit, Less Explicit; More Intelligent, Less Obvious

"The space your luxury brands 'play in' [i.e., the store and store environment] are the last frontier and possibly most effective for brand differentiation," Ken Nisch believes. As brand marketers strive to rise above the fray and achieve a meaningful point of difference, they will increasingly turn to experiential marketing. The reason why the shopping experience is gaining such critical importance in today's retail environment is simply that you can't mass-produce an experience. Each shopping experience is personal, and retailers will be rewarded as they strive to enhance those individual shopping experiences. Nisch says, "If you think about the shopping environment, experience is the one thing you can't deliver through the magic of camera."

Because an experience can't be mass produced, luxury is added into the exchange through the very "perishability" of the experience. Nisch explains: "The human reaction that is built into the exchange makes the experience and, therefore, the product more luxurious. If you can deliver the same experience in exactly the same way a hundred times, it probably isn't all that luxurious."

When consumers shop, there are cues and codes that signal luxury to the consumer; Nisch's expertise is manipulating those signals to send a consistent brand message. He shares some of the challenges in branding in the retail environment for a Jaguar dealership:

> When you think of Jaguar, you have a brand that differentiates itself through its iconic styling. Then it differentiates itself by price. In the design intricacies of the showroom, we created an experience that was thoughtful and intelligent, not pretentious. The intangible value of the Jaguar showroom is ultimately one of the important elements of luxury, not an obvious use of fine materials. The discovery of intelligent luxury then becomes the complement to the consumer.

Today luxury is about being less obvious and more intelligent. Nisch explains:

> There is luxury on the outside and then luxury on the inside. Ultimately, the more "insider" the luxury is, the more exclusive it is. If it is more intelligent and takes more expertise to know it, appreciate it, and understand it, then it is a little less obvious and has less mass appeal. Like the connoisseur of wine, you become the connoisseur because you understand the nuance of what is on the inside, in the bottle, not in the wrapping or outside.

"There is luxury on the outside and then luxury on the inside. Ultimately, the more 'insider' the luxury is, the more exclusive it is. If it is more intelligent and takes more expertise to know it, appreciate it, and understand it, then it is a little less obvious and has less mass appeal," says Ken Nisch, JGA.

The cues and codes of luxury are very much culturally conditioned, so a company should not transplant a luxury retail concept from one culture to another without attending to those cues. Nisch explains some of the finer points of culturally coded luxury:

We are working with a fine confectionery group and discovered how different luxury is perceived in Japan, North America, and Europe. In North America there is a certain abundance associated with luxury. If you have a plate with only five chocolates in a case here, people will say, "Those must not be fresh." If you go to Japan, and you have a whole plate of chocolates abundantly displayed, they would say, "Those must not be exclusive." And in Europe if you put the chocolates in a box instead of displaying them on a plate, they say, "Those must not be handmade." So much of luxury is culturally driven, and design must reflect that.

For the future, Nisch sees shopping as becoming more integrated in our life, less often a destination and more frequently something that happens when you are just living. He concludes:

Most luxury goods that are consumed by consumers are as a texture of their life. They are a by-product of going somewhere without a great degree of premeditation, but on the way to and doing something else. That's also why quite often you see luxury retailers, not in malls, but out on the streets where people walk and live. People are traveling, they are in airports, they are doing business. They are not exclusively shopping but rather living.

WHERE THE AFFLUENTS SHOP
FOR THEIR LUXURIES

Shopping is the act whereby consumers put their desire and passion into action to search out that something special to buy. For more luxury consumers today, as Ken Nisch says, shopping is more incidental to life rather than something planned and pre-

"Whoever said money can't buy happiness simply didn't know where to go shopping."—Actress Bo Derek

pared for. Although it is becoming more incidental to everyday life, shopping is becoming an important destination activity associated with travel. Many travelers use their trips to far-off places as an opportunity to buy mementos like gems, jewels, and arts and crafts where they can get good prices for things hard to find at home. About 20 percent of luxury travelers in the American Express Platinum Survey said that shopping was very important in their travel planning.

How luxury consumers go shopping, how much time they spend considering and planning a purchase, and how much effort they make in comparison shopping is largely determined by how much an item costs and how long they expect to live with the purchase. For example, fragrance, beauty, and cosmetic purchases and fashion apparel and accessories are more likely to be bought on a whim without a lot of consideration, whereas furniture and home decorating purchases are much more likely to be the subject of heavy research, lots of comparison shopping, and delayed gratification.

Department Stores Are Favored Places for Luxury Consumers to Shop

When it comes to shopping for luxuries, consumers turn first to department stores. Figure 11.2 lists the first, second, and third choice for luxury shoppers in each luxury home and personal luxury product category. Department stores are rated as one of the top three choices in 11 out of 14 different product categories. Tied for the second most popular place to shop for luxuries are specialty home furnishings and furniture stores (rated in the top three in eight categories) and on the Internet, by mail-order, or through television (also the top three choices in eight different categories).

Luxury shoppers' preference for the department store channel is an extremely important finding for the managers and own-

FIGURE 11.2
Where People Buy Luxuries

	FIRST CHOICE	SECOND CHOICE	THIRD CHOICE
Home Luxuries			
Art & Antiques	Other Stores/Art Galleries (27%)	Internet/Mail-Order/TV (26%)	Spec. Home Furnishings/Furniture (18%)
Electronics & Photography Equipment	Electronics Spec./Computer (59%)	Internet/Mail-Order/TV (40%)	Warehouse Club/Discount (15%)
Furniture, Lamps, Floor Coverings	Spec. Home Furnishings/Furniture (50%)	Warehouse Club/Discount (17%)	Department Store (16%)
Garden, Outdoor & Lawn	Warehouse Club/Discount (38%)	Spec. Home Furnishings/Furniture (28%)	Department Store (26%)
Home-Decorating Fabrics, Window & Wall Coverings	Department Store (27%)	Spec. Home Furnishings/Furniture (22%)	Other Stores (14%)
Kitchen Appliances, Bath & Building Products	Spec. Home Furnishings/Furniture (29%)	Other Stores/Hardware (29%)	Department Store (25%)
Kitchenware, Cookware, Housewares	Department Store (32%)	Internet/Mail-Order/TV (28%)	Spec. Home Furnishings/Furniture (22%)
Linens & Bedding	Department Store (40%)	Spec. Home Furnishings/Furniture (25%)	Internet/Mail-Order/TV (23%)
Tabletop, Dinnerware, Flatware	Department Store (47%)	Internet/Mail-Order/TV (27%)	Spec. Home Furnishings/Furniture (24%)
Personal Luxuries			
Clothes & Apparel	Department Store (63%)	Spec. Fashion Boutique (47%)	Internet/Mail-Order/TV (16%)
Fashion Accessories	Department Store (57%)	Spec. Fashion Boutique (33%)	Other Stores (14%)
Fragrances & Beauty	Department Store (58%)	Internet/Mail-Order/TV (25%)	Other Stores (17%l
Jewelry	Jewelry Store (59%)	Internet/Mail-Order/TV (17%)	Department Store (16%)
Watches	Jewelry Store (44%)	Internet/Mail-Order/TV (20%)	Department Store (18%)

ers of department stores, because it points the way toward a success strategy, even survival strategy, for this rapidly failing channel
of distribution. The fact is, luxury shoppers, the most affluent
shoppers, the ones with the most money and the most willingness
and ability to buy, in many instances prefer to shop and buy in a
department store. It just behooves department stores to pay very
close attention to the needs, desires, and passions of their luxury
consumers and strive to serve them better in every way possible to
build loyalty and repeat purchases.

FUTURE VISION OF LUXURY—LUXURY MUST EXTEND THROUGHOUT THE ENTIRE BUYING CYCLE

We have already seen the critical role that a store's brand plays
in influencing the luxury consumer purchase. As marketers, we
need to look more closely at the entire buying cycle that begins
when the consumer feels a need or desire to get something new;
extends throughout the purchase research cycle where the consumer evaluates different options, thinks about brands or designs,
and compares prices; then on to the store where the purchase is
made; then back home to admire and enjoy the purchase. In the
research we found that a lot of the pleasure derived in luxury purchases stems from the anticipation and buildup of excitement sur-
rounding the purchase. So even at the needs identification and
research phases, the feeling and experience of luxury must infuse
the entire buying cycle.

Also important is the role of in-store customer service in the
luxury purchase. Luxury consumers expect greater levels of attention and service, paradoxically even when they also expect to
get a bargain. They demand more service from their favorite
stores and look to the stores to provide higher-level service than
they find in more ordinary stores. Sometimes they are even willing to pay for the extra service that often comes with a higher

price tag at the luxury store. Here are comments related to the buying process and role of the store in enhancing luxury:

- "It feels better to get something at a better store like Bloomingdale's, especially when you are buying clothing. There is such a difference when you are buying clothing from a good store. You will find clothes that are better tailored. It's better brands, you are getting higher end."
- "It is all about the experience that you have when going to a more luxurious store like Bloomingdale's."
- "I bought Hunter Douglas blinds, and I paid more for them because they would put them up for me. I knew about the 800# but I wanted the service of someone else doing the work. That was a luxury for me."
- "If I had to choose between stores, then it's the service that matters. Even if quality [of products] is the same, you go with the store that is better known because they are going to stand behind the item more. They are going to take care of you better. I think service and reputation is important."

Sometimes the sales cycle can cover an extended period. Often at the end of the waiting and researching period, consumers are emboldened with a strong feeling that they deserve a reward for all the time that they waited and all the research that they did. They want a reward (i.e., they want to feel like a winner), and the retailing environment can do much in satisfying the consumer's desire to be rewarded with the purchase.

Buying luxury is rarely a do-it-yourself process. One of the defining characteristics of luxury retailing is that luxuries need to be "sold" and "presented" by a competent and knowledgeable sales professional. The sales professional plays a critical role in informing the consumer how to distinguish the superior features of a particular luxury brand. One only needs to think about the mystery of buying diamond jewelry. You can't just walk in off the street and buy a diamond. You have to learn about the cuts, the clarity, the color, and how all those other attributes translate into the price per carat. It takes someone experienced and knowledgeable to explain the grading system for diamonds. Even though the retailing of diamonds is clearly more technical than that of retailing handbags, the same principles apply across all categories of luxury. Somebody knowledgeable and trustworthy must explain the finer points of quality to the uninitiated. Through the sales process, the consumer becomes initiated into a select group of the special and privileged. This is critical to the success of luxury selling, luxury-brand building, and luxury consuming.

Because luxury extends throughout the entire sales and buying cycle, the luxury marketer must carefully control every point of customer contact throughout that cycle and make sure to flavor all contact with luxurious messages. That means the choice of advertising vehicle is critical to setting the stage for luxury indulgence. Your product needs to see and be seen by the right audience, among the right group of luxury peers, and surrounded with the right editorial message. Next it has to be in the right stores where the sales staff is trained to present the luxury product in the right light.

What sales alternatives are available to the luxury marketer that wants to explore nonstore retailing? Although the Internet is in the top three retailing choices for many luxury goods, it still has a way to go before it is a really effective retailing vehicle for luxury, though it is wonderful as a research and informational tool. I am probably one of the more experienced Internet shoppers around, but I can't tell you how many times I have gotten stalled at checkout or unable to complete my transaction. Sometimes it simply doesn't work as well as it should.

But what really seems to be limiting the Internet as a shopping vehicle is that it tries too hard to mimic the catalog-style, paper-based form of shopping in which the user has to turn the pages, follow a linear path through the site, and fill out an order form. Typical Internet Web sites today aren't taking advantage of the tremendous interactive possibilities that the Internet can make available.

A company on the forefront of a new and more interactive Internet experience combining commerce and entertainment is sevenEcho (http://www.sevenecho.com). It is taking the Internet e-commerce platform into a new dimension by adding what it calls a "personalized entertainment platform." Their software enables customized, content-driven stories to be combined with specific product placement that enhances brand image and grows sales. Kenneth Olsho, senior vice president of channel development for sevenEcho explains: "Simply put, through personalization on your Web site you build connections with the consumers and add strength and sales to your brand. Also, with our online entertainment platform, a brand gets specifically detailed and measured consumer market research. By providing focused entertainment, we help *marketers personally connect* with their customers and *customers personally connect* with a brand. An online brand relationship is traceable, long lasting, and unlikely to be 'TiVoed' out of the picture. Also, once an emotional bond is established an audience can be called to action, such as product purchase."

Still in its development stages, sevenEcho aims to enhance the Internet selling experience through storytelling. SevenEcho's platform combines a game-style interactive experience with a personalized story, so each viewer receives a made-to-order narrative and becomes part of the action. I picture some 21st century amalgamation of my kid's computer games with my shopping for a new pair of shoes on neimanmarcus.com, where I can see my shoe selection in the red color I want rather than the black color they want to show me, where I can pick the shoes up to see if the insoles have a pattern, talk to someone who has the same shoes, and maybe imaginatively walk around in them to see how they feel. Olsho says, "Entertainment transports the viewer to a different motivation level. As you wrap your brand within an interactive entertainment form, the marketer will get a better sense of their audience and understanding of their preferred behaviors. Also, because of the consumer interaction, the brand gets a precisely measured market response to their selling efforts. In summary, while entertaining their target consumer, a brand gets greater affinity, tactical marketing information, and increased sales!"

THE INTERNET IS RIGHT AT THE TOP OF PLACES WHERE LUXURY CONSUMERS SHOP

If you are looking for growth and excitement in serving the luxury consumers, then look no further than here. The Internet, along with sister direct-marketing channels that include mail-order and television shopping, is where the real action is for the future of luxury retailing. In the latest Neilsen/NetRatings survey, the super-affluent consumers were found to be the fastest-growing segment in the online world. See Figure 11.3. Internet users with incomes of $150,000 grew 31 percent in the previous year to reach 7.9 million individuals. The $100,000 to $150,000 and the $75,000, to $100,000 segments also grew rapidly, 24 percent and 27 percent, respectively. As the number of affluent Internet users rises, so does the importance of the Internet as a channel of distribution for luxuries.

The Internet or related direct-marketing channels rank among the top three shopping choices in 8 out of 13 luxury product categories: art and antiques; electronics and photography equipment; kitchenware, cookware, and households; linens and bedding;

FIGURE 11.3

At-Home Internet Users, March 2003 to March 2004

AT-HOME INTERNET USERS IN MILLIONS	UNIQUE AUDIENCE 2003	UNIQUE AUDIENCE 2004	% GROWTH
<$25,000	7,961	9,399	18
$25k–$49.9k	33,074	37,826	14
$50k–$74.9	38,165	42,473	11
$75k–$99.9	20,732	26,393	27
$100k–$149.9k	14,356	17,786	24
$150k+	6,010	7,873	31

Source: Nielsen/NetRatings, April 2004

tabletop, dinnerware, and flatware; watches; jewelry; and clothes and apparel.

Anyone who thinks that the Internet isn't an important channel of distribution or one that can be ignored until some future date is sadly mistaken. Luxury consumers are taking to the Internet like a duck to water. They value its convenience as time is increasingly precious in the world of luxury consumers. They appreciate the ability to comparison shop without wearing out their shoes going from store to store. They simply like it and will continue to favor it as one of their top shopping choices for luxury in the future.

P erso n a l **P** *e r s p e c t i v e* *o n* **L** *u x u r y*

Cooking.com's Tracy Randall
Luxury Delivers Enhanced Cooking Experience

Founder and president of Internet-based kitchen and housewares retailer Cooking.com, Tracy Randall contends that "luxury isn't something we tend to think a lot about. Cooking.com is a Web site that sells 6,000 SKUs [stock-keeping units] of kitchen-related merchandise. Most of what we carry are items that are a necessity for your kitchen. When we ask our customers what they consider basic items, they tell us a food processor and a standing mixer are necessities. Some folks might look at these as luxuries. But because the kitchen has become more of a central focus of the home, those items are considered basics today for our customers."

Although housewares are more necessity than luxury, many of the brands Cooking.com offers, such as All-Clad and Calphalon, deliver superior performance that sets them apart from the everyday or ordinary. Randall goes on to define the typical Cooking

> "Having nice equipment is an aesthetic concern, but the attention is also on quality equipment that provides a higher-quality cooking experience," says Tracy Randall, Cooking.com.

.com customer, and the company's focus on the luxury market becomes clear: "Our average customer is 45, has an income right at $100,000, and tends to be on her second round of purchasing for the kitchen. Her kids are older, and she has more time to spend in the kitchen and a little more money, so she is more established and chooses a step up as far as quality is concerned. She aspires to upper-end goods. Having nice equipment is an aesthetic concern, but the attention is also on quality equipment that provides a higher-quality cooking experience."

As cooks become more experienced and sophisticated, they are turning to authorities like the Food Network with celebrity chefs, including Emeril and Wolfgang Puck, to provide guidance for the more technical aspects of products. "The Santoku knives have been something that the chefs on the Food Network use, and they are among our best-selling items the past 12 months. Folks like to have an authoritative person that they respect endorse a product; it gives them confidence," Randall says.

Being an Internet-only kitchen retailer, Cooking.com has competition coming from all directions, as you can buy housewares and cooking products from every discounter, department store, or home specialty store. Even Home Depot and Lowes go head-to-head with Cooking.com in some categories. How is a fledgling Internet retailer to compete? Randall says, "We aim to provide the maximum choice to our customers and offer a good price. The online shopper really wants selection and a lot of information to compare and contrast and understand the different features and benefits of different products. Cooking.com specializes in providing that information."

Being a leader in the Internet space for kitchen and housewares, Cooking.com has a unique vantage point in the evolution of the Internet:

We were founded in 1998, so we have been at it for a while. Changes we have seen include selection becoming wider, as Viking launches cookware lines. Vendors are also going more luxury, like KitchenAid, which has a line of high-end waffle irons. We are also selling lots of high-end ice cream makers and espresso machines. But the biggest change we see is how rapidly the Internet is evolving along with the way the consumer shops online. The best example is Google. Three years ago, nobody had heard of Google, but today it is the biggest part of our marketing mix.

For now, however, Cooking.com will just continue to hone in on delivering the kind of shopping experience their customers have come to depend on. And that is offering the widest possible selection and the insider, expert information to guide consumers in their selection of products. Every now and then the company hits the jackpot when an order is placed by one of Cooking.com's affluent customers who is retrofitting her entire kitchen. Randall says, "Once a week or every other week we'll have someone getting a whole lot of pans, great knives, and some beautiful countertop appliance to set out, so it is pretty obvious someone is either redoing her kitchen or buying everything for a second home. Those are exciting orders."

TELEVISION SHOPPING IS BREAKING THE MASS-TO-CLASS BARRIERS

Both Lucy Ricardo and Ralph Kramden back in the 1950s pioneered the television infomercial, but the business of television home shopping didn't really take hold until a minimum baseline of American homes was wired for television cable. So it wasn't until 1982 that the Home Shopping Channel was launched to bring the convenience of shopping through television right into your living room. With QVC, which stands for Quality-Value-Convenience, following close on Home Shopping's heels, television's shopping revolution was at hand.

Today, the television shopping industry is said to have grown to its current $7 billion range with a number of new entrants emerging, notably NBC Shopping. Further, all the leading shopping channels have fully integrated live television presentation with Internet Web sites, yet the basic premise of television shopping hasn't changed all that much in the past 20-plus years. Each television cable network employs a gaggle of personable hosts who viewers invite into their home for a couple of minutes to a couple of hours. While the hosts "visit" in the home, they present viewers with an array of merchandise, usually themed around fashion, beauty, home, cooking, and cleaning, that viewers can order by telephone or online. Product presentations last for several minutes and the best-sellers get a very thorough review, so only about a dozen or so unique items can be featured over the course of any hour. A key selling feature in television shopping circles is celebrity spokespeople brought in for special shows to explain the key benefits and features of specialty products.

But the provenance of television shopping—its roots in the marketplace—has been traditionally downmarket. The image of the typical television shopper is not me but rather some credit card–addicted, overweight housewife living in a trailer park somewhere in Kansas. Today, however, more luxury marketers, such as Estee Lauder and Bose, are finding success in television shopping, and more are surely destined to follow.

Today, a fledging network is making a strategic move from the masses to the classes in television shopping. The Luxury Television Network (LuxTV) is a dig-

> Today, a fledging network is making a strategic move from the masses to the classes in television shopping: the Luxury Television Network (LuxTV).

ital cable channel set to be launched in the fall of 2005 and will be the first channel dedicated to entertainment programming about the luxury lifestyle. Back in the early 1990s, Ivana Trump made a stab at launching a luxury television shopping network with her Fifth Avenue Channel, but the timing just wasn't right. But now might be the perfect time for LuxTV to make a go of it. The network is backed by Mitchell Cannold, 30-year veteran in entertainment and cable; Marvin Traub, chairman and CEO of Bloomingdale's; Robert Quish, advertising executive most recently with Lowe-NY; Jeffrey Stier, online and direct-marketing entrepreneur; and Nancy Robins, an executive with experience building partnerships with such luxury brands as Cartier, Coach, Tourneau, Saks Fifth Avenue, and Bulgari.

LuxTV will marry traditional television formats of how the rich and famous live and play through news, magazines, biographies, series, reality, movies, and sports programming. It also plans to "tastefully and seamlessly weave into the fabric of every show" high-end products and services from fashion, travel, food, art, home decor, society, and celebrities. The focal point of LuxTV is its "concierge" service that allows viewers to immediately purchase or get more information about the luxury lifestyles and products they see on the channel.

Fully integreated with telephone and the Internet, the network aims to provide its retail partners and brands with "a cost-effective way to expand retail reach into areas not currently served by stores." The brains behind LuxTV conceive the network as not just another television shopping channel on the order of QVC or HSN or another specialty network like the Food Channel or Travel Channel. They are launching a new television genre they term "transactional entertainment," which is an intersection of entertainment, branded content, and commerce.

QVC's Doug Rose
Luxury Is Pleasure Shopping

As vice president of merchandising brand development at QVC, Doug Rose is chiefly responsible for identifying brands that are a good fit for QVC's distribution model. Once identified, Rose then brings them into the fold. Starting from "very humble roots," as Rose describes it, QVC has evolved in the home shopping arena through its reputation for product and service quality and its focus on the fun of shopping. As Rose says, "We tap a large audience of people in the world for whom the act of shopping is inherently entertaining. We aspire to be a destination retailer for people who are in the mood to escape and want to give themselves a little reward."

When it comes to finding brands that will entertain QVC's viewers, it applies a criterion that steers viewers away from broadly distributed brands that are necessity-driven purchases toward brands that are highly discretionary, even luxurious. It aims for brands with the ability to excite passionate enthusiasm from consumers, as well as brands with a compelling story to tell. Rose points to brands like Bose electronics and Estee Lauder's Prescriptives cosmetics line as outstanding partners for QVC's special breed of retailing. "With these kinds of brands, that are more deep than broad, we can spark a lot of interest in people who may be curious about the brand but haven't experienced it directly. We can bridge that gap and explain what makes it unique. We make it real and accessible for our viewers," Rose says.

Brand storytelling is an essential part of the QVC package and what makes it

"We aspire to be a destination retailer for people who are in the mood to escape and want to give themselves a little reward," says Doug Rose, QVC.

great, as Rose explains: "Part of the marketing mix on QVC is there is no intermediary. For example, Estee Lauder's Prescriptives brand has broken through for us, and that is one of Lauder's most prestigious brands. When we feature Prescriptives products on air, Lauder puts its absolutely best national salesperson on our floor. At the same time, he or she would be able to speak to a dozen people in Bergdoff's, now he or she is able to reach thousands, even millions, of consumers coast-to-coast." And QVC never discounts Prescriptives cosmetics but usually offers special configurations or combinations of products unique to QVC and unavailable through traditional retail channels.

A guiding principle behind the brands that work for QVC is recognition that they have an inherent entertainment value. The story must be entertaining and compelling to lots of people when it is communicated on air by an engaging spokesperson. Pleasure shopping also involves the social experience of shopping, which the television medium can do better than other media, like the Internet. Rose continues: "We work to develop a level of trust in our relationship with our viewers. Trust is a very human emotion and it's something you reserve for other people. You can't really trust a Web site the way you trust a human being. So when Bob Bowersox, a former restaurant owner, professional chef, and now QVC spokesperson, explains the features and benefits of a line of cookware, you trust him. He is a very reassuring voice of credibility. Humanity and connecting socially with other people are critical ingredients in pleasure shopping."

For the future, Doug Rose and QVC will continue to explore the potential for new brands with interesting stories and distinctive value propositions. A recent experiment in selling a Saturn automobile with a customer care offer over the airwaves suggests just how far television shopping can ultimately extend:

For years we wondered whether there was room for us in the car-shopping world, because it is an area of retail that is most encumbered with intimidation and with all the power appearing to reside on the side of the seller. So we found a partner and tested a program with Saturn. The premise was that you bought an exclusive special care package through QVC and in order to take advantage of that, we sent the buyer to fulfill it at his or her local Saturn dealer. Our first test was quite successful. In about 90 minutes of air time, we took calls from 16,000 people and ultimately sold about 3,500 Saturn cars.

12

LESSONS FOR MARKETING LUXURY TO THE MASSES AND THE CLASSES, AND EVERYONE IN BETWEEN—IT ALL STARTS AND ENDS WITH CONSUMERS' EXPERIENCE

Throughout the preceding sections of this book, we have deconstructed the marketing equation for luxury. With reference to findings from a two-year survey of luxury consumers, we explored in detail the traditional five-Ps of marketing luxury: people, product, pricing, promotion, and placement. We looked at each P from the point of view of the consumer, how consumers interpret the marketing messages and meanings in the marketplace. We also seasoned our investigation of luxury marketing with profiles of key executives in companies that best exemplify the new luxury marketing paradigm. From companies that many might not associate with luxury—Best Buy, QVC, Aerosoles— to established and recognized luxury marketers—Crystal Cruises, American Express, Starwood, Polo Ralph Lauren, Saks Fifth Avenue, Herend Porcelain—we have tried to gain new insights and new perspectives on what luxury marketing is all about in this new millennium.

Now it is time for us to pull all the disparate pieces of information together and draw conclusions and action-based recommendations for greater success in marketing luxury to the masses, the classes, and everyone in between. But first, let's review key findings from the research about our target: the luxury consumer and the aspiring luxury consumer.

KEY RESEARCH FINDINGS

The luxury consumer is driven experientially; it's not about the money. The luxury consumer primarily interprets and participates in the luxury market experientially. Luxury isn't just about the thing; it is about the special experience the consumer feels in buying or owning that thing. For these consumers, luxury is about achieving a comfortable lifestyle in the material realm, having those things that make life easier, more pleasant, and more satisfying. But the real meaning in the luxury comes through family, friends, and experiences that deepen one's understanding and appreciation of life. In other words, the luxury lifestyle is not necessarily about money; it's about the experiences and feelings that having enough money can buy.

Luxury transcends the physical and material. It is interpreted personally and experientially and not about what one has or owns. As a result, it transforms the individual, it enhances his or her appreciation of life. Almost 90 percent of luxury consumers agree with this statement: "Luxury doesn't have to be the most expensive thing or the most exclusive brand."

Luxury consumers are democratic in their approach to luxury; Americans value individuality over exclusivity. Although much is made in the luxury goods industry about maintaining the exclusivity of goods, usually through high prices and limited distribution, luxury consumers don't particularly buy the idea that luxury is better when it is something exclusive to them. Rather, they have a very democratic view of luxury, revealed when 77 percent of luxury consumers agreed with this statement: "Luxury is for everyone and different for everyone." Because luxury is not really about money, it is something that everyone from the highest to the lowest income can, and surely does, participate in. It's about the feeling, not the thing.

Exclusivity, in and of itself, brings very little luxury value to today's democratically attuned luxury consumer. That said, luxury consumers also yearn for more "specialness" in their experience of luxury. Exclusivity for the sake of exclusivity is not what American luxury consumers value; rather, it's exclusivity derived from one's ability to express a personal point of view, an attitude, and one's uniqueness. So the challenge for luxury marketers in the American luxury market is to deliver greater exclusivity by making the luxury consumer feel special and unique, but never let that morph into class snobbishness or arrogance. It is a delicate balance that is very hard to pull off successfully, but those marketers that do it will achieve great rewards.

Luxury goods are better; quality counts. When we draw luxury consumers back to discuss the thing—the product—they share a widely held view that items called "luxury" are noticeably a cut above the average. They have an expectation of better quality, finer details, superior workmanship, and materials that go along with the purchase. Nearly 90 percent of luxury consumers agree with this statement: "When you buy a luxury item, you expect it to be a cut above the average."

It's this expectation of higher quality that makes luxury consumers willing to dig a little deeper into their pocketbook or wallet to buy that extra feeling of confidence. But that extra quality doesn't always have to cost more.

Luxury consumers are bargain shoppers always looking for a good deal. Even though luxury consumers appreciate superior quality, they also get an experiential thrill out of paying less for the best. Over 80 percent of luxury consumers agree with this statement: "I enjoy the feeling of buying luxuries on sale and usually search out the lowest price or the best value." The irony of this finding is that these luxury consumers who can afford to pay full price in every category that they participate in are unwilling to. They get a kick out of buying on sale, getting a bargain, and winning at the shopping game.

The luxury shoppers are ready, eager, and always willing to search out the best price. They don't feel compelled to pay the highest price or shop at the full-price, full-service store, when they know they can get the same thing somewhere else cheaper. They are savvy shoppers and know how to find a bargain and get a good price.

Luxury consumers are highly invested in their lifestyle; they put little at risk. One characteristic of luxury is clear: Luxury is always evolving, changing, and moving. Once consumers achieve a certain level of luxury, that level becomes the ordinary, and they seek out some new higher plane of luxury. Thus, what was once the extraordinary becomes the ordinary, and they seek out a new luxury fulfillment.

Luxury is something that consumers strive for. It also is something that luxury consumers are heavily invested in maintaining and keeping. For luxury consumers, you can't go back once you have experienced luxury. It's a divide a consumer crosses that says, "I have made it." Because luxury is tied up with creature comforts and feelings of comfort, consumers who achieve a luxury lifestyle are not likely to make do with less or give up continued luxury. They buy and continue to buy luxury because they can afford to and appreciate the enhanced experience of luxury, but they are not buying luxury to impart status or achieve social advancement.

Luxury consumers don't buy because of the brand; brand justifies the purchase. The brand is not the arbiter of whether a specific product is a luxury. Neither does it play the deciding role in whether to buy. Rather, the brand becomes a justifier for the purchase. It assures consumers of the superior quality of the item and that it will last for years. The brand and its reputation encourage consumers to dig a little deeper into their pocketbook to buy. It's the "Good Housekeeping Seal of Approval" that confirms the product is worth the extra investment, so it plays a critical role in the buying decision. The brand transmits the value and quality messages so important for consumers who participate in the luxury lifestyle.

Luxury consumers exhibit differences of degree, not of kind. The differences we find within the luxury market are primarily behavioral, not motivational. Behaviorally, different luxury consumers might buy more or less of a certain type of luxury product; for example, the more affluent buy more luxuries and spend more when they do simply because they can. But as far as the motivations for buying luxury goes, the differences are slight because all luxury consumers up and down the income scale gain their greatest luxury thrills from experiences. The differences among the four types of luxury consumers—Butterflies, X-Fluents, Cocooners, and Aspirers—identified by different points of view are subtle. But they express subtle motivational differences behaviorally in the luxuries those consumers buy and how much they spend. For example, the X-Fluents spend more on luxury; the Cocooners devote most of their luxury budgets to home; and, predictably, the iconoclastic Butterflies are less materialistic than any of them, though they spend just about as much money buying luxury things as the X-Fluents do. But though we can identify four types of consumers, it is important to remember they are far more like each other in basic approach and values than they are different from each other.

LESSON #1—LUXURY MARKETERS NEED TO ADD A NEW MARKETING "P"— PERFORMANCE—TO GAUGE THE SUCCESS OF THEIR MARKETING EFFORTS

The traditional four or five Ps' approach to marketing was invented in the middle of the last century. Although the marketing Ps inform and guide tactical marketing decision making, they give very little direction from a strategic point of view to today's experientially driven market. The four Ps, in particular, keep us focused on the thing, the noun, and as a result render us basically passive in our approach. Sure, we lob out advertisements or marketing communications, but we have to wait to see how the market responds. So marketing becomes an exercise in frantic activity directed toward the thing followed by periods of waiting and watching to figure out the next action that needs to be taken, sort of like a slow-moving tennis match.

But the world has changed, and the marketing paradigm has gone experiential. Consumers don't buy things any more; they seek experiences and feeling. They aren't particularly concerned about the thing that you want to sell them; rather, their overwhelming concern is how the thing will enhance or improve the quality of their life; they want transformation. They are looking for a performance value in the luxuries they buy. In other words, they want to make the luxury part of themselves experientially and emotionally.

Our concept of luxury marketing must shift from a more or less passive, linear game of tennis conducted between the marketers and the consumers to a fully interactive, real-time interchange of experiences, feelings, and emotions. We must involve them, interact with them, connect with them every day in every way. We can't wait and see but must continually mix it up. We must persistently act and react to the consumers' actions and reactions. This new experiential consumer equation demands greatly enhanced performance on the part of our brands, our products, our marketing communications, our retailing, and our selling. Performance becomes the new P in the traditional marketing model for the experientially driven marketing world.

Everything in marketing turns on performance. The word *performance* has a diversity of meanings, including an artistic presentation as well as the effectiveness

> Performance becomes the new P in the traditional marketing model for the experientially driven marketing world.

of what one does or actions taken. But the definition of performance that luxury marketers need to focus on is the manner of functioning, or how something or somebody functions, operates, or behaves. It's the action of the thing, the product, the service that is delivered, no longer the thing itself. The shift that marketers need to make in their thinking about their business is to expand from an overriding concern with product, pricing, placement, and promotion to the following Ps interpreted experientially:

- *Product* performance (i.e., what it does for the consumer; how it makes him or her feel)
- *Pricing* performance (i.e., how price interacts with the consumer's perception to encourage the consumer to buy; how price makes the consumer feel)
- *Promotion* performance (i.e., how the brand connects with the consumer and the consumer's expectation of performance)
- *Placement* performance (i.e., where the consumer wants to buy and what kind of experiences they want when they shop)

It is through performance that the connection between the marketer and the consumer is experienced.

Figure 12.1 summarizes the performance values that need to be delivered to the consumer through the traditional four Ps of marketing. As we move through the other lessons of luxury marketing that follow, these performance values as each relates to product, pricing, promotion, and placement, will be explored in more depth.

FIGURE 12.1
Performance Values

Product	• Add value to make unique, more special, and different so that the luxury value is enhanced. • Deliver wonderful use experience to consumer. • Transmit cues and clues through the product that signal specialness. • Continue to add luxury value as luxury expectations continue to inflate. • Reject exclusivity in favor of more individuality and personal specialness.
Pricing	• Price conveys meaning, so price high enough to communicate specialness. • Make consumer feel like a winner, so price low enough so that value equation is stacked in consumer's favor. • Ideal luxury price is less than the price consumers expect to pay but more than the price they want to pay.
Promotion	• Involve consumers by telling stories about the brand. • Use stories to communicate brand values. • Develop dialogue with consumers so they can tell stories to you; Internet becomes focus of storytelling. • "Once upon a time" enhances the fantasy of having and owning.
Placement	• Enhance the shopping experience to deliver luxury throughout the buying cycle, from initial consideration through purchase to after the sale. • Brand stories have to be part of the retail experience. • Enhance fantasy experience of having and owning.

LESSON #2—LUXURY IS AN EXPERIENCE EVERYONE WANTS AND BELIEVES THEY DESERVE, SO GIVE IT TO THEM

After a little reflection, it may not appear so revolutionary that today's luxury consumer market has gone experiential. After all, the luxury consumers are at the top of the income ladder, blessed with high incomes and the ability to buy just about anything their hearts desire. Because their wealth didn't accumulate overnight, they have spent years steadily improving their standard of living, so they live in well-furnished houses with closets full of clothes, and they drive fairly new cars that take them from place to place. Material purchases for many of the luxury consumers are more likely to be replacement items or things they might want or take a passing fancy to, but these objects are not likely to be something that these luxury consumers have scrimped and saved for. Affluent consumers' high incomes give them considerable consuming power that they use freely in today's marketplace. Because, for these highly affluent luxury consumers, material things are fairly easy to acquire, don't demand a lot of sacrifice, and are not really filling any deep-seated need, then it just intuitively makes sense that the luxury consumers derive their greatest feeling of luxury satisfaction from experiences.

Assuming this logic holds—that for the affluent the ready availability of material things makes them value experiences more—then it also intuitively makes sense that people who have less material wealth would find greater happiness in acquiring material possessions than in experiences. But that isn't the case. Consumers at every income level and every age range across the board favor luxury experiences over home or personal luxuries.

Wanting to see just how extensive this experiential market shift is, we ran a nationwide omnibus survey among a representative sample of over 900 consumers 18 years and older. Screened only for their purchase in the past year of all three types of luxuries—personal, home, and experiential—we asked from which purchase they gained their greatest personal satisfaction and happiness. See Figure 12.2. We didn't ask anything about their spending nor did we define or quantify what their specific luxury purchase might entail. For example, one person might define experiential luxury as eating dinner at Red Lobster; home luxury as buying a votive candle; and personal luxury as shopping for a pair of shoes at PayLess. But no matter what their luxury might be, the consumers reported getting their greatest luxury satisfaction from the experience.

> Consumers at every income level and every age range across the board favor luxury experiences over home or personal luxuries.

FIGURE 12.2

Source of Satisfaction from Luxury Shopping

Source: Unity Marketing Omnibus Survey, June 2004

In my research with consumers, I have found that no matter who they are or where they live, no matter how much or how little money they make, no matter how much or how little money they spend buying something, all consumers want the same basic things. They want to feel special. They want to buy the very best quality thing, whatever that is, that they can afford. At the same time, they want to make sure they paid a good price and didn't get gouged or paid too much. They want the item they buy to work right, to look good, to last a long time, and to perform as expected and as promised. They want to be treated well and with respect by the sales personnel in the store. They want the reassurance of knowing the company that is producing their special product has a good reputation, is known for quality, can be depended on to stand behind their purchase. Regardless of whether they are spending $1, $10, $100, or $1,000, they all want the same special feeling about their purchase.

This is the underlying motivational dimension of today's consumer market: Everybody everywhere wants to feel special. Maybe we don't get those special reinforcing feelings from our loved ones, our friends, our coworkers, or our bosses; or we get them, but we still want more.

> This is the underlying motivational dimension of today's consumer market: Everybody everywhere wants to feel special.

So we turn to the commercial world and reach out to get our deep-seated needs for confirmation and feeling special and cared for met in the store, in the mall, and in the restaurant. No matter how much money is in our wallet, that cash represents some measure of power in the commercial world. Thus it becomes fairly simple and straightforward to get personal reinforcement by buying something. You become the hero or heroine of your personal "specialness" fantasy when you shop.

The lesson then is to make your customer feel special in every way, every day. The special feelings play out, in particular, in personal interaction, so the way the customer is treated is crucial. Crystal Cruises has internalized this learning to great benefit of the company. Saks also embodies the value that the way shoppers are treated when they cross the threshold is paramount. And Best Buy is fashioning luxury retreats staffed by entertainment experts to serve the luxury consumers that wander into their big-box stores. The lesson is to focus on enhancing the specialness feelings of all the consumers, from the masses to the classes.

LESSON #3—THE AFFLUENT MARKET IS SWEET, BUT THE MASS MARKET IS SWEETER, SO LOOK BEYOND YOUR TRADITIONAL MARKET SEGMENTS

Over the past years I have had a number of discussions with executives running traditional, heritage luxury brands. Inevitably, the discussion turns to new luxury, mass-tige, democratization of luxury, trading up, and all the other keywords that stand for cheap luxury and less affluent luxury customers. They define their customers as people with incomes of $250,000 plus or whatever number they think is the right one, and they clearly differentiate themselves from the peddlers of "cheap luxury" like Victoria's Secret, Starbucks, Target, or any of the other brands they think is not in their league.

I don't think they really mean to sound so snobbish, but they come across as believing if a potential customer doesn't look, act, dress like or have as much cash in their wallets as their current customer, then that potential customer isn't a particularly good fit with their brand. I try to remind them that if their typical customer has an average income of $250,000, that means they have a bunch of customers making less money as well as a bunch making more, so they do indeed have less affluent customers already participating in their brand or shopping in their stores.

Luxury marketers need to open their minds to the tremendous marketing opportunities that exist at the lower fringes of their traditional market. They don't need to make themselves or their products any less luxurious or lower their standards or cut their prices to attract new customers with lots of market potential. The math very simply shows that the luxury market potential of consumers at the upper mass-market income level, incomes $50,000 to $74,999, represents a target market of even greater potential to the luxury marketer than do consumers with incomes of $75,000 and above.

During our most recent luxury survey (results shown in Figure 12.3) we captured data on the upper mass market (household incomes of $50,000 to $74,999) and its purchases of luxuries. These data were not included in survey results reported in the previous chapters; however, we did plug in the upper mass-market's purchase incidence and spending on luxuries into a spreadsheet to calculate its luxury market potential. And the findings are astounding. The total luxury market potential for the upper mass market, those households with upper middle incomes, is $497.3

FIGURE 12.3
Upper Mass-Market Luxury Market Potential in Millions (Total Households = 20,315,000)

	UPPER MASS-MARKET % PURCHASE	UPPER MASS-MARKET TYPICAL SPENDING	UPPER MASS-MARKET LUXURY POTENTIAL IN MILLIONS	AFFLUENT LUXURY MARKET POTENTIAL IN MILLIONS	% DIFFERENCE AFFLUENT VS. UPPER MASS MARKET
Home Luxuries			**$137,857.6**	**$126,030.6**	**-8.6%**
Art & Antiques	6%	$560	6,825.8	20,030.5	193.5
Electronics	26	750	38,852.4	33,946.5	-12.6
Home Fabrics, Window & Wall Coverings	9	380	6,947.7	7,727.3	11.2
Furniture & Floor Coverings	11	1,750	39,106.4	31,036.0	-20.6
Garden & Patio	9	750	13,712.6	3,660.7	-73.3
Kitchen Appliances, Bath & Building	10	750	14,474.4	16,894.5	16.7
Kitchenware, Housewares, Cookware	13	380	10,035.6	4,631.5	-53.8
Linens & Bedding	15	120	3,656.7	4,403.2	20.4
Tabletop, Dinnerware, Stemware, Flatware	6	380	4,245.8	3,700.5	-12.8
Personal Luxuries			**$248,533.7**	**$193,799.0**	**-22.0%**
Automobiles	4	27,500	223,465.0	170,362.5	-23.8
Fashion & Fashion Accessories	15	380	11,193.6	9,351.8	-16.5
Fragrances, Cosmetics, Beauty Products	21	120	4,997.5	2,430.2	-51.4
Jewelry & Watches	12	380	8,877.7	11,654.5	31.3
Experiential Luxuries			**$110,859.0**	**$148,726.4**	**34.2%**
Entertainment & Dining	23	1,070	48,908.4	42,325.4	-13.5
Travel	14	1,860	51,011.0	82,754.7	62.2
Spa/Beauty	5	670	6,125.0	12,243.4	99.9
Home Services	2	120	4,814.7	11,402.9	136.8
Total Luxuries			$497,250.3	$468,556.0	-5.8%

billion, or about 6 percent larger than the potential of the affluent market, which is $468.6 billion.

It is true that upper mass-market consumers spend less money
on the luxuries they buy, and they may well purchase little luxuries like costume jewelry from Kohls, Isaac Mizrahi outfits at Target, bed linens at the outlet store, and dinner at Panera, as opposed
to big luxuries bought at Neiman Marcus, Barneys, and Saks Fifth
Avenue or dinner at Tavern on the Green. They also tend to buy
at a lower-incidence level, but the fact that there are over 20.3 million households that fall into this income range pushes their total
market potential over the top.

It all comes down to the number of households at each income level. Out of the nation's 111 million households, some 18
percent fall into this upper mass-market segment, or 20.3 million;
11 percent are near-affluents, or 12.2 million; 9 percent are affluents, or 10.1 million; and the remaining 5 percent, or 5.7 million,
are super-affluents.

Luxury marketers will be well served in the future if they think
much more seriously about the market potential of the consumers on their borders and at the fringes. Through research we have
found the differences at each stage of affluence is one of degree,
not of kind. We also found that the traditional perspective that affluent consumers participate in luxury in all aspects of their life is
just a lie. Maybe 1 or 2 percent of affluent households go the luxury route all across the board, but the vast majority pick and
choose their luxury indulgences from moment to moment and
from one category to another.

The same dynamic is going on every day in shops all across
America. For one purchase, luxury consumers might opt for the
full-priced designer model at Saks; for another, they shop at Target or Costco, going for price. The lesson is that luxury marketers
need to be much more expansive in how they view their target
market and its overall potential. I don't care where a marketer de-
cides to draw the line in the sand and say that "everyone on this
side of the line is our target customer and everyone on the other
side is not." There is a gray area where a "not-quite" consumer can

reach up to your brand of luxury, and the marketer will gain big benefits from reaching down just a little to attract and capture that consumer. The simple fact is the rich don't become rich overnight. They attain wealth and affluence over time and progress through different income levels at different life stages. Cre-

> The lesson is that luxury marketers need to be much more expansive in how they view their target market and its overall potential.

ating a loyalty bond with less affluent consumers, who tend to be younger, will pay off in the long term as their incomes grow and their affluence rises. Recognizing this life stage progression of luxury, Volkswagen is following its traditional customers from their counterculture, starving grad student roots to their current affluence as doctors or lawyers. Likewise, Mercedes is moving downmarket to offer a model priced right for consumers' evolving life stages and income levels.

With an expansive view of the luxury consumer and his or her true spending power, we also must recognize that income is only a number, and it really doesn't tell us a whole lot about the individual market potential of that consumer. For example, a single 35-year-old female lawyer living in Des Moines, Iowa, and making $75,000 is a card-carrying member of the luxury class and is likely to remain so throughout her adult life. Especially after she marries another lawyer and they both make partner, their income will place them in the financial stratosphere. On the other hand, a single mother of four making the same income and living outside New York City is nowhere near as affluent, but she can budget and save for a yearly trip into Tiffany to buy a silver charm for her bracelet. And as soon as she remarries, she may well be catapulted right into the Tiffany customer sweet spot too. Luxury marketers that firmly target the classes need to seriously study the luxury potential within the masses that are on their borders or already shopping in their midst. Best Buy woke up to this potential and is starting to reap the rewards.

The same learning goes for mass marketers but in reverse. The luxury shoppers in their midst, although lured primarily by a discount shopping experience, may well spring for pricier goods or higher-quality brands if mass marketers offer it to them. Clearly Target and Costco have learned this lesson well.

LESSON #4—GIVE YOUR LUXURY CONSUMERS AN EXIT RAMP OFF THE MASS TRACK

I know at first glance this seems to contradict lesson #3 that the mass market is sweeter, but it doesn't really. Everyone wants that feeling of specialness and uses shopping and buying as an important means through which to achieve that feeling. But that feeling of specialness is totally unique and different for each individual. The mass track is this incredible sameness you find in stores and malls all across America, from the national retailers who are taking over the retail landscape—companies like Gap, Talbots, Restoration Hardware, Pottery Barn, Victoria's Secret, Ann Taylor, and Ann Taylor Loft—to the big boxes like Bed Bath and Beyond or the mass merchants like Target, Wal-Mart, and on and on. So Gap's clothes may be very different from those offered at Talbots, but once you've shopped one Gap or one Talbots store, you pretty well have shopped them all. Consumers everywhere, and especially luxury consumers with ample means to buy where and whatever they want, are craving a unique expression of their individuality. You don't get that if you see yourself coming and going on everybody else's body.

Everything, every store, every mall or strip center, is becoming a little too much the same . . . same stores, same products, same brands, same look, same layout, same-same. People want different, new, unique, and special, and although sameness provides a certain comfort level and predictability that shoppers might opt for in certain situations (such as when they are grocery shopping and want to get in and out fast), they often crave a thrill of surprise when they shop. And when was the last surprise you got shopping at any one of the national chains?

In the marketing circles that I run in, the knee-jerk reaction to getting off the mass track is to become more exclusive; in other words, exclude certain customers from the product or exclude their participation as shoppers in the store through price, limited availability, and the like. But I think we need a new vocabulary, because the word *exclusivity,* or *more exclusive,* just doesn't resonate with the luxury consumers. They get no greater or lesser thrill from something *just because* it is more exclusive. It has to come with more values than just exclusiveness.

In Unity's latest luxury-tracking study—our quarterly study in which we survey luxury consumers about their most recent luxury purchases, where they buy them, how much they spend, and what luxury brands they have been made aware of in the past quarter—a battery of terms describing motivators for making luxury purchases was included and shown in Figure 12.4. Exclusivity sinks right down to the bottom along with status as one of the least important luxury motivators. *Exclusivity* is just not a word that luxury consumers associate with anything positive, so therefore it isn't a word that we in the luxury marketing arena should throw around as freely as we do.

We should replace this concept of exclusivity by focusing on the positive expression of individuality and personal identity of the consumer rather than on the negativity of exclusiveness. Luxury consumers want something unique to themselves, special just for them, that makes them feel special and unique, that expresses one's personal style and identity. We must reject the concept of exclusivity because at its root it is a negative expression. It is about excluding someone, and that doesn't feel nice when you are the one excluded. It violates the entire concept of democratic luxury that runs through the veins of the American luxury consumer.

But you can turn exclusivity to a positive concept. It is not about excluding someone from having an item, a brand, or shopping in a certain store; it is about turning an item, a brand, a store into something unique and more special for the individual. It is a subtle shift in emphasis from the negative-leaning *exclusivity* to the positive-trending *individuality*. It is the difference between putting

FIGURE 12.4

Motivators for the Luxury Consumer

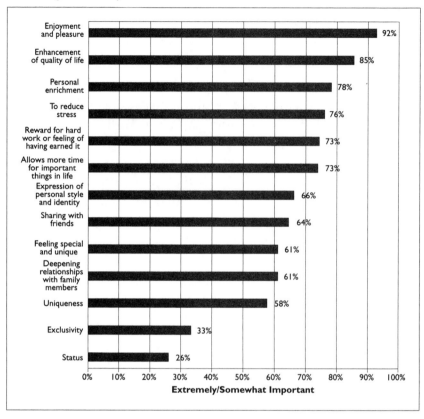

up a stop sign that says Do Not Enter and putting up a sign that says Turn Here for Something Really Special. This shift in emphasis is so important when you think about the independently, democratically, nonmaterialistic Butterfly consumers who are coming to dominate the luxury market. Their value system simply rejects snobbishness or anything that resembles it, such as the idea of exclusivity.

> But you can turn exclusivity to a positive concept. It is not about excluding someone from having an item, a brand, or shopping in a certain store; it is about turning an item, a brand, a store into something unique and more special for the individual.

LESSON #5—NO MATTER WHERE YOU MARKET ALONG THE MASSES-TO-CLASSES CONTINUUM, YOU CAN ALWAYS ADD MORE LUXURY VALUE

Back in my days working at The Franklin Mint, the now defunct luxury marketer of collectibles and desirables, research uncovered a fact that became a rule of thumb in product development. Products we called mixed media—in other words, products that combined different types of materials, such as porcelain with feathers, crystal, or fabrics—got a significant boost in consumer response rate. The simple fact was by adding $5 of additional cost to an item, you could charge $25 more for it and sell more of the item as a result. Enhancing the luxury value of an item made it more attractive to a wider base of consumers and gave them a justification to pay more for the item than for the standard issue.

This is a very simple, but critical concept, that luxury marketers must embrace: They have to strive to add luxury value to the things they sell and the way they sell them. What is luxury value? It's the "bling-bling" factor . . . anything that makes something more unique, more special, more distinctive, more to-die-for. It is the unexpected, the nontraditional, what breaks the mold, makes you take notice—the feature that takes you off the mass track onto a track all your own. Think about the patterned insoles used to enhance designer shoes. It's unexpected, imaginative, enjoyable, and makes the consumer smile as she shells out $450 for that very special pair of shoes. The value-added luxury is the cues and clues that transmit to the consumer that he or she deserves this extra level of specialness.

If you want to learn more about adding luxury value to the product, just look at the couture fashion industry. It's all about the details, finer-quality fabrics, more distinctive patterns and designs, more dynamic shades of color, or unusual combinations of color. Couture fashion takes the ordinary and makes it extraordinary, the essential challenge for every luxury marketer.

Marketers simply need to take it up a notch to transform the ordinary to the extraordinary. We must go against the discounting tide and rather than trying to find creative ways to cut costs in our product offerings—in other words, give the consumers less value for less money—we need to find innovative, creative ways to add value to our products and services to justify a slightly higher price tag. The more luxury value you add, the higher your price can go, but even at the bargain basement price range of Target, an Isaac Mizrahi design justifies a couple of dollars more than the standard issue price.

When is added luxury value enough and how much of a premium can you charge? That will depend on your customers and where their value systems lie and the basic competitive standards that operate in your particular market space. Talking to the consumer is critical to finding the "right" added values, so you can leverage added value for a higher price. Sometimes companies stake their entire product line's value equation on a faulty premise and never take it to the street to find out if they are right.

This same concept of adding luxury value applies equally to experiential luxury service providers. You need to find out what luxury values are really key to the consumer, then work to enhance those values above and beyond the present level. The lesson from learning that the food is only a small part of what makes for a luxury dining experience points to areas of weakness and opportunity in the restaurant business. If a restaurant owner focuses most of his or her attention on the food at the expense of staff training and supervision, that may well be a fatal mistake.

The luxury value proposition may not be the most obvious or straightforward thing at all. For example, Crystal Cruises has discovered that a key value for its luxury customers is sheer space, and it uses this luxury value to set itself apart as a more luxurious cruise line. Guests don't feel crowded and because of the higher staff-to-guest ratio, they never have to wait in line for service. These are key luxury components of the cruise experience. Further, the service staff pays attention to gaining more than a passing acquaintance with guests and their personal preferences. Just saying "Good morning, Mrs. Danziger," goes immeasurably further than "Good morning" in the luxury service business. And how hard is it really to make a more personal connection?

LESSON #6—LUXURY MARKETERS NEED TO STRATEGIZE FOR "LUXFLATION" TO COUNTERACT THE DOWNWARD GRAVITATIONAL PULL OF LUXURY FROM THE CLASSES TO THE MASSES

The natural evolution of all luxury concepts is to first be introduced to the classes, and then translated down to the masses. Inevitably, all luxury concepts are reinterpreted for the masses, and if in the past this evolutionary progress may have taken decades, today the transformation of luxury from the classes to the masses is happening at an incredibly fast pace.

Any number of factors are in play in the rapid progression of products from indulgent luxuries to basic necessities. Think color televisions, DVDs, VCRs, cell phones, home computers, air conditioners, dishwashers, and jet travel, all of which started their product life cycle as a luxury available to a few, only to be transformed over time into a standard of living basic for most Americans. Propelling the rapid transformation from luxury to lifestyle necessity is the wealth effect. More and more Americans are enjoying greater disposable income, as the cost of the basic necessities of life take a smaller and smaller share of the family paycheck, and personal income tax levels continue to decline. Along with increased affluence and an ability to spend more on desire-based purchases, the rise of mass media, 24/7 cable news channels, and the Internet have brought new awareness to the masses of how the rich and famous live. Thus, as the masses are exposed to what the rich have and how they live, it has given people everywhere a growing appetite for the good life and the feeling that it is within one's grasp.

Luxury is a constantly moving target. Consumers become more familiar with one standard of luxury, so what was once extraordinary becomes ordinary and the luxury feeling of specialness is lost. As luxury moves downmarket to the masses, luxury marketers must continually reach up and extend the bar of luxury higher and higher to bring freshness, newness, and something altogether extraordinary to the ever-aspiring luxury consumer. It's this trend toward "luxflation"—the need to deliver greater and greater luxury value to consumers—that is the ultimate marketing challenge for all luxury marketers.

Luxury marketers and service providers must continually strive to refine, define, enhance, and enrich the luxury value proposition that they offer their customers. And today they have to make this transformation happen at a faster and faster pace. The luxury fashion industry is the pacesetter in rapid and continual luxury enhancement and transformation. The industry develops entirely new collections (often based on totally new concepts) twice a year and it does this year in, year out. Few other industries run at such a fast pace, but if you are in the luxury market, you better try to pick up the speed, because luxury consumer boredom is just around the corner if you let your luxury edge slip from the extraordinary to the ordinary.

Being equipped to constantly change and adapt to the changing needs and desires of the luxury marketplace must be hardwired into the structural "DNA" of the luxury company. Luxury marketers must be constantly evolving as their market is evolving, and it is evolving faster and faster every day under the powerful influence of the media and the Internet. Luxury marketers must keep out in front of their markets, anticipating their needs and designing innovative products so that the products are ready and waiting when the consumer goes shopping to find them.

> Luxury marketers and service providers must continually strive to refine, define, enhance, and enrich the luxury value proposition that they offer their customers.

This need to keep upping the ante on luxury becomes the mirror image of the trading-up phenomenon, whereby the luxury market devolves into the masses, resulting in virtually no distinction between mass or class, luxury or ordinary. Devolving from class to mass represents a real and present danger for individual luxury brands. Fifty years ago, Revlon was a luxury brand of cosmetics. Today, it is relegated to blister packs in supermarkets and drugstores. The lesson for luxury brand managers is that they must be vigilant in maintaining the luxury allure of their products by continually pumping up the luxury value of their brand to reverse the inevitable downward pull of gravity toward the common and everydayness.

In addition to being responsive to the change in fashion, luxury marketers must continually look at new luxury opportunities that present themselves as the results of advances in technology. This year's number one most purchased luxury product, electronics, owes its leadership position to technology developments. Luxury marketers will be rewarded as they anticipate and plan for the next luxury innovation, the next new desire that will sweep through the luxury market. And, of course, after it transforms the luxury market, the next big thing will expand to the mass market.

LESSON #7—LUXURY MARKETERS MUST EMBRACE A LUXURY-BRANDING PARADIGM THAT COMBINES PRODUCT FEATURES AND BENEFITS WITH CONSUMERCENTRIC LUXURY VALUES

The business of creating, building, and communicating a luxury brand just got more complex in the new experiential consumer market. Today, marketers must make the quantum leap beyond thinking only about luxury product benefits and features to delivering luxury performance at the experiential level.

We have seen how for the Butterfly consumers, who are coming to dominate today's luxury market, luxury consumption is driven by a desire for self-actualization, as described by Abraham Maslow in his hierarchy of needs. Self-actualization is the need that is expressed only after the other lesser needs in the hierarchy, such as physiological, safety, love and affection, and esteem, are satisfied. This need is described as "the desire to become more and more what one is, to become everything that one is capable of becoming." It explains the pursuit of self-fulfillment through spiritual enlightenment, greater knowledge, peace, appreciation of beauty, culture, art, and aesthetics. Retailers like Ten Thousand Villages have found innovative ways to connect with this self-actualization desire in their customers, and Crystal Cruises meets this need in its on-board educational programming.

The luxury-branding challenge for the future is to connect all the different dimensions of luxury—luxury features and luxury experiences—with the consumer. The luxury-branding message is simple and it is clear: The message must reflect the consumer's experiential dimension. Product features and benefits are the foundation on which the experiential dimension stands, but the new branding equation must enter into a new realm of performance and delivery of luxury values. The obvious isn't always the reality in luxury branding. As we have seen, buying a meal is only a small part of what makes up the luxury dining experience. Far more important than just the food is the totality of the dining experience—the restaurant's lighting, music, atmosphere, and the way the customer is treated from walking in the door to leaving.

The role of luxury branding in persuading people to buy cannot be separated from the other primary influencers on purchase: the retailer's or dealer's brand and the price-value equation. All three influencers, which make up the luxury-branding triple play, engage the consumer on the experiential plane. The retailer's brand encompasses the shopping experience, the thrill of the hunt, the fun of finding something wonderful in a wonderful store environment or, conversely, finding something wonderful in the quickest, most convenient fashion. The price-value relation is also experiential, such as the thrill of finding an outstanding bargain on the sale racks. Old luxury retailers like Saks Fifth Avenue are transforming themselves into new luxury retailers by upping the ante in the experiential side of the shopping equation, from a spa or massage to a wonderful cosmetic shopping experience. Matterhorn Nursery has turned shopping for a petunia into an experience by inviting shoppers into a whole village of wonderful garden-shopping experiences and inviting them to stroll through its display gardens, which are a restful retreat from the hubbub of today's fast-paced world.

The true measure of a luxury brand today is how well it performs or delivers luxury satisfaction to the consumer. As we have described, the greatest luxury satisfactions are achieved experientially. Therefore, the luxury brand becomes the means through which corporate strategy connects with consumer psychology. This is the new paradigm for luxury branding in the 21st century. It's all about the experience. For Cooking.com, part of the experience is using the product, but an even bigger part of the experience it sells and on which its brand is based is the experience of honest, truthful information so the consumer can make an informed purchase decision. QVC is tapping the unique television paradigm, whereby viewers feel up close and personal about the television personalities they invite into their homes every day. Those virtual guests who share our time watching the tube become powerful spokespeople to sell us all kinds of new stuff.

The challenge in brand building in the future is breaking through the increasing cluttered airwaves to connect on an emotional level with the consumer target market. It has been said that the typical weekday edition of the *New York Times* contains more information than the average person was likely to ever have been exposed to during a whole lifetime in 17th-century England. The best way to cut through the advertising pollution is by communicating emotionally with consumers through storytelling, using consumers' terms and imagery so that the advertising resonates instantly with them. This is what M&C Saatchi achieved in its commercial for Crystal Cruises, in which the luxury of space, peace, and beauty was communicated through a story that built a fantasy the viewer could participate in.

In communicating their brand to the consumer, advertisers must not just talk to the consumer; they must create a dialogue with the consumer. They need to understand why people buy a specific brand . . . what qualities, attributes, values the consumer associates with the brand . . . what imagery the brand evokes . . . what fantasies, what feelings, what experiences it fulfills for the consumer. Then these concepts need to be translated into advertising that will connect with the consumer.

For a luxury brand, it is important to be seen where similar brands are seen; therefore, the selection of distribution partners is a critical component for brand image. As we have seen, the reputation of the store is second only to the reputation of the brand in the consumer's purchase decision. Best Buy understands this synergy between brands and the store and is enhancing the shopping experience to present a friendlier environment for its luxury customers. Luxury manufacturers must choose their retail partners carefully because of this synergy between product brand and the store. It is also a reason why so many luxury brand marketers are increasingly controlling all aspects of their brand by setting up dedicated brand retail stores that control the entire presentation process.

At the retail level, the standard of customer service is critical to the proper presentation of luxury goods. The salesperson plays a critical role in transmitting brand values and brand identities (e.g., in telling the customer why this item is worth three to five times more than a comparable item at Sears or JCPenney). An important opportunity for building one's luxury brand is to select only those retailers that are committed to the brand. Marginal and unfocused retailers should be dropped to improve the brand's franchise for its other dealers. The investment in flagship stores like the Polo Ralph Lauren store on New York's Fifth Avenue pays off in augmenting the brand's prestige, providing a venue to showcase the entire product line, and presenting the brand as a lifestyle.

LESSON #8—NURTURE BRAND EVANGELISTS TO SPREAD THE WORD ABOUT THE LUXURY VALUES YOUR BRAND DELIVERS

Word-of-mouth advertising is entirely too powerful to leave up to chance, but too many marketers think it just happens. Right behind the luxury-branding triple play (i.e., the brand/company reputation, the store's or dealer's reputation, and the price-value relationship) in influencing luxury consumers in their last luxury purchase is the recommendation of friends (i.e., word of mouth). Word of mouth is important in home and personal luxuries but is even more magnified in encouraging experiential luxury purchases. See Figure 12.5.

FIGURE 12.5
Luxury Purchase Influencers' Index

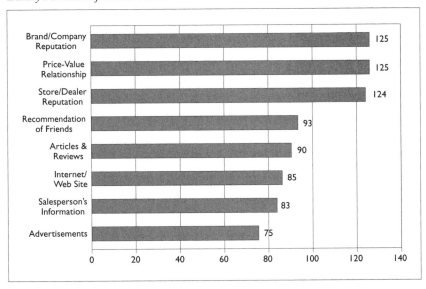

What people say about the product, store, or service brand and its reputation is critical to managing the brand. Part of the magic of QVC and other home-shopping and infomercial models stems from how they incorporate the look and feel of true person-to-person communication about the product in a nonselling, informational way; in other words, they employ word-of-mouth selling. How can luxury marketers harness the power of word of mouth and use it as a meaningful marketing strategy and not leave it all up to chance? Here are the keys to implementing a word-of-mouth strategy:

- **A unique, innovative concept.** The first key to laying the groundwork for a word-of-mouth program is to have a new, innovative, truly different concept. If it isn't new, it's old, and people don't want to talk about last year's news. They want to talk about what's hot, what's new, what's innovative. That way they become part of an in-group, a select group that is in the know and has some kind of secret insider's information. When they chat up your concept, they share secret special information and bring new members into the in-group. For example, Aerosoles offers a totally new concept in shoes that not only look good but feel good and are affordable.

  What if yours isn't a new concept? Simple: You must keep reinventing your brand, your store, your concept. After all, your market is always changing, your competition is always evolving, so you must keep moving too. You have to keep your brand fresh, as KitchenAid does. It keeps reinventing its standing mixer—an icon ever since it was introduced 80 years ago—with funky new colors that command a prominent place in any luxury kitchen.

- **A simple, immediately understood concept.** In my consulting work, what I find even harder than discovering a unique and innovative concept is making it simple, easy to explain, and easy to understand. Let's face it, you have only a fraction of a second to attract the attention of the consumer on the shelf, on the page, or on the screen. Your only hope to lay the groundwork for word of mouth is to dumb down the concept enough so that ordinary people with no special training can immediately understand and communicate your concept in a split second.

The concept of Aerosoles shoes is basic for anyone who has ever suffered from wearing an uncomfortable pair of dress shoes. If your feet hurt, everything else hurts, so Aerosoles offers an experience of comfort and fashion at an affordable price.

Matterhorn Nursery, too, offers a simple concept: The ultimate garden experience that includes the best of everything and anything you need for your garden, from the plants to the tools to decorative accents to clothes to garden in and hot tubs to soak in after you are done, plus the insiders' knowledge that gives you an edge in designing your garden space and growing beautiful plants and flowers. Or Cooking.com, the Web site where you can buy literally anything for your kitchen; and when it arrives at your home, it is sure to work as well as promised. Or Sub-Zero, experts in refrigeration.

- **Identify and cultivate passionate consumers.** So now you have a unique, innovative concept that is made simple so that anyone can understand and communicate it effectively, but there is one more factor that is critical to the success of a word-of-mouth strategy: You have to identify and develop a dialogue with the most likely prospects to be your brand's ambassadors. The secret is to find the customers who are the most passionate about your product and your brand. Let's face it, a successful word-of-mouth program must find and cultivate those customers. Marketers and retailers must come into the 21st century and put information technology to work to learn as much as they can about their customers— their passions, their dreams, their desires. The next step is to create a meaningful dialogue with those best-of-the-best customers.

Some retailers are beginning to test these waters with membership loyalty programs that don't insult the customer by making them pay a membership fee to join the club. Chicos, the woman's clothing specialty retailer, has a free passport club that members earn themselves into based on how much they spend. The club gives them some modest discount off every purchase as well as special sales offers and a gift certificate on their birthday. The Ulta stores, an innovative but simple beauty store concept that sells all kinds of cosmetics, makeup, fragrances, and beauty accessories with a full-service hair and nail salon and beauty spa in the back, has its free Ulta club card that also offers discounts after a certain amount is spent. These programs can help retailers identify their most passionate (i.e., biggest-spending) customers, who are most likely to chat up the store.

Brand marketers and retailers need to establish a foundation on which to build word-of-mouth programs. Word of mouth is entirely too powerful to leave to chance. The keys to getting word-of-mouth programs going are fairly straightforward and will ultimately help all of us build better businesses: Create an innovative but simple-to-understand concept and then identify, communicate, and develop meaningful dialogue with the most passionate customers, who are most likely to become your unpaid word-of-mouth ambassadors.

LESSON #9—THE PRICE COMMUNICATES ON MANY DIFFERENT LEVELS; KNOW AND UNDERSTAND THE EXPERIENTIAL DIMENSIONS OF LUXURY PRICING

With so much emphasis on price at the consumer level, from the simple fact that the majority of luxury consumers made their last product purchase in nearly every category of luxury goods on sale to the ranking of price/value at the top of purchase influencers for luxury, you can easily make the mistake of thinking price has something to do with money. But make no mistake, price is only a concept that represents many different dimensions in the luxury purchase transaction, about the least of which is how much something costs. When it comes to the price of luxury, it isn't about the money; it is all about the meaning.

> When it comes to the price of luxury, it isn't about money; it is all about the meaning.

The meaning is the luxury value, those sometimes tangible but often intangible qualities of a product, brand, or service that communicate specialness to the consumer. The price is one of the cues and clues of value, so it can't be too low to signal "cheap" or too high to signal "exclusivity" or "I am excluded from considering this purchase." The average amount luxury shoppers spent buying their last luxury purchase can provide a valuable guide to understanding the emotional dimension of pricing. Those average prices represent what luxury consumers perceive as the "right price" for those items, as that is what they finally chose to pay. Chapter 9 explores in more depth the research findings on price.

Consumers never think of prices as a single number; rather, prices are always expressed in a range. What luxury marketers need to do is understand the price ranges that apply to their products and then make sure they fall somewhere just under the top of the typical price range if they want to hit the right price for the largest number of luxury consumers. For example, if the average price paid for luxury linens and bedding is $200, then a sheet set priced two or three times that amount will appeal to a very narrow range of buyers. On the other hand, if you price your sheets at $250 or $275, maybe as high as $300, you might just find the right price range to appeal to a broad range of luxury consumers. The higher price tag signals superior quality; at the same time, it doesn't make consumers feel they are being taken for a ride. A product priced at a premium over the average signals greater quality, whereas pricing it close to, but slightly above, the average transmits a value message.

As soon as we forget all about the money and focus on the experiential value of the price, we are on our way to turning pricing into a powerful strategy in our luxury-marketing equation.

It is in this range of acceptable prices where the luxury marketers need to seek their official price. It has to offer significant luxury value but be priced below, but not too far below, what the consumer believes that level of luxury value is worth. As I explored in Chapter 9, price transmits powerful emotional messages that resonate on many different levels with the luxury consumers. Finding a good price and paying the right price reinforce the consumer's self-perception of being a good shopper, a smart shopper. Finding a bargain means the shopper has won at the shopping game, so he or she gets the experiential thrill of being a winner. Luxury consumers know the value of a dollar, and they aren't about to put their luxury lifestyle at risk to acquire more stuff; thus their frugalness is an expression of emotional security. And they know the price really isn't the price, because in a day or two that price is likely to change; and when it changes, it always goes down, never up, in today's economy. As soon as we forget all about the money and focus on the experiential value of the price, we are on our way to turning pricing into a powerful strategy in our luxury-marketing equation.

LESSON #10—BRAND AWARENESS IS NOT ENOUGH ANYMORE; WE NEED TO CONNECT MORE PERSONALLY WITH CONSUMERS

Branding, building a brand, communicating the brand's values, and using the brand as a conduit to connect with customers will continue to grow as the pivotal axis on which effective marketing is based. Using the brand to connect with consumers is about creating a dialogue, involving them with the brand and making them active participants with our brands.

The key challenge for brand managers used to be building brand awareness, with the assumption that trial and use would follow. However, just because virtually everyone knows brands like Clorox, Tide, Crest, Colgate, Coca-Cola, and Pepsi doesn't mean people actually use them. Today, just plain brand awareness isn't enough. People want a real connection with their chosen brands. Because luxury brands are even more value packed with emotional resonance, consumers' desire to make an even deeper connection with luxury brands is pronounced. They want to know the brand is really "for me, about me, understands me, fulfills me, in essence *is* me," whether it is Polo Ralph Lauren, Sub-Zero, Volkswagen, KitchenAid, Aerosoles, or Saks Fifth Avenue.

Personal consumption as a means toward self-actualization is a new concept on the commercial landscape. It is finding its first expression in the luxury market, where the consumers' affluent lifestyles provide all the material goods needed for life. A drive for self-actualization takes buying and shopping into a new experiential realm. But the trend toward searching and finding self-actualization through buying and shopping is already encroaching on the mass market as well, as evidenced by the fact that at all levels of income, consumers everywhere rate the experience of luxury more satisfying than owning and having home or personal luxuries.

This business of luxury marketing and branding has taken a quantum leap into a new experiential orbit. As a result, we must transform all the basic suppositions on which old luxury brands were based. We need to find new ways of communicating brands and brand values with our customers. We need to take our communications to the next level by incorporating two-way interaction with the consumer, whereby we don't just throw out our branding messages in a one-way barrage of noise but instead establish new ways to gain feedback and dialogue with the consumer. The home-shopping channels have figured this one out by encouraging viewers to call in to chat on the air with their favorite host or celebrity product sponsor.

> Today, it is through the Internet and company Web sites that the platform for all branding and marketing communications should begin, so marketers waste much of the power of the Internet and minimize the effectiveness of their Web sites if they simply transfer traditional marketing communications from print or TV to the Web.

The technology of the Internet offers intriguing hints about the possibilities of establishing meaningful two-way communications between brands and their customers. Luxury marketers must look to a future where their Web sites become the central hub of two-way communications with customers. Today, it is through the Internet and company Web sites that the platform for all branding and marketing communications should begin, so marketers waste much of the power of the Internet and minimize the effectiveness of their Web sites if they simply transfer traditional marketing communications from print or TV to the Web. They should start all marketing and branding communications on the Web first, using all the tools, facilities, and capabilities of 21st-century computer networks and then transfer that to traditional media as needed.

Web sites must include the data and tools required so consumers can make an informed purchase decision. Luxury marketers, in particular, need to actively pursue a dialogue with consumers, inviting them to communicate back to the company and making sure someone responds in real time to incredibly valuable consumer input. Companies that are truly connecting with consumers in a new electronically enhanced way include eBay and the two leading cable home-shopping networks, QVC and HSN. Aeorsoles, too, deserves a nod for making its multichannel retailing strategy seamless and invisible to the consumer.

Every point of contact between the luxury brand and the consumer must be reconfigured for two-way communication. New methods of communications must be established between and among the luxury brand's customers, retailers, distribution partners, and the company, as sevenEcho is trying to do. The challenge becomes connecting why consumers buy with how and where to reach them, and at the same time providing the means and opportunity for consumers to connect back to the brand. The Internet is tailor-made to do this, but remember to design for multiple means of connection, including telephones.

In addition to exploring new mediums of communications, luxury marketers must also find new messages to communicate. If brand awareness is no longer enough, if simply knowing the name doesn't do it, we need to develop more conceptually based means of communicating brand values and experiences. And that is through stories and storytelling. Think about those brand names we all know—Clorox, Crest, Tide, for example—that have no story that personalizes or gives meaning and dimension to the brands. On the other hand, a brand like Polo Ralph Lauren is incredibly rich in story content and allows consumers to make the story part of themselves through the purchase of the goods.

Stories are the new message of luxury branding, and through this very basic human medium of communication, consumers will come to make the brand part of their personal identity. In our branding communications, the stories that are most compelling and will best connect with the consumer are the stories in which a person, not a thing or an entity like a company, is the central character. Think about the power of the personal story and how it has become intertwined indelibly around these brands: Martha and Martha Stewart Omnimedia; Bill and Microsoft; The Donald and The Trump Organization; Warren and Berkshire Hathaway; Michael and Dell Computers; Steve and Apple Computers; Ted and Turner Broadcasting. We don't even need their last names to make the connection.

The real power in business is the people: the people running the companies, the people in the stores, and the people

> If brand awareness is no longer enough, if simply knowing the name doesn't do it, we need to develop more conceptually based means of communicating brand values and experiences. And that is through stories and storytelling.

making the purchases. What we really care about and ultimately relate to most closely are people, so our brands need to be presented as stories about people. It doesn't necessarily have to be the founder like Ralph Lauren or some iconic personality like Martha Stewart. The branding story could be built around someone else, such as a customer; for example, look at the effectiveness of Jared Fogle as Subway Sandwich's diet guru. It can even be a made-up person, like Betty Crocker, as long as a fully developed persona is at the heart of the brand.

The key to a brand's story is not necessarily who the story is about, though nobody in a company is ever as passionate or more fully embodies the values of the brand to the extent of the company founder, but the story has to be centered on a person with whom people can identify and relate to in a personal way.

LESSON #11—LUXURY IS ALL ABOUT THE FANTASY; HELP YOUR CONSUMERS CREATE AND LIVE THEIR PERSONAL FANTASY

The last takeaway lesson I want to leave with those of you who are marketing luxury to the masses as well as the classes is to remember that luxury is ultimately all smoke and mirrors. Luxury is the dream, the aspiration, the hoped for, the fantasy. Luxury operates in the human psyche as a metaphysical construct that transcends reality. The reason why experiences so fully embody luxury to the consumer is that experiences are laid down as memories or stories about one's life that he or she creates. Memories are never remembered in their reality. Rather, they are embellished and polished and recollected with the soft focus of nostalgia.

A material thing, no matter how longed for or dreamed about before it is obtained, is still a concrete thing. It can't ever transcend itself to become a luxury fantasy. The luxury fantasy happens instead before the thing is actually acquired, and it may well keep its luster for a few days, a few hours, a few minutes. But then that once extraordinary thing simply becomes the ordinary. It is only in the mind and imagination where luxury can ultimately reside. Luxury is in the anticipation, the planning, the researching, the saving, and to some extent the purchasing. But once a material object is bought, the luxury fantasy ends and the object of that elaborate luxury fantasy becomes just another ordinary thing.

For an experiential luxury, however, the fantasy never stops because you go from one fantasy—the anticipation and planning fantasy—to another one—the recollection and nostalgia fantasy. In between the fantasies you live the experience, but that is swift and fleeting whereas the memories linger forever. This is why experience will always trump material goods in the luxury market. That is also why marketers of material goods and services need to study and understand the many different dimensions of the luxury service provider's art. Luxury marketers and retailers must transcend the physical, material world and become a character in the consumer's luxury fantasy.

So it is with the metaphysics of luxury that our story of the luxury market began and where it ends. Luxury is no longer about the thing anymore; it is all about the experience.

> For an experiential luxury, however, the fantasy never stops because you go from one fantasy—the anticipation and planning fantasy—to another one—the recollection and nostalgia fantasy. That is why experience will always trump material goods in the luxury market place.

I find the act of writing a solitary pursuit during which I hole up in my home office with the phone turned off and a big Do Not Disturb sign on the door. But even though writing is a solo effort, preparing a book for publication and doing the research so that you have something meaningful to say takes lots of help from very generous people.

First, I want to recognize the tremendous support received from Condé Nast's *House & Garden* magazine as the initial sponsor of the first round of luxury research, including both quantitative and qualitative studies. Its early support of my theories and hypotheses of the new experiential paradigm shift in the luxury market was instrumental in getting this book written and directing my company in a whole new research direction toward luxury.

Second, I thank all the fine people who shared their valuable time and gave me wonderful new insights into the depths and dimensions of the luxury market. These people include:

Sylvia Bass, American Express, http://www.aexp.com
Kimberley Grayson, Aerosoles, http://www.aerosoles.com
Barry Judge, Best Buy, http://www.bestbuy.com
Robert Passikoff, Brand Keys, http://www.brandkeys.com
Ariel Foxman, *Cargo* magazine, http://www.condenast.com
Tracy Randall, Cooking.com, http://www.cooking.com
Gregg Michel, Crystal Cruises, http://www.crystalcruises.com
Dominique Browning, *House & Garden* magazine, http://www
    .condenast.com
Jo Tyler, EdD, Humanizing Business, http://jo.tyler@verizon.net
Kim Kiner, Hunter Douglas, http://www.hunterdouglas.com
Ken Nisch, JGA, http://www.jga.com
Brian Maynard, KitchenAid, http://www.whirlpool.com

Lisa Behe, Martin's Herend Imports, http://www.herendusa.com

Matt Horn, Matterhorn Nursery, http://www.matterhornnursery.com

Dr. Paul Glat, Plastic Surgery Associates, http://www.drglat.com

Jeffrey Morgan, Polo Ralph Lauren, http://www.polo.com

Doug Rose, QVC, http://www.qvc.com

Robin Domeniconi, *Real Simple* magazine, http://www
.realsimple.com

Maximillian Riedel, Riedel Crystal, http://www.riedelusa.com

Kimberly Grabel, Saks Fifth Avenue, http://www.s5a.com

Ken Olsho, Seven Echo, http://www.sevenecho.com

Paul Hooker, Sferra Fine Linens, http://www.sferrabros.com

Doug McKenzie, Starwood, http://www.starwood.com

Paul Leuthe, Sub-Zero, http://www.subzero.com

William Taubman, The Taubman Company, http://www
.taubman.com

Doug Dirks, Ten Thousand Villages, http://www
.tenthousandvillages.org

Leaf Van Boven, University of Colorado, http://www.psych
.colorado.edu/~vanboven

Karen Marderosian, Volkswagen, http://www.vw.com

Finally, I must acknowledge the wonderful support my husband and business partner, Greg, gave me throughout the process. He stepped in to clear me of so many home and work responsibilities so I could focus my efforts on this book. Thanks to Len Stein of Visibility PR, who was instrumental in helping me fashion the critical luxury messages coming out of the research in order to get the widest exposure to the largest number of people. Thanks also to Michael Cunningham and the Dearborn folks, who supported this and my previous effort *Why People Buy Things They Don't Need*, as well as to Jane Wesman Public Relations, which is directing its efforts toward both books. My first publisher, Doris Walsh, along with her partner, Jim Madden, at Paramount Market Publishing is greatly appreciated for her ongoing support and advice. Thanks to Ellen Coleman for her advice through this whole process. And special thanks to Susan Peterson, who has helped every step of the way to refine my thinking and sharpen my ideas.

RESEARCH OBJECTIVES
AND METHODOLOGY

The research studies included in this book attempt to understand why consumers buy luxury, what they believe luxury is, and how their emotions and feelings related to luxury impact their buying behavior. This is the second annual study of the luxury market by Unity Marketing—the 2002 study conducted in association with Condé Nast's *House & Garden* magazine and the 2003 survey updating the most volatile data contained in the original survey. By understanding the "why" that drives luxury purchases, luxury marketers will gain new understandings about how to build their brands, target the emotional needs of their target market, and sell more products. Today, as the consumer's approach to buying luxury goods has changed, it is critically important for luxury marketers to understand the new, emerging dynamic of the luxury market.

Specific objectives of this research study:

- **Luxury-buying behavior:** To conduct a national survey of affluent consumers to discover what luxuries they buy, including luxury home products bought specifically for the home; personal luxuries, such as automobiles, apparel, jewelry; and experiential luxuries or luxury services that provide experiential pleasures. To track changes in luxury purchases from year to year.

- **Spending on luxury:** To benchmark their spending on luxuries (i.e., luxury home products, personal luxuries, and experiential luxuries) and track changes over time.
- **Demographics of the luxury market:** Primary demographics of the luxury households, what types of luxuries they buy, how much they spend, where they shop for luxuries, and key demographic segments within the luxury market (e.g., HHI, size, composition, ethnicity/race, education, etc.).
- **Luxury market psychographics, or why people buy luxuries:** To understand the influences on people's luxury purchasing, what they look for in luxuries they buy, and how they shop for luxuries. To understand how luxury consumers' attitudes about luxury impact their purchases and spending on luxuries. To discover why they buy luxuries and what the key motivators and drivers are for luxury consumption.
- **Actionable marketing recommendations:** To put insights, understandings, and discoveries about the luxury market to work in actionable marketing recommendations and insights for luxury marketers.
- **Trends in luxury:** To identify the key trends that are transforming the luxury market now and into the future.

RESEARCH METHODOLOGY

Unity Marketing's research methodology for this luxury study entails two different types of research with different methodologies. First is a qualitative research phase, conducted using focus groups, that helps to develop hypotheses and concepts about the luxury market. These hypotheses are then tested and validated in the second phase of the research project that encompasses quantitative research. Two consecutive years of qualitative research have been conducted for this study and is described below.

Phase 1: Qualitative Focus Groups

A total of seven focus groups was held in four major markets (Philadelphia, Chicago, Atlanta, New York City Metro) in the second and third quarters of 2002. Respondents were recruited based on subscribing to one of the leading home/shelter magazines; having income levels of $100,000 or higher; and the value of their housing falling within the top 20 percent of the local housing market.

Only women were recruited for the focus groups after the first two groups were conducted in Philadelphia. The focus groups' screening criteria were tightened after two initial groups in Philadelphia with a male and female mix were recruited. Based on the dynamics of the groups, we felt female-only groups would be more relaxed and open in discussions about luxury. We also believed that women represent significant direct purchasers or influencers in luxury purchases.

Phase 2: Quantitative Online Survey Research

2002 Survey: Hypotheses resulting from the focus groups were tested in a quantitative telephone survey conducted August 2002 among a total of 866 homeowning households. This survey was conducted in association with *House & Garden* magazine. The following sampling strategy was used:

- Higher-income households with incomes of more than $50,000 but less than $100,000 for a total of 239 respondents
- Affluent, high-income households with incomes of $100,000 or more for a total of 627 respondents

2003 Survey: The 2003 survey was conducted by Unity Marketing with no corporate sponsorship. A highly reliable Internet survey-polling firm was used to conduct the 2003 survey. This company also conducts research for *American Demographics,* among others. The different methodologies from year to year appear to have had little overall impact on the survey results.

The 2003 survey instrument was designed to record the most volatile luxury consumer data, such as purchase incidence and total spending, and to provide comparative links with survey results in 2002. Although the 2003 survey was not so extensive as the previous year's survey, we did expand on questions about places where luxury consumers shopped for products and the role of branding in the purchase of each luxury product. We asked about luxury consumer purchase incidence and total spending within 13 different categories of products defined in the same way but arranged in two major categories: luxury home products and personal luxuries. We combined recreational vehicles with automobiles because of the low purchase incidence.

Rather than ask about luxury services, we defined such purchases as experiential luxuries. In this section we also eliminated party-planning services because of low incidence and slightly rephrased the term describing luxury entertainment and dining experiences. Some attitude questions used in the 2003 survey were also slightly rephrased.

Besides differences in survey methodology, we found differences in the sample that responded to this year's survey. The 2003 sample of 634 respondents has a slightly lower average income, $135,000, as compared with the previous year's survey, $152,000. Because of this skew toward a lower average income, we have stripped out the $50,000 to less than $75,000 income sample from the survey totals and compared only respondents with incomes of $75,000 and above with last year's results, which amounts to 443 respondents. As a result of stripping out the lower-income segment, the survey sample from year to year averages $152,000.

Another important difference between the 2002 and 2003 survey samples is the significantly higher participation of male respondents in 2003—50 percent as compared with 32 percent in 2002. In some instances, the greater participation of men in the survey sample may impact overall findings, which will be noted in the survey report that follows.

The total survey sample for the 2003 survey included the following:

- Above-average income: $50,000 to less than $75,000 and 121 survey respondents (not included in survey totals)
- Near-affluents: $75,000 to less than $100,000 income and 143 respondents (32 percent)
- Affluents: $100,000 to less than $150,000 and 143 respondents (32 percent)
- Super-affluents: $150,000 and above and 157 respondents (35 percent)

Demographic Profile, 2002 compared with 2003

In the 2002 luxury survey, a total of 866 consumer surveys were completed compared with 443 luxury consumers surveyed in the 2003 survey. The average income for both years was the same, approximately $152,000 overall. It is important to note that the 2003 sample does *not* include any consumers with incomes less than $75,000, whereas a comparative sample of these consumers was included in the 2002 survey.

Although women respondents dominated the survey in 2002, representing nearly two-thirds of the total sample, the most recent year's survey included a far higher percentage of men. The gender breakdown was 50 percent male and 50 percent female. Men were more highly represented among the most affluent consumers with incomes of $150,000 and above. This difference in the sample's gender makeup may well account for differences in purchase incidence and will be noted throughout the survey. See Figure A.1.

Key Demographic Characteristics of the Luxury Consumers Surveyed

- **All respondents purchased luxury:** Only affluent consumers (i.e., incomes of $75,000 and above) who purchased any luxury—home luxuries, personal luxuries, and/or experiential luxuries—were included in the survey. In 2003, home luxuries were purchased the most (82 percent), followed by experiential luxuries (72 percent), and personal luxuries (61 percent). See Figure A.2.
- **Highly educated:** A key demographic characteristic of the luxury market is high educational levels. This goes along with high income levels. Among the 2002 survey sample, 72 percent had completed college or more, such as taken postgraduate courses or completed a postgraduate degree. Another 17 percent had some college experience. In the latest 2003 survey, 68 percent completed college or achieved high

FIGURE A.1

Demographic Profile

	2002 AVG. INCOME: $152,000			2003 AVG. INCOME: $152,000			
	% Total 2002	% Income >$100,000	% Income <$100,000	% Total 2003	$75,000 to less than $100,000	$100,000 to less than $150,000	$150,000 and Above
Male	32%	36%	40%	51%	45%	46%	58%
Female	68	64	60	49	55	54	42
Income							
<$100k	31		31	32	32		
$100k to $150k	36	64		32		32	
$150k to $200k	17			19			19
$200k to $250k	5			7			7
$250 or more	11			10			10

FIGURE A.2
Luxury Purchase Incidence, 2002 and 2003

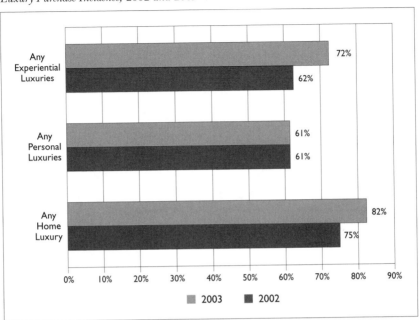

levels of attainment. Some 24 percent had some college, and 8 percent had completed high school.

- **Live in households valued from $250,000 to $349,999:** In 2003, the median household value was in the range of $250,000 to $349,999. In 2002, the median value of luxury consumers' homes was $250,000, so the median value of luxury consumers' homes skews slightly higher in 2003. Just under 10 percent of the 2003 sample reported a household value of $1 million or more. Among the respondents with incomes of $150,000 and higher, the median household value was in the lower end of the $500,000 to $749,999 range.
- **About 90 percent of the sample are white:** In both survey years, white Americans make up about 90 percent of the survey sample (93 percent in 2002 and 90 percent in 2003).
- **Only one-quarter of the total sample own a second home:** In both survey years, the majority of respondents (79 per-

cent in 2002 and 75 percent in 2003) do not own a second home, vacation home, or other residence. About one-fourth of the survey sample in 2003 own either a second home, vacation home, and/or another residence.

- **Live as married couple:** Some 74 percent of the luxury consumers surveyed in 2003 reported being married. Just over 10 percent lived together as a couple, and another 10 percent were single. The remainder of the sample were divorced, separated, and/or widowed.

- **Majority of luxury consumers have no children under 18 years living at home:** In the 2003 sample, some 55 percent of luxury consumers had no children under 18 years living at home. Of the remainder, some 34 percent had either one or two children. Some 11 percent of luxury households have three or more children living at home.

- **Average age of respondent is 44:** The average age of a luxury consumer surveyed in 2003 is 44 years, making these consumers a member of the baby boom generation. The luxury consumer population tends to skew toward the more mature, middle-aged consumers age 35 and above. Fewer than one-fourth of the luxury consumers surveyed in 2003 were under 35. This compares to the luxury survey of 2002 in which less than 10 percent of the sample were under 35 years old. In 2002, just under half were 35 to 49 (48 percent), whereas 44 percent were a more mature 50 to 69. See Figure A.3.

FIGURE A.3

Age Distribution, 2003

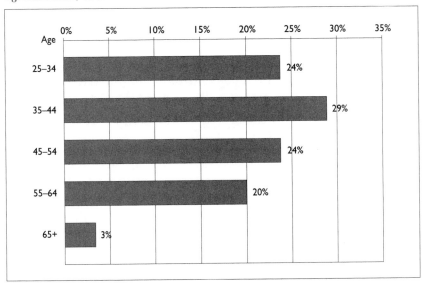

Danziger, Pamela N. *Why People Buy Things They Don't Need.* Chicago: Dearborn Trade Publishing, 2004.

Davis, Melinda. *The New Culture of Desire: 5 Radical New Strategies That Will Change Your Business and Your Life.* New York: Free Press, 2002.

Easterbrook, Gregg. *The Progress Paradox: How Life Gets Better While People Feel Worse.* New York: Random House, 2003.

Hall, Doug. *Meaningful Marketing: 100 Data-Proven Truths and 402 Practical Ideas for Selling More with Less Effort.* Cincinnati, OH: Brain Brew Books, 2003.

LaSalle, Diana, and Terry A. Britton. *Priceless: Turning Ordinary Products into Extraordinary Experience.* Boston: Harvard University Press, 2003.

Maslow, Abraham H. *Toward a Psychology of Being.* 3rd ed. New York: John Wiley, 1999.

McConnell, Ben, and Jackie Huba. *Creating Customer Evangelists: How Loyal Customers Become a Volunteer Sales Force.* Chicago: Dearborn Trade Publishing, 2003.

Nunes, Paul F., and Brian A. Johnson. *Mass Affluence: Seven New Rules of Marketing to Today's Consumer.* Boston: Harvard Business School Press, 2004.

O'Shaughnessy, John, and Nicholas Jackson O'Shaughnessy. *The Marketing Power of Emotion.* New York: Oxford University Press, 2003.

Pine, B. Joseph, and James H. Gilmore. *The Experience Economy: Work Is Theatre and Every Business a Stage.* Boston, MA: Harvard Business School Press, 1999.

Postrel, Virginia. *The Substance of Style: How the Value of Aesthetic Value Is Remaking Commerce, Culture and Consciousness.* New York: Harper Collins, 2003.

Schwartz, Barry. *The Paradox of Choice: Why More Is Less.* New York: Harper Collins, 2004.

Silverstein, Michael J., and Neil Fiske. *Trading Up: The New American Luxury.* New York: Portfolio/Penguin Group, 2003.

Stanley, Thomas J., and William Danko. *The Millionaire Next Door.* New York: Pocket Books, 1996.

Twitchell, James B. *Living It Up: Our Love Affair with Luxury.* New York: Columbia University Press, 2002.

Van Boven, Leaf, and Thomas Gilovich. To Do or to Have? That Is the Question. *Journal of Personality and Social Psychology* 85, no. 6 (2003): 1193–1202.

Zaltman, Gerald. *How Customers Think: Essential Insights into the Mind of the Market.* Boston: Harvard Business School Press, 2003.

Zyman, Sergio. *The End of Advertising as We Know It.* New York: John Wiley, 2002.

Share the message!

Bulk discounts
Discounts start at only 10 copies and range from 30% to 55% off retail price based on quantity.

Custom publishing
Private label a cover with your organization's name and logo. Or, tailor information to your needs with a custom pamphlet that highlights specific chapters.

Ancillaries
Workshop outlines, videos, and other products are available on select titles.

Dynamic speakers
Engaging authors are available to share their expertise and insight at your event.

Call Dearborn Trade Special Sales at 1-800-621-9621, ext. 4444, or e-mail trade@dearborn.com.

Dearborn™
Trade Publishing
A **Kaplan Professional** Company